HIGHER AND TECHNICAL EDUCATION

HIGHER AND TECHNICAL EDUCATION
Book of Knowledge

B.M. Naik
and
W.S. Kandlikar

GYAN

Higher and Technical Education : Book of Knowledge

Rs. 790

ISBN: 978-81-212-1088-1

Published in 2010 in India by
Gyan Publishing House
23, Main Ansari Road, Darya Ganj
New Delhi-110002
Phones : 23282060, 23261060
Fax : 011-23285914
E-mail: books@gyanbooks.com
Website: www.gyanbooks.com

Laser Type Setting by: Rudra Computer Graphics, Delhi
Printed at : Chawla Offset Printers, Delhi

Contents

Preface 9

1. **Autonomy Policy for Higher Education in a Changing World** 21
2. **Changing Role of Higher and Technical Education Under Globalization Pressures** 41
3. **Gap Analysis between Indian Institutes and Their Counterparts Abroad** 57
4. **Privatization of Technical Education Identification of Risk Factors and Their Management-Making Education Affordable** 75
5. **India Dreams To Build A Knowledge Society** 91
6. **Continuing Engineering Education (CEE)** 99
7. **Management Education for Inservice Engineers** 111
8. **Training And Development of Professors New Approaches** 119
9. **Science and Technology - 'Guru Killy' For The Development of Any Backward Region Like Say Marathwada** 129

10.	**Needed - Innovation and Entrepreneurship in Higher and Technical Education Institutes for Employment Generation**	139
11.	**Operating Manual For Systems Improvement in An Educational Institute**	157
12.	**Private Universities - End of Monopoly Regime**	169
13.	**Quality Assurance System in Higher and Technical Education**	181
14.	**Science Park Valuable Tool To Tap Knowledge**	195
15.	**Expanding Horizons in Higher and Technical Education To adopt new visions of new world A Challenge**	217
16.	**Strategic Planning – A New Tool For Creative Management of Institutes**	237
17.	**Find a Worthy Purpose and Means Will Follow**	247
18.	**Performance Planning and Appraisal: Why and How?**	253
19.	**Students Need to Acquire Innovation and Entrepreneurship Skills for Global Competitiveness**	263
20.	**Engineering Education: Where And How It Should Reach**	273
21.	**India Needs Industry Oriented Technical Universities to Win in World Economy**	283
22.	**Higher Education : Lessons From Japan**	295
23.	**A Case for Initiatives in Technology Transfer**	301
24.	**Innovation and Technology Transfer Practices and Policies in Germany Lessions of Experience**	307
25.	**Technology Revolution How To Make Most**	327
26.	**Technical Education for Tomorrow**	339

27. The Challenge of Globalization for Indian Universities **349**
28. Vision 2020 and Institutes of Technical Education **357**

Conclusion **375**
Bibliography **387**
Index **403**

Preface

Universities and colleges are assuming key role in global economic systems, where new knowledge and highly skilled people are perceived as fuel for economic and social development.

Demand on talent is rising. The demand on higher and technical education is rising exponentially. It is mainly because knowledge has become the dominant economic force. More and more students of all ages are appearing at the doors of institutes to be diversely and repeatedly educated in a growing array of subjects. Students are expecting world class education. Many wish to make a career on international plane. Some want to become entrepreneurs to start new technology based firms. They are ready to pay the necessary costs. But unfortunately not many institutions in India are able to give. Thousands of students, who are denied admission, are going abroad.

Knowledge based enterprises, research companies are creating job market for which institutes are expected to provide competent manpower. Nations have ambitious plans for development. They look towards institutions as suppliers of national and international leaders. Employment and self employment market is not limited to India but extended to whole world. Talent has become far more mobile. Demand is from across the world, so is also the supply. Nations like Australia, Canada, and New Zealand etc have designed schemes to attract brains from everywhere and anywhere. They aim, to produce global leaders, leaders for human civilization. Is this an opportunity for Indian youths? They may fill up the job positions especially in advanced countries where the population is aging. Where would the institutions find necessary guidelines to make students fit for global career? They are here in this book.

Millions deserving and willing are denied admission. So as to meet the rising demand a large number of universities, colleges and polytechnics, have come up in the recent past. Some however feel that the number is too big, and ask a question, does India really need so many? Studies conducted elsewhere indicate, nations like Japan, Germany, US have progressed faster at a time when the output of graduates in their countries went up. It is observed that India has only 5 engineers per thousand populations where as advanced countries have around 60. They progressed mainly on the strength of scientifically educated skilled work force. Millions of students in India who are qualified and willing for various reasons are denied admission. The enrolment ratio of eligible youths is only 10, whereas world average is 30. It is observed that educated people do not consume jobs, but create. They contribute to "knowledge based economy", that is to say a society which is driven by knowledge. Production, use and distribution of Knowledge are now critical to economic and social progress. India should have to move ahead vigorously in higher education to avail the chances in world. The authors concur with the finding of the National Knowledge Commission (NKC) report in respect of expansion in higher education. Government of India has kept a target to raise enrolment ratio from 10% to 15% by the year 2012. This requires systematic effort. Randomly putting more money or more men on the job will not solve the problem. Where do you get appropriate strategies? The readers will find them in this book.

Skill set is critical. The skill set of the vast masses in India is far too low by international standard. India is categorized as a lowly educated, low skill, low income economy. GDP is low and so is the standard of living. In the absence of educated people, they tend to be followers and driven by others like bogies. To make most of the global opportunities it is necessary to upgrade people's knowledge and skills. Hence many institutes are wanted. Not all, but some are expected to be world class. Otherwise institutes from foreign will come here and capture our vast education market. Indian management and education entrepreneurs would then become unhappy. Goods from China and other east-west countries will flood Indian market. We will keep buying and they keep selling. **So as to combat onslaught from foreign, it is necessary to upgrade institutes urgently. Transforming technical institutes to world class standard is not now an option but compulsion. Foreign institutes are waiting at our doors to enter. If we delay transformation they may displace Indian education entrepreneurs easily.** This is the fear, and so the bill presentation in parliament is being delayed. Delaying entry of foreign universities is not in the interest of the students. This is the time characterized by skill revolution. Rapid transformation of institutes to world class standard is the crying need. Where do you get the strategies? The strategies include adaptability to change and many more. You will find them here in this book.

Knowledge is Prime Mover. Education institutes in competitive world are expected to teach not only known knowledge but also to germinate brand new ideas, new knowledge, and new technologies. Ability of society depends on capacity to create a stream of continuously flowing graduates with newer knowledge. It depends on capacity to change with respect to time. It is this capacity which is crucial for the creation of India's future. Knowledge has become the prime mover. Science and technology represent the driving force. Institutions now should spend more time and energy on developing new hi-tech required for the creation of brave new India rather than preserving the past. They must become innovative in character. Is there a need to change the academic culture? The answer is certainly, yes. Good teaching in class rooms and labs is necessary but not enough. The institutes should have to become enterprising to teach creativity. How to go about it? The book shows new directions for the thought and action of the key people involved in management and governance.

Institutes are expected to strike roots, grow tall and sturdy. Institutes are a place where creative minds converge; established notions of truth are challenged, brainstorming takes place. The greatest teachers prefer hard truth to comfortable fiction and self respect to popular esteem. They do not yield to popular pressures but stand up with courage for truth. Public good is uppermost. For this they have to be autonomous in nature, with freedom to think and freedom to act. They ought to have organic links with surroundings. Institutes function as a stepping stone to job market. They are the knowledge organizations meant for creativity and innovation. The book presents their status analysis vis-vis elsewhere in the world. It is urged that they grow soon to international standard.

Research Park provides a common platform for industry and academics. It is a place where industry personnel meet academicians to exchange ideas and give birth to new products, processes and firms. It is a platform where new technology based activities by innovators are conducted, employment and self employment is generated. World experience tells us that institutes of higher & technical education function like an engine. They are the drivers of regional and national innovation leading to industrial development. Previously they were on the periphery, now in this period of knowledge society, obviously being knowledge organizations they have moved to the center. It is observed that institutes acting entirely on their own cannot do much to boost quality. Teaching oriented institutes are good but not enough. They ought to have focus on regional innovation, a multifaceted entrepreneurial infrastructure in place locally like Research Park, technology incubator, patent and IPR centre, entrepreneurship development centre etc. This requires a complex and subtle set of complementary physical, political and organizational inputs. There is no precedent in this respect. How to become a path finder? You will find steps in this book.

World class institution takes the nation forward primarily by playing the role as a trainer. It primarily makes the people employable. It provides the economy a steady and ample supply of skilled young graduates. They are needed most to adopt changing technology. It is a proven theory that GDP grows faster where people are more educated. Secondly, an institute provides new products, new processes, new knowledge and theories, which when commercialized leads to enrichment. An Institute may work also as a partner, develop joint ventures of professors with entrepreneurs to commercialize their researches, and earn royalties. This increases attractiveness of the region as a whole to talented innovative people. An Institute functions also like a magnet to attract competent people from anywhere and everywhere. It also plays a role of networking to form clusters. Hi-tech clusters grow now a day's around knowledge centers. How to make college a magnet for industries? The book explains this exceedingly well.

World class institutes spin-off Hi-Tech companies. World best institutes now have become birth places for hi-tech firms. They are known as the maternity homes for safe birth of New Technology Based Firms. Institutes are engaged in spin-off of start ups, and generation of jobs. This has become an important performance indicator. 30 to 40 companies are born each year in each institute in countries like U K, Australia, Germany and USA. Government of China has given a target of 1000 start ups each year to universities. Where do you get world trends in spin-off? The book illustrates with examples how an institute can play a key role in enterprise development transforming the region into a hi-tech region.

How to set up a world class institute

IITs were designed as world class institutes. From beginning world best institutes in countries like USSR, Germany, UK, USA were entrusted the responsibility to install them. They remained under foreign collaboration for 20-30 years. Exchange of faculty, research collaboration, world class systems and procedures gave them global orientation. Establishment of universities even in developed countries like Limerick University in Ireland and Harburg University in Germany and many more elsewhere in the world have been set up under the close supervision of world best professors in world class universities. From very beginning these universities are associated with almost 15 world best professors. They supervised them from their respective universities and visited frequently to plant high class academic culture. Frei University in Berlin was set up on these lines. Here the university purchased existing residential colonies along with existing telephone lines, electricity, water supply, drainage, roads etc. This saved lot of time. Should we adopt such innovative strategies?

Integration of Indian institutes with their counterparts in world is a must. Technical Education now a day is frequently in news. It is often discussed and debated in parliament and state assemblies. Governments are becoming aware of the important contribution that world class institutes make to the competitiveness, economic growth and harvesting the opportunities world over. World class approach in establishing and running is becoming essential, lest institutes and students will be thrown behind. People are giving top priority to the education of children. They are taking loans from bank, selling gold, property in favor of education. Engineering education is believed to be creating the people's future. Governments consciously bear this in mind while designing the policies and allocating resources. India government has increased its budget allocation ten times for the year 2009-2010. The economic and political security of India now critically depends on scientific and technological capability of people, and hence the role of technical education. Where do you get basic principles of networking? The book explains the challenges and opportunities involved in making institutes globally competitive.

Have students become profit centers? Private institutions are seen dominating the scene. Eighty percent graduates are coming from private self finance institutions. Turmoil is however, breeding everywhere because of rising fees in self finance colleges. Pretty strong signals that something is not quite right are being received. Frequent agitations from poor and disadvantaged people for whom it is difficult to pay have become common. The policy makers and educators need to listen to their voice. It is feared that majority of the bottom half population are not able to send their children to college. Nation in the effort of development is losing their talent. Second grade but rich are becoming doctors and engineers. Education has become a commodity on sale. Education institutes in private sector have gone in the hands of mostly politicians who do not understand deeper purposes of education. Court decisions on admission are given go buy. Admissions are being made on capacity to pay for rather than merit. The book examines this aspect in proper perspective. It is the government's legitimate responsibility to make education affordable. The book deals with these aspects and makes appropriate recommendations.

Are institutes under global pressure to reshape? The knowledge business is already exploding in size, becoming global in scope, and intensely competitive. If institutes in India are to be successful in this huge new global market, they will have to adopt sweeping changes in governance, leadership quality and organization structure. The way they performed in the past, the strategies of yesterday would not suit any more. This book explores what challenges are involved and what strategies are needed in making institutes globally competitive. Governance and leadership is the first and foremost valuable input needed to make institute world class. Today it is far from adequate. It is mainly on account of this that the Indian institutes do not stand high in the world list. This needs detailed examination. Those individuals and nations, who lag behind in knowledge, will face a heavy penalty. Why are people ready to pay any cost for knowledge? The book attempts to address the question.

Prime Minister Dr Manmohan Singh while appointing National Knowledge Commission in the year 2005 said **"Time has come to create a second wave of institution building to achieve excellence in the fields of education, research and capability building. He further said the present frame work of higher education needs to be altered to make it globally competitive."**

How to bridge the gap between Indian institutes and their counterparts abroad? The book is an outcome of research done by the authors over a period of years. It is written out of intense passion to improve the state of affairs and close the gap between Indian institutes and their counterparts abroad. India, in the recent past has made a gratifying progress. Yet there are too many inadequacies and there is a great scope for improvement. The book makes introspection. Really, India lagged behind not because of shortage of resources but because of lack of proper visions and missions. The same are presented in this book for adoption and implementation. It is pertinent to note the observations of National Academy of Sciences of USA, given in the book, "Rising above the Gathering Storm: Energizing and Employing America for a Brighter Economic Future."

"Civilization is on the brink of new industrial order. The big winners in the increasingly fierce scramble for supremacy will not be those who simply make commodities faster and cheaper than the competition. They will be those who develop talent, technologies, techniques, and tools so advanced that there is no competition."

These observations are addressed to US government to invest more in R&D, and attract best brains from the world over, so as to rejuvenate the economy. They are pertinent to Indian government as well. **Higher and technical education in India needs intellectual capital more than financial capital.**

Does India need entrepreneurs to generate and commercialize new technologies? Improving quality and relevance of education is not now a matter of only putting more money or putting more men on the job. It is not a matter of just improving teaching in class rooms and laboratories. It is more a matter of imaginatively creating an environment to build synergy of industry with academics. Units like Research Park, technology incubator, entrepreneurship etc. facilitate taking technology out of labs to industry to improve productivity and competitiveness. Students learn in them innovation and research skills needed lifelong. Institutes are expected now to produce not only graduates but also innovative entrepreneurs and technology pioneers. They are expected to turn out engineers who do not do only what they are told to do but use imagination to do what they are not told to do. Those professors, planners, administrators and industrialists who account for this trend win. Others may work hard, may have all the resources to draw on, but for scientific approach in commercialization of new technology, will lag behind. The book deals with winning strategies in technical education.

Invest in Big Bang ideas. Waves after waves of scientific discoveries are sweeping the world. Technological innovation is found to be driving the growth. Discoveries in the past like steel, steam engine, computer, internet, airplanes, penicillin etc changed the face of the world. Nations have advanced who harvested S&T. Now organizational innovations like technology incubators, Research Park, Patent and IPR, etc., which lead to thriving entrepreneurship, are bringing about a marriage between industry and academics. They are said to be cracking brand new careers, unheard a few years before. World experience tells us that they create bright future with high pay and fine conditions of jobs. Where do you get them? They are here in this book.

Is higher education about to be deregulated? Yes

The universities, world over are about to lose monopoly control on higher education. Information technology, internet, corporate vendors, for profit companies from across the world are giving on demand, any time learning on line. What Peter Drucker said a few years back was :

"Thirty years from now the big university campuses will be relics? Universities will not survive. Already we are beginning to deliver more lectures and classes off campus via satellite or two way video at a fraction of the cost. Today's buildings are hopelessly unsuited and not needed. However, universities which provide leaders are less likely to be replaced by IT and internet".

Universities are the conservators of the human experience. They have also to be the creators of new knowledge, fresh insight, novel techniques, and creative approaches. Institutes must accept both the roles. The task of the university is to deserve to be the book of knowledge for tomorrow.

Indian higher technical education is far too behind the world

It needs to be upgraded forthwith, otherwise India may loose on global plane, so warned Narayan Murthy. Technical education has expanded well in the recent past and there are more than 2300 colleges [2009], and around 8 lakh students studying. However, quality is not up to the mark. Only 30% are employable. Finishing Schools are started to make up the deficiencies. Students are not very happy with the quality. They want world class education. Thousands are going abroad. Foreign universities are knocking doors to permit them to install campuses. Chinese goods due mainly to their technological superiority are flowing in large numbers in Indian market.

Conventional wisdom in technical education now in global competition does not suffice. Traditional system of education which at one time served well is not enough. Autonomy, flexibility, innovativeness is wanted. Creative solutions on the lines of world class institutions are needed. Only teaching and learning in class rooms and labs although wanted is not enough. Expansion in scientific infrastructure like incubator center for wannabe entrepreneurs is needed. Igniting the minds of students for innovative entrepreneurship is the need of the hour. Silent revolution is observed to be taking place, but much more at fast rate is needed.

The book covers a large number of topics involved in planning and management of engineering education, like manpower planning, strategic planning, international experience along with policies and practices, visions and missions, systems and procedures. Students look at institutions as spring board to obtain high quality, knowledge intensive and high paying jobs in global market. Government has started Technical Education quality Improvement program [TEQIP] for up gradation to world class level. Many new IITs, IIMs, universities are being started. Need and importance of knowledge based economy is well realized. Now is the time to use innovative pathways to reform.

The book is addressed primarily to thinkers, practitioners like principals, directors, board of governors, professors and all those who seek reformation. It draws heavily on my experience as founder principal for seventeen years in the distinguished institute Shri Guru Gobind Singhji Institute of Engineering and Technology at Nanded. It is a compilation of articles written and published by the authors. It is hoped that readers will find the book useful.

The authors acknowledge with sincere thanks colleagues, officers, and managers with whom they had discussions.

B M Naik & W S Kandlikar

1

Autonomy Policy for Higher Education in a Changing World

"If we grant autonomy to colleges, our efforts and investment are likely to be fruitful. If we don't grant, and even provide abundant financial and other resources, all that is not going to be much useful."

Statement of Problem

Absence of autonomy is found to have created almost a complete lack of competitive environment in institutions and loss of spirit of academic leadership. In the absence of autonomy colleges have become like bogies, having no authority to steer the direction by them selves. They have become too much dependent on Universities. They do not have authority to self monitor and self control and hence do not move with the times. There is a time lag between the action initiated by university and action taken at college level. This slip is a cause of worry. It is this slip which is avoided in autonomous structure. When institutions become autonomous, they become self actuating, self driven, shaping future on their own, and not depending on university.

In India, autonomy is talked more but little practiced. Government, universities, colleges and policy makers in public interest need urgently to act together with dedication and not merely provide lip service. They ought to consciously chart the road map for installation of autonomous structure.

Educating and training the concerned persons for effective use of autonomy, and changing their mind set, is the need of time. Learning to use autonomy is relatively easy, but unlearning the old style of working in affiliating system is difficult. Hence brain washing, is necessary. It is therefore advisable to make colleges autonomous right at birth.

Autonomy is effective in increasing the response ability of an institution to the changing situations. It requires consistent efforts over a period of ten to fifteen years to learn successfully to use autonomy. Mere declaration of autonomous status to institutions does not bring autonomy. People have a tendency to cling to old systems. The leaders of the institutes must have to change their mind sets, and consistently practice democratic functioning as is demanded, in autonomous structure.

They should have to abandon bossism or bureaucratic culture, and refrain from autocracy. So as to enable youths to make most in globalize world India needs urgently to initiate steps to adopt and implement the policy of autonomy.

Introduction of autonomy is not like a magic wand. Its successful use is a long drawn process, which requires patience and consistent efforts. Once perfected it lasts longer.

Concept of Autonomy

An autonomous institution signifies its overall ability to act by its own choices in pursuit of its chosen mission. Autonomy is a dynamic participative model of governance based on continuous evaluation of performance. The evaluation need be done at regular intervals by internal as well as external agencies.

Every stake holder's view point is valuable and this needs to be respected and cared for. Autonomy means freedom to think and freedom to act but freedom implies accountability and responsibility. Greater autonomy means greater accountability and greater flexibility, relating to budgets, admission of students, degrees awarded, quality of teaching and research. Autonomy means self determination, self control, and self regulation, with least interference from external sources. It means greater economic freedom, to raise the resources. Autonomy implies going away from government closer to its own students and faculty, who are the main stake holders in an institution. Autonomy means internal debates, discussions, continuous improvement for the public cause of education. Autonomous institutions are found to be innovative and innovating non stop. Autonomy enables to make best utilization of available resources, available ideas to harvest opportunities.

Stimulant of Excellence: Institutions by practicing autonomy over a period of years are found to become innovative and rich in terms of knowledge. Knowledge and decision making are distributed throughout the organization. An autonomous institution is characterized as a knowledge organization. Creativity and innovation; trust and confidence, are the main pillars on which institutions rest. They attract brains from anywhere and every where. Scholars dream to study in them. They tend to become creative by keeping role models of internationally known institutions before eyes. The professors in these institutions not only teach and research but think great in global context and provide guidance to government, corporations, and other public bodies in respect of public policies. Autonomy provides freedom to professors to enable them to be equal to world class professors. An academic institution is not only a teaching institution but a knowledge source for the society; a think tank, it ought to be so in public interest. However, government which is least qualified in academics is found occasionally to interfere in these institutions even in academic matters. This kind of over stepping by government is required to be stopped forth with. This is in public interest.

An autonomous institute has an in built mechanism for continuous reformation.

It should be allowed to function; even if it fails for failure teaches important lessons. *In any case freedom which is the main strength of an institution ought not to be curbed.* Government has a tendency to interfere unnecessarily, and to kill its self improvement ability. Institutions ought to have immunity from arbitrary exercise of disturbance from external authority. It should be allowed to enjoy self ruling and ought to have exemption from external control. It is like learning how to ride a bicycle. It takes some time and requires self effort to learn. But once learned one keeps on refining it. Autonomy signifies the state of being free or at liberty rather than in confinement. It has the power to determine action without restraint. Pursuits of truth, innovation, discovery, creativity which are the main functions of an institution require minimum interference, demanding more autonomy. This is for larger good. Government and its other agencies, should consciously avoid interfering. But autonomy does not mean monarchy. Institutions must have to follow the law of the land.

Leadership Distributed: The concept of autonomy is intertwined with decentralization and privatization. Powers are not centralized at one level but distributed at various levels with various persons. Financial resources and newer ideas available in private sector besides in government need to flow in education. Hence private sector leadership with continuous experimentation, in autonomous structure is the accepted way of working.

An academic institution is a knowledge organization, consisting of innovative people. The academic leadership in the institution is scattered through out. Leaders create leaders. This is their distinguishing feature from other organizations. The people are worthy and autonomous structure enables them to become further more worthy.

These autonomous institutions by virtue of self control are a security for the economic future of people and the nation, so said Mr. Jefferson former president of US.

The autonomous institutions, public and private both, tend to make full utilization of the knowledge available in the society. Education needs of the people can not fully be visualized by people only in government. It needs to be assessed at every institution level, both in public and private sectors. Knowledge available out side government must be allowed to flow in the system.

History

The first autonomous college in India "Hindu College of Calcutta" came in existence in the year 1817. This was followed by Agra College in 1827, Poona College in 1833, and Elephantine College, Mumbai in 1834. Eight autonomous colleges came in existence before the universities like Bombay, Madras were set up.

Education Commission under the chairmanship of Dr D S Kothari in the year 1966 recommended grant of autonomy to colleges. National Education Policy of 1986 recommended granting autonomy to colleges. World over, colleges and universities by law are autonomous. In India today there are more than 18000 colleges, but they are not autonomous, mostly affiliated to universities, offering stereo type, irrelevant and standard courses. Only about 200 colleges are autonomous. Affiliating system has resulted in a huge waste of intellectual and physical resources, besides misdirection to younger generation.

Government of India, with a view to make education responsive to people's needs recently had appointed the committee under the chairmanship of Kanti Biswas, which submitted *"Report of the Central advisory Board of Education on Autonomy of Higher Education Institutes, in 2005".*

The terms of reference were

(a) To suggest measures for enhancing the autonomy of higher education institutes, especially those with potential for excellence.

(b) To institutionalize regulatory provisions for promoting autonomy and accountability of higher education institutes.

The committee has strongly advocated the implementation of the policy of autonomy to make education flexible keeping in tune with world wide latest developments.

Some of the important recommendations are

(a) Freeing higher education from unnecessary controls and regulations and withdrawing avoidable state interventions.

(b) Institutes need to be insulated from internal and external pressures, of political, bureaucratic and other groups.

(c) UGC/AICTE and government should evolve strategies to achieve this end.

(d) There is a need to grant autonomy for designing curriculum.

(e) To bring innovative approaches in teaching and research.

(f) To make more funds available for education.

(g) To start self finance courses.

(h) To set up internal quality assurance cell.

(i) To improve PG courses and research.

(j) To fix number of posts of professors, assistant professors etc.

(k) To train academic administrators.

(l) To provide block grants.

The report observed with surprise that the associations of professors, like MFUCTO are objecting for the implementation of autonomy. Autonomy empowers professors. Then why do they not want autonomy? The government administrators and universities are perhaps not serious about releasing authorities to professors. For small little things they have to take approval from government. Today, professors have many responsibilities and no authority. Who will take responsibility with out authority?

National Knowledge commission, Government of India in its report of 2006 has analyzed the problems in higher education, and said,

"most obvious solution is to provide autonomy to colleges either as individual colleges or as clusters of colleges"

World Experience

International association of university presidents [IAUP] in its meeting December 8-9 2006 in Thailand discussed the issue,' *the anatomy of autonomy"*

Views were expressed on institutional autonomy in this meeting by experts from various countries. They differ considerably from country to country. Perceptions of autonomy change over time as well. Governments in almost all countries have been interfering not only by the power of purse; but they have been interfering in respect of rules of admission, recruitment of staff and faculty, courses and deciding how an institution should be governed. Interference from Government of India in IIM Ahmedabad is a well-known recent case. The ideal situation IAUP recommended is that,

"Government should put trust in institutes to carry out their designated public roles without government intervention."

They should be permitted to fight out for themselves and evolve solutions. But unfortunately this does not happen. *Institutions are given freedom with strings attached*. This should be avoided by government.

American Council on Education

According to the report,

"Shifting Ground- autonomy-Accountability and privatization in public higher education" of 2004,

it is observed that demand for higher education in US is increasing. The report recognizes that

"Good *health of higher education is a necessary condition for good economic health of USA*".

The relationship between higher education institutes and their states is undergoing a profound restructuring. States are funding less and less, leading to increase in tuition fees. Financial grants are being converted in to loans. Some feel public purpose of education is at stake. Autonomy and privatization are not mutually exclusive concepts. Privatization in all sectors is found to yield higher productivity; in higher education also it should be so. Debates are going on how autonomy is useful or how it is hurting the ability of higher education institutes to serve public interest. Some look at autonomy especially in financial respect and privatization as a threat to academic success. Some fear that the changes will lead to negative social consequences. Autonomy however is in practice in varying proportions in various states. *In sum total, significant trend is observed in favor of autonomy and privatization.*

It is realized that it is the autonomous status of universities and colleges which has elevated the scholarship, and economic performance of US ahead of European counterparts. Greater autonomy is being perceived as the strategy to cater to increasing number of students in higher education. Freedom from state regulation is often exchanged for increased accountability, demonstrating how the institute will meet state needs in a fiscally responsibly manner. Rigid regulation is being replaced by a focus on performance and learning out comes, with smaller share in funding from states. The report applies to both public and private institutions.

University of Massachusetts in its report of the year 2000 says autonomy means ability of institutes and particularly of faculty-to carry out the primary mission of higher education in a manner with shared visions. That mission is to educate, [not just train, as politicians and others urge], the general population for intelligent participation in the public realm and to contribute to the understanding [not just of knowledge, as urged by those who think education as marketing of ideas], of how physical, aesthetic, political and social worlds work.

If some one comes along proposing a change in an institute, public policy or ways of doing education business, the institute does not compromise on academic freedom. The central question to be answered is, whether the change will preserve or enhance the autonomy of the academy? Whether the professors are involved more in academic or administrative matters? If the answer is not yes, the institute says people should resist the change, and fight tooth and nail.

Council of Europe Conference in the year 2003 prepared and adopted a report,

"Institutional Autonomy and Higher Education Governance"

It said that institutions have to be autonomous at the heart, to be able to meet the needs of world around it. Its research and teaching must be morally and intellectually independent of all political authorities, and economic power. Academic freedom to students and faculty it said is the integral part. It advocated student's participation in governance of the institutions. Freedom was related to academic matters, and not organizational and economic. It recommended self governance with invited external participation. It advised the academic community

"To elect its own offices like vice chancellor, director, dean, professors etc with little or no external interference".

Hidden interference of political persons is discouraged. Autonomous institutions are expected to open up new sources of income, as the state is not able to meet the demands fully. It is expected to co-operate with business and international agencies. Increase in efficiency with the association of business is expected.

It further said, law must delegate the necessary decision powers to the institution, for changes in curricula, teaching and research, interaction with their counterparts nationally and internally and for economic transactions. Transparency in transactions is prescribed. Quality assurance system should be independent of political system. Autonomy is desired to set the institution in motion. We must see continuous improvement, not uniformity, but variety. It further said realization of fruits of autonomy will depend on co-ordination between government and institutions for change, and willingness in national interests.

With the emergence of globalization, fantastic opportunities have opened up, requiring higher knowledge, and hi-tech skills to perform the jobs. A knowledge based economy in the whole world is being pursued. Higher education institutes are obviously at the center and going to play a key role in meeting the challenges of globalization. Consequently, every one in every country is for changing the higher education.

A report from Germany, *entitled "Financial Autonomy of Higher Education institutes, the necessity and design of Institutional frame work"* recommended autonomy for only academic purposes. It suggested giving flexibility in budgets and lump sum grants to institutions is necessary. It recommended authority to institutions to raise resources from several other sources. Absolute financial autonomy it said is not desirable. Government, ultimately should bear the financial burden, yet grant liberty to the institutions in operations. Total autonomy may do more harm than good. Decentralized decisions are better characterized by better knowledge of problems and needs greater flexibility. Hence it recommends autonomy.

Bulgaria in 1993 has made an act of academic autonomy for higher education establishments. According to which the state has granted autonomy to higher education and research establishments. The act delineates the relations between the institution and the government, other establishments, in the country and outside. The act empowers the institutes to define independently operative rules and regulations. It prescribes methodology for up gradation of faculty and staff. It empowers them to create their own funds. Rights of IPR, patents are granted. It empowers fundamental rights to students and faculty. Mobility of professors and students is encouraged. An opportunity for training and retraining for faculty and staff is prescribed by law.

A report from **Japan** says autonomy has played an important role in promoting life long education. The corporate education in Japan is rising, mainly because the institutions have been granted autonomy. Education only once in initial stages is good but not enough. People change jobs 3 to 7 times in service career, for which they need retraining, which the institutions are providing. **But for autonomy this would not have become possible.**

Vietnam has recently accepted the need for a comprehensive transformation of its higher education system. In 2005, the Ministry of Education and Training developed a Higher Education Reform Agenda (HERA), a blueprint for reform of the system by 2020. The Government of Vietnam recently approved the main elements of the *Agenda, including a proposal to give universities and colleges the right of autonomy*. Measures supportive of institutional autonomy in higher education now need to be addressed. In particular, there is a need for legislative and regulatory reform, the establishment of appropriate accountability relationships, the development of leadership and managerial expertise at the institutional level, and the *building of confidence and trust in the processes of institutional self-governance*

U K recognizes autonomy as an essential tool for success. The strength of U K higher education is founded on its autonomy and funding structures that support universities and institutes ability to respond flexibly and according to institutes priorities. There is a shared responsibility of funds. All those who benefit from higher education contribute to its cost, including individuals, employers, and the public purse. Universities and government have a shared responsibility to protect the reputation of UK higher education at home and abroad. Higher education continues to expand in response to changing student demand and also to respond to the needs of diversity of markets in which it operates. Public funding in UK fell by 37% in the year 2002. But the total budget of each higher education institute has increased. Institutes are earning money from multiple sources. Block grant scheme is in practice. There is a commitment from government to funding through block grants. Institutions have mobilized funds from various other sources with almost no control from government.

China:

In the recent past a tremendous change is noticed in higher education in China. This is solely on account of decentralization and autonomy and granted to them. Institutes lacked autonomy and flexibility in the past. Now administration has been decentralized, and local private participation has gone up. Provincial governments have been given more decision powers. Institutions have now more rights for decision making.

Incentives have been designed for the institutions which use autonomy to the advantage of students and the economy.

Internal management of the institutions has substantially improved. More number of courses with flexible curriculum has been introduced. Moral of professors and students has gone up. Management of education and research is according to the market demands, and needs of society. The institutions are giving a much different look than in the past.

Autonomy and decentralization have put more enthusiasm in the education domain. Consequently, the number of students studying has gone up. Post graduation and doctoral courses have been increased. State funding has gone up. The number of publications, patents earned companies spin-off from universities has shot up. **Undoubtedly, one is conspicuously struck by the impact of autonomy and decentralization**.

Policy Implications for India

Do we want the education to be relevant and purposeful? Do we want education to be innovative, creative and flexible enough suiting to the current global needs? Do we want it to be qualitative and cost competitive? Do we want institutes to produce pioneers in technology and world class leaders in industry? Should the institutes be producing new technologies, patents, and first mover entrepreneurs? This will not happen unless the institutions are autonomous.

"Government should put trust in institutes and empower them to carry out their designated public roles without government intervention."

Solution to improve higher education does not lie in providing more funds, but in making effective utilization of provided funds, which essentially requires autonomy. But for autonomy, public and private investments in higher education are used less productively. Autonomy, at the moment, is the single most solution to many ills in higher education.

Autonomy is a world proven model of governance. There are however, problems in its adoption and implementation. Teething troubles like every where are here in initial stages. They need to be identified and solved with determination by concerned through teaching, debates and discussions.

Once used to affiliating system, an institution finds it difficult to abandon it and switch on to new. It is easier to introduce autonomy at start of college. New institutions should there fore be permitted only with autonomous status. IITs were born autonomous and hence they could shine in world.

Autonomy is a world trend. Debates and discussions for refinement are however going on; they are not limited to India. Academicians in India ought to hold many conferences and seminars, to discuss pros and cons. Key persons in government, universities, and colleges need to take initiative.

US economy is reported to have advanced mainly because of its world best higher education system, which owes credit to its autonomous institutes. Students all over the world dream to study in US. Why? It is mainly because the professors in institutions are teaching the latest. This attracts best and brightest brains from every where and any where in the world. Many of them settle there adding to intellectual capital.

World class institutions are using autonomy with higher degree of success. They are managed and maintained by local trusts, on which scholars, scientists, industrialists, educationists, noble laureates are represented. They have much less of bureaucracy and much more decentralization, and autonomy.

Today, in India higher education is over administered. Decisions which matter most are in the hands of bureaucrats in, UGC and AICTE. The engine of development of academics must move out from distantly located administrative bodies to professors close to students.

Government by legislation should grant autonomy and permit the institutions to use autonomy in right spirit. It should not stifle the autonomy. Government is neither designed nor capable to steer higher education, it should there fore not interfere. It should leave it to academicians and the governing board. Interference is found to kill the internal curative strength.

Presently, in India there is an over regulation from government in higher education. Institutions and universities have become mere tools in the hands of bureaucracy. Institutions badly need liberation from government clutches. Too many controls from unqualified have spoiled education.

Interference in academics by government is however observed in almost all the countries, more so in developing. It is being resented by academicians. Frequent interference by government is observed to be damaging public good.

World over, a gap exists in perceptions on autonomy between the law makers on one hand and the academicians on the other.

It is up to the leaders in education to explain to legislators and convince that lack of autonomy threatens the economic security of the nation. This must be realized by both. Initiative must come from academicians.

IITs and IIMs have become world class because they are autonomous right from birth. More money and more autonomy is the right kind of solution to problems of higher education in India. Government should only give adequate funds and yet not interfere in their administration. Simply because it gives public funds, it does not get authority to interfere. It should appoint a professional body, neither political nor bureaucratic to monitor. This is in public interest.

Autonomy means ability of institutions especially of faculty to carry out the primary mission of higher education. A professor is a hero. Autonomy should enable him to be so. He should be permitted and enabled to have freedom to be innovative and creative. Then and then only autonomy is meaningful and it delivers expected results.

Institutions are now at the core of knowledge based economy; hence they have assumed the position of drivers of development. To be a winner in global competition India has no way other than making its universities and institutions autonomous.

Indian institutions and economy have a high potential to leap frog their counterparts in developed countries, which is hindered by lack of autonomy.

Autonomy is the only way to achieve excellence in higher education, which unfortunately today in affiliating system is blocked. The blockage needs to be removed urgently. Grant of autonomy will enhance the chances of India becoming a world leader.

"If we don't step up the challenge of creating autonomous institutions, we undermine every thing else we are trying to reform higher education."

Traditional regulations by universities and government in today's stormy weather of globalization do not suffice. Higher and Technical education must remove constraints, and introduce flexibility, and autonomy. Virtual and for profit universities from across the world are on the horizon, and posing a serious threat.

SYSTEMS IN AUTONOMY

Currently There Is Over Administration in University

Today we are living in fast changing world. The influence of ever emerging new knowledge and new technology on various walks of life is growing. It is shaking the foundations of economy, commerce, trade, industry and culture. In liberalized economy and single global market place, survival of the fittest has become the Law. Only those nations and organizations win in a world economy which is flexible knowledge based and decentralized.

Autonomy Empowers College

Autonomous college is a decentralized form of organization. This model as compared to affiliated college is more efficient, avoids waste of time, waste of money, effort and is more productive. It empowers the College, principal, Professors. The conventional affiliated University model is a bureaucratic less efficient model where administration over powers the academic. It is like a three legged race where legs of several colleges are tied with each other, for syllabus, examination etc. It takes away the freedom from college. In industry "Inspection Raj – License Raj" has gone out. Situation has changed from total control to total decontrol. In higher education decentralization is the crying need of the hour. Shall we not say goodbye to Local Inspection Committee?

World over only autonomous colleges exist. In India we still have this old affiliating college model of 1950 in 2008, Education Commission in 1986 prescribed autonomy. IIT's have been set up from beginning as autonomous. Tamil Nadu, Karnataka, Kerala have made many (200) colleges autonomous.

We have long experience in Higher Education Institutes (HEI). It is a ripe time for us like a worthy son of 25 years to become independent. India had to fight to earn independence. Here independence is being given, should we sit back silent? Or we should grab the opportunity, as a golden chance.

Systems Matter More

Without autonomy our Colleges, our professors, and students will not grow. They will remain pygmies. We will do disservice than service if we remain affiliated. Systems are very important. Once "Peter Drucker" was asked, how come Japan's economy is better than American, when Japanese man is less impressive than American. He replied Japanese systems are superior to Americans systems. The systems matter 80%, individuals matter only 20%. Autonomous system is structurally more efficient, so says "Deming" principle, of ISO series.

The College in autonomous structure would have like in University, academic council, executive council, Board of Studies. The syllabus is designed in college, many professors can participate in policy making and strategic thinking. Question papers are set in College – Assessment is done in College – result is declared quickly and for which students are happy Professors empowered. This is the Privilege of academicians to teach, research and examine. They do associate experts from outside in syllabus making, exam. etc.

College Grants Increase

Grants to the College continue as they are, rather more grants are given to run on autonomous basis, to have academic, examination, affiliation, sections, plus dean of academic, dean of research and dean of extension.

Institutes are not for only teaching. More importantly they are like a heart to body to educate people in all walks of life the "Lifelong education" to make and retain people competitive.

In globalised situation, foreign Universities are coming in India. American, English, and Australian Universities have become aggressive to capture the education market. Shall we the leaders in Higher education sit silent, remain blaming the University and not rise to make our institutes customer oriented, more innovative, competitive by world standards.

Way To Deemed University

When an institute functions for 5 years as autonomous, it qualifies to become a "Deemed University". Principal becomes Director in higher scale like Vice Chancellor. Several other additional posts like Dean, Registrar as in University are created.

The student's population in Higher Education is swelling at 15% per year, although our population is growing at the rate of 2%. To cope with this increasing demand, the existing colleges will have to show vision to grow in terms of organizational capacity for which Autonomy is a gift. Who does not want gift and powers? We have to be visionary.

Autonomy is beneficial to all stake holders, namely, students, teachers, society, industry and people at large. Region can become forward only through education. Shall we not realize and respond. If we don't do this we will be obstructing the regional development, and future generation may not pardon us.

We all have high capability which for want of autonomy cannot be put to fuller use. Here is a golden chance. Hurry up! let us show the way to others.

Experience in Foreign Countries

I have visited Universities in Germany, USA, UK, studied their organizations and management practices in depth. When I visited Karlsruhe University with 25,000 students, I found only seven clerks to maintain examination and certificate record. A Professor conducts examination of his students, on the day convenient, declares marks, shows answer books to students and after satisfaction of students mark sheet is sent to office for record. There is no sealing of bags, transportation, Central Assessment, Dy. Registrar examination, vehicles to run here and there. From experience in foreign countries, I feel this is the only way for each of us as an individual to grow to national and international levels. I have no doubt that you will consider seriously to become autonomous, talk to your colleagues in

College and apply to University forthwith without losing time. I have a conviction that each college will succeed and serve the society in a better manner.

Are there any disadvantages? Are there disadvantages in India becoming independent? There are no disadvantages, whatsoever.

Global Pressure

With wasteful methods in centralized organization we cannot compete with rest of the world. In order that we do not buckle under global external pressures we need to overhaul our systems and do "Reengineering" for which the first step is to become Autonomous.

How satisfied our students, industry, people are about higher education? Let us make a search, the answer will be found in becoming Autonomous. Let us change ourselves else we may be changed. The external threats in liberalized economy are very serious. Let us aim at making our institutions globally competent.

Some Myths

Common fears are expressed that teachers in autonomous structure will-not teach and give more marks to students. They may distribute degrees at cost to students. They may be partial and victimize students. This has not happened anywhere else. It is less likely that it will happen in India. This is a false fear. Do you think students want only degrees? We should make a survey and find answer.

The teachers in autonomous structure are found to care more for self reputation, because those who do not get exposed. Today, they have a place "University" to hide. When the College and professors have no chance to blame anyone else, they always safeguard their own credit and avoid unhealthy practices.

Government Blessings Are There

Our Honorable Minster for High Education and Technical education and Secretary both are keen on Colleges becoming autonomous. Vice Chancellors are also keen to pave the way. Let We all throw out the old model and adopt new and initiate steps.

Professors and Students are the Main Players of Autonomous College

References

1. Report of Council of Europe conference, Strasburg, "Institutional Autonomy and Higher Education governance" December 2-3 2003, Bologna Secretariat, Dr Per Nyorg.
2. Bulgaria, Academic Autonomy for Higher Education Establishments, 1993.
3. Report of the central advisory Board of Education [CABE] Committee on autonomy of Higher education, government of India 2005, under the chairmanship of Kanti Biswas.
4. BM Naik, New Vistas in Technical Education, vivek Publication, Aurangabad, 1999.
5. American Council on Education, "Shifting Ground-Autonomy-Accountability and Privatization in Public Higher Education", 2004.
6. Report of National Knowledge commission, government of India, 2006.
7. Higher Education in Australia, Structure, policy, and debate by Jim Breen Monash University.
8. Report from International Institute of Education Planning, 7-9 Rue Engne, 75116 Paris.
9. Financial Autonomy of Professional Higher Education institutes, comparison Between Finland and some European countries, By Voukko Kohtamki, Finland, 2003.

2

Changing Role of Higher and Technical Education Under Globalization Pressures

"The power of research is demonstrated not only by the single isolated innovation but by the ability to create new technology based industries, some of them becoming the most economic power drivers."

Synopsis

The paper outlines in brief, the need and importance of building a **knowledge based economy** in India, in the context of globalization. This is with a view to enable people to be more competitive to make most of global opportunities. Strong higher education system is however, a pre-requisite for development, without which India in spite of potential can not hope to become a strong economy. Urgent steps for strategic changes in creating entrepreneurs, new knowledge, new technology, patents, IPR, establishment of new technology based firms etc. are recommended. Conventional wisdom, of institutes as "teaching shops" in present stormy weather of globalization falls too short of purpose, and does not suffice. Teaching with out research base and with out innovation is found to be ineffective, outdated, irrelevant and obsolete. From experience in the world it is recommended that India should harvest its untapped research, innovation and entrepreneurship potential lying idle in higher education institutes. Brilliant students and faculty are eagerly waiting. The new roles have a potential to convert, brain drain in to brain gain.

Introduction

Pressures are mounting on higher education institutes like colleges, polytechnics and universities to play a key role in creating knowledge based economy and bringing about integration of the Indian economy with global. Corporations, governments, and international organizations like UNESCO, World Bank are calling for a more prominent role for education from basic literacy to life long professional education. OECD defines :

"Knowledge based that is to say knowledge driven economy is one in which the production, use and distribution of knowledge and information are critical to the process of economic growth".

Not surprisingly the role of university is central to the emerging knowledge based economy. World experience tells us that those regions/ nations whose institutes can quickly adapt to the rapidly changing economic, political, technological and social climate will have much greater prospect of success. They are identified as major drivers of change to achieve economic growth. A region where more enrolment takes place in institutes, and liberal, broader, quality education is offered, globalization at faster pace takes place. Higher education has considerable potential to reduce adverse effects, and increase impact of globalization in stimulating economic growth. Knowledge inculcated by institutes can enable people to derive maximum benefits from entry in global market. India has the potential to leap frog the educational infrastructures and effectiveness of developed countries. Raw talent of Indians is good and anxiously waiting to be nursed well.

Colleges and universities in India after independence have made a laudable progress, yet they are observed to be poorly equipped and woefully unsuited to the demands of globalization. They are far too behind their counterparts in developed world. Thousands of students every year are going abroad for higher education. Institutes emphasize memorization that is "rote learning," and do not offer innovation, entrepreneurship and leadership skills needed in world market. Institutes, in globalization have to play a key role in developing knowledge society. They need to be repositioned, and restructured in terms of their relationship with people, government, industry, private sector and the world. Our true wealth resides in educated citizenry. Most profitable investment lies in education. People who are willing to learn, rich as well as poor, need to be educated to fit them in today's complex globalize world. They need to be allowed to grow to the level they are capable for. Otherwise they tend to become a liability and threat to the national as well as world peace. It is being realized that lack of education is closely linked with unemployment and in turn to crime. India should have now to invest with priority in colleges or else it will have to spend more on building prisons for those who do not get education, and wind up in committing crimes. If investment in colleges by choice does not take place government will be forced to invest more on prisons? Should the state therefore not be investing adequately in building institutes? Public Investment in education will have to increase for it is the best use of tax payer's money.

Need and Importance of Building a Knowledge Society

In globalization, intellectual capital has become more important than land, buildings, equipment etc. Intellectual skills of people in modern job market have achieved more significance than hand skills. Colleges, Polytechnics, universities have come to be known as power houses producing new ideas. They increase brain power and enable the nation to win in brain race. They generate and disseminate new knowledge needed to keep the people competitive. Institutes have moved from periphery of development to the center.

Institutes Produce National Leaders and Captains for Industry

Development to take place fast and remain sustainable requires educated people and visionary leaders. More educated people are observed to choose better leaders. Institutes are now called upon to produce leaders for industry, and leaders for economy, society and every walk of life. They could produce world class leaders for which essentially institutes would have to be world class by themselves, which is so essential to win in world economy. We know that today's leaders in politics, industry, economy etc were yesterday's students. We must look at today's students as tomorrow's leaders, and institutes as generators of visionary and creative leaders.

Each one is affected by globalization and each one is impacting globalization. We are now the citizens of one world. We have to be competent by world standards. The boundary lines between the nations are becoming thinner. Students and people in globalization would have to develop international perspectives, tolerance and negotiation skills needed in world market. This is essential so as to keep pace with the world development. World over, this is found to be a winning strategy. We should not delay in its adoption. Else, expert leadership, critical skills, professional services, and new knowledge on which its future in globalize world depends would remain subdued.

More Students Entering the Pipeline

More students entering the education pipe line in India is a welcome sign. This is the critical input for development. As the world due to globalization, is getting more and more interconnected, the higher education which is meant to drive knowledge, creativity, and innovation, in human society is becoming more crucial. Colleges, polytechnics and universities all over the world have always been the creators of new knowledge and its keepers. They have sought to prepare new generations with the skills, cultural and scientific literacy, flexibility and capacity for critical inquiry and to make their contributions to society. Development of a nation today is said to depend on its capacity to educate people in relevant knowledge and state of the art technology.

No society, region or nation will prosper without good institutes of higher and technical education.

They form the core of development and hence need to be reformed with priority. It is the well educated people, people with capability and competency, who make the investment and efforts in development projects fruitful. It is this interaction between education and development that shapes our collective future as global citizens. World Bank in its report of 2002 has underlined the importance of higher education for creating able leaders for development of nations. A close coupling exists between 'education and competitiveness of human force 'which needs to be kept in view, in today's stormy weather of globalization.

In India proportion of students entering the pipe line of higher education of the age 17 to 23 is around only 7%. This proportion in USA is 55 %. World average is 23.4 %. It is observed that countries with higher levels of education will be least affected due to shift taking place in employment. In globalization people are found to change jobs 3 to 7 times in service career. The proportion of older students for upgrading skills world over is therefore increasing. U K has declared recently skills revolution, and urgent action taken to up grade people's competitiveness. Most successful nations shall be those who invest in life long learning, and create a learning society. Getting educated only once is not enough. Higher education has become critical to win in business. India would have to work and match with its competitors. Are our students and faculty aware of importance of education for economic development? What our institutes are doing to promote life long education?

Institutes Build Knowledge Society

A central theme is emerging in which significant social, economic transformations are taking place on global level. They are challenging the traditional role and traditional position of universities in society. It is argued that these institutions now are a "think Tank". They need to find ways of addressing these important complex challenges facing the nations with imagination. India has many hidden jewel professors. It is necessary to explore, reward and felicitate them Professors are expected to be equal to their counterparts in developed world. How are they enabled in India to be so? They should be enabled to establish alliances with world best institutes, political system, social system, and world economic system. They should not be merely teaching but influencing public policies and society. They should be researching themselves and guiding students for research. There is tremendous positive impact on the transfer of science and technology from institutes to private sector and then to economy, thereby creating marvelous number of jobs with high pay off. Institutes now stand for creating a learning society and a learning economy. Institutes in globalization can and should bring about a cultural revolution, and contribute to collective wisdom, so essential for bright future of our children and grand children. Questions are being asked, are we educating students to understand global systems? Do the students understand that they have to have tolerance for the culture of others? Knowledge society will give kick start to Cultural Revolution.

Protect Civil and Political Rights for Knowledge Society to Thrive

Protection of civil and political rights is a prerequisite for establishment of knowledge based economy. There is a close and inseparable relationship between the quality of higher learning on one hand and the quality of effective and democratic governance on the other. Economic development depends on level of education of the people and level of education depends on quality of governance of the nation. Just as it is very hard to imagine sustainable and democratic development without higher education, it is futile to promote higher education in a society where civil and political rights are systematically suppressed and denied. Experience shows that countries that thrive best in global economies are those which are truly open. Openness means open trade, open investment, open borders. It also refers to open societies that invite new ideas, show a high tolerance and open descent and criticism and rethinking, reworking of their own governance. True development occurs when knowledge is owned and operated by communities, and by women and men who form those communities. Higher education is not a luxury for the rich it is a necessity especially for the poor. E-governance is said to provide solutions. Openness and transparency is consciously promoted by state government through, Right to Information Act. What kind of e-governance? What are the limits? Who will out line the strategies? It is the well educated who can show the way

Privatization Accelerates Arrival of Knowledge Based Economy

While the importance of higher education world over is increasing, state budget allocated to higher education per student is observed to be decreasing. In countries like USA, UK per capita public investment on education is reported to be falling. Tuition fees are therefore rising. Private and public investment taken together is however observed to be rising. In India the situation is not different.

Increase in tuition fees is resented by students. They are however paying, because higher education is bringing to them benefits like higher salaries, and an opportunity for better jobs which weigh far more. Private investment by philanthropic organizations, industry, and fees paid by students are found to make education responsive to market needs. This is a great advantage. Privatization leads to stimulate competition to get good students, good faculty thus improving relevance and quality of education. Privatization leads to quick response of education to market forces, which the students and economy needs.

The internal rigid structure of government, universities and colleges is a major obstacle to quick changes needed in education. Private institutes have flexible structure Privatization has an edge over government regulated institutes in this respect. As such there is no substitute for privatization. But privatization may not protect students coming from low income families. Government would have to cover them by scholarships, bursaries etc. There is no substitute for public funding. Almost 70% of the students in USA are taking education in government funded institutions. In Germany all institutions are Government funded, and education from KG to PG is free of cost.

Funding alone by government even if it can leads however to mismatch and waste of resources. Therefore both public and private funding must simultaneously go on. Funding by government for poor and deserving is essential. Can we afford to lose students because of high fees? This has to be viewed as an investment in creating leadership from weaker sections of society. All needs of education however can not be visualized by government. It is the inherent weakness of the government regulated systems.

Many times advanced education of superior quality by government is neglected, Privatization makes up the gap. Public funding alone leads to over centralization, and increase in overheads without commensurate gains. These weaknesses are overcome in privatization. Where lays the golden mean of public and private funding? Who will find? This requires well educated people.

The model of private and public funding is found to be more rewarding.

Globalization Brought Opportunities

Some view economic globalization as inevitable, and therefore advocate to focus on necessity of institutional reforms to harvest benefits arising out of globalization. Others view economic globalization as unnecessary evil where economic interests have displaced broader social, human and democratic concerns. The later argue in favor of resistance while the former says resistance is futile. Globalization can benefit human civilization as a whole. However some may benefit more while others less. People in India to benefit more will have to upscale the skills and knowledge of its people. India is a developing country. It remained less developed so far, by world comparison because its economy was localized and less globalized. The region can be richer if the digital divide between the region and developed world is reduced. We must wake up to this reality and act fast with our full strength to accelerate international trade and commerce, which demands more knowledge of the world. Do we share the same planet, same environment? Then we must nurse globalization.

Opportunities are not Risk Free

There is however more uncertainties and more risks involved in global opportunities. So as to harvest them demands new knowledge new skills, and positive human attitude to go round the world. Survival of fittest is the law. There is an impact of new technology on jobs and business. Are our institutes preparing youths to cope with? Are they providing skills required in global market? Globalization means mixing of cultures, shrinking of time and space. Globalization means business at the speed of thought, instant communication and instant decisions. Globalization means abandoning traditional methods, systems and procedures in favor of modern, which requires education. Keeping the risks to a minimum and harvesting opportunity requires education. Who provides the scientific approach to harvesting opportunities? Higher and technical education will.

Institutes as Drivers of Change

Student's and entrepreneurs in search of new knowledge tend to migrate else where because good institutes are inadequate in number. Good institutes are found to function like magnates to attract intellectuals. Institutions in India except IITs are observed to be far too behind their counterparts in US, UK. Thousands of students are seen migrating for admissions elsewhere. After studies many of them do not return. India to that extent looses talent. USA has gained lot of intellectual capital from foreign countries like India, China by creating world class universities. If India creates world class institutes it can reduce brain drain if not eliminate, and attract brains from other developing and developed countries.

Wealth of a region now depends upon knowledge possessed by the people. He who possesses knowledge becomes well to do, hence is its importance. Is it the local people who posses technological knowledge? We must ensure this. Development is said to primarily aim at acquisition of the intellectual capital. It is not merely construction of roads, bridges, factories etc. Institutes in the state will have to grow to the level of their counterparts in rest of world. Winners are not those who manufacture goods, but those who develop talent.

New Role of Higher Education

To produce captains for industry, to commercialize new knowledge, generate new technology, patents and IPR, Starting New technology Based Firms, research parks? It is high Time for institutes to become enterprising and to give kick start.

Institutes can and should derive financial advantage of innovation capacity of students. Institutes ought to be autonomous to do that.

Indian higher education institutes are late starters but now after independence, observed to have made lot of progress. The number of universities, colleges has substantially gone up.

They are found to be doing a good job. A revolution is noticed in every state and in the whole country Students are coming to institutes in larger numbers. People are giving high priority to education. Even if they do not have money enough, they are found borrowing from banks, selling land and houses. The job opportunities in globalization are large enough that they get more than they spend on education. Many are taking jobs abroad in countries like USA, UK, and Japan etc.

Universities abroad are now highly enterprising in creating knowledge based society. There is a world wide wave in this respect. There is however, a serious deficiency in the institutes in India. They are observed to be too weak in research, innovation, patenting & IPR, and spinning off of new technology based firms. If we make bench marking of our institutes with their counterparts in developed countries a big gap is noticed. For example USA universities are spinning off new technology based firms very large in number. MIT Boston is obtaining more than 150 patents every year. The royalty earned from patents is 20 % of the yearly budget of the institution. It is spinning off around 50 companies every year. A study conducted in the year 1994 found that 4000 companies owe their origin to MIT. They employ 1.1 million people, and generated 232 billion dollars in world trade. In the United States companies employed 733000 people or one out of every 170 jobs in the country. Indian institutes have not taken any financial advantage from creating innovations. Higher education can not grow where R & D is absent.

The universities in Australia are also quite active in this respect. Each university is spinning of as many as 50 new technology based companies. Chinese universities are also not behind. Each university in China has set up technology incubator, business incubator and they are pumping new technologies and innovations in industry. Countries like Germany, UK, and France are far too ahead. From 1980 universities in Germany have set up technology transfer and patent centers. The author was given a fellowship by the ministry of education government of India, in the year 1996 to visit patent and technology transfer centers in universities of Germany. He has personally visited six universities and observed that students acquire innovation, patent skills. They sow the seeds of entrepreneurship while studying.

How many of the universities in India have obtained patent and IPR? How many companies have been born in universities? Do the students learn innovation skills? How much commercial exploitation is done of the PhD thesis? Are they just lying on library cupboard? They are being exploited by foreign companies, for obtaining patents. Many Indian traditional researches like of Haldi, Wheat, Basmati, Ayurvedic medicines etc are being exploited by foreigners. It is because our institutes have so far ignored patenting. There is vast untapped potential available for exploitation. Shall we not hurry up in this regard?

Prof Terman of Stanford University in the year 1950, gave the principle for establishment of research parks, that "University professors need access to industry to make application of the findings of research, so also industry need access to University research to keep industry globally competitive." Based on above Silicon Valley was born, with the backing of Stanford and California university, research Triangle Park at North Carolina is set up with the lead of Duke University, 128 street in Boston with the initiation of MIT and a large number of university related parks have come up in Japan, Germany, and UK, with a view to induct new knowledge and new technology to make industry globally competitive.

Department of Science and Technology Government of India have started a similar scheme of Science and Technology Entrepreneurs Park [STEP]. Twelve such parks are operating in universities in India. University of Pune, Cochin University, IIT Kharagpur etc parks reports are encouraging. IIT Mumbai has started a technology Incubator. TIFAC is set up to give fillip to patenting. The schemes need to be driven further with greater strength and vigor.

Transnational Linkages Essential to Build Knowledge Society

Securing the connections between the developing and developed institutes to build capabilities of knowledge generation is essential. We can not afford to ignore good policies and practices developed else where in the world. IITs were developed in collaboration with foreign. So they are found to shine in world. Rests of higher education institutes were disconnected and although they spent more they lagged behind. Now we can not afford to ignore the global scene in education. Why our institutes do not stand in the world list? Why thousands of students are going abroad? Strategic international partnerships have a great potential to bring new knowledge and relate knowledge to local conditions. Who will give directions in this respect? Who will caution the government of fatal consequences of not adequately interacting with world? It is the educated galvanized people who can.

Examine Hold Ups

Higher education institutes world over are declared as primary engines of economic and social development. Our industry has under nourished the relationship with applied research, innovation, in engineering colleges and universities. Synergies in their relationship like in foreign are yet to be achieved. Inventors, discoverers, creators in colleges and polytechnics must have to be respected, honored and rewarded if these activities are to flourish. We must examine why such activities are not being conducted satisfactorily? Not many professors do research. What are the factors holding up? Policies and practices, visions and missions need reconsideration. Who will do it? There are thousands of eligible students who desire to take admission in higher education institutes, but due to various reasons they can not. The factors need to be identified and solutions evolved, to make accessibility easy.

What can we Conclude?

Demand for higher education in decades ahead will grow exponentially. Advanced education will become even more pressing both for individuals and society. Education will change in profound ways; much of the change will be driven by market forces. We have to develop capacity in institutions to change. This is a big challenge before the nation. Universities must remove constraints. We can not afford to waste talent.

"Think globally, Act locally", is the first and fore most new role and responsibility of higher education institutes in the present stormy weather of global changes. They should not think routine way like bygone days. Globalization offers new opportunities and is a strong driver of change. Institutes have to perform differently. What is the new role institutes have to play? They have to look beyond instruction in class rooms become enterprising to generate new knowledge, new technology, patents and IPR so as to make knowledge society effective. Institutes should have to volunteer to show leadership in this noble cause.

Another new role is to **"Dream Big" Jump start technology clusters** attached to institutes using youthful talent for research and innovation. They are found to act as major contributors to regional development. Incubators, technology parks act as spark plugs for development. Institutes now should *have to produce not only graduates but produce entrepreneurs using New Technology.*

Thirdly, higher education in global circumstances has to aim at "**corporate development**." They must produce captains of world class industry. Building synergy between the education and business for national growth is essential. New technology is driving business to greater heights, requiring more skilled and flexible graduates. *Universities and corporate presidents should establish a new forum of partnership to achieve synergy.*

Fourth role is to take a special drive for advanced education. It is becoming ever more pressing both for individuals and society. Much of the change in higher education is being driven by research in technology and market forces. Institutes must take a new look at it, and on mass scale start M Tech and doctoral courses.

Fifthly, Indian Industry can no longer do all the research; it needs to survive by itself. Engineering colleges/ polytechnics, universities in partnership with industry may have to conduct research more vigorously. Leaders in education and leaders in industry must have to walk hand in hand together for national cause.

Last but not the least, Traditional regulations by universities and government in today's stormy weather of globalization do not suffice. Higher and Technical education must remove constraints, and introduce flexibility, and autonomy. Virtual and for profit universities from across the world are on the horizon, and posing a serious threat.

If higher and technical education is not revitalized in the light of above, opportunities will slip out of our hands and economic stagnation may result.

"If you solve the education problem, then you don't have to do any thing else. If you don't solve education problem and do every thing else, nothing is going to matter as much."

References

1. What Business wants from higher education, By Diana. G Oblinger and Anne-Lee Verville published by American Council of Education.
2. The Creation of the Future By Frank H T Rhodes, published by Cornell University Press.
3. Higher Education in Canada, Edited by Charles M Beach, Robio W Broadwayand R Marvin Melnnis published by Queens University press.
4. Universities for Sale, by Niel Tudiver, A Canadian Association of University Teachers Publication.

5. The Crisis in Canadian Universities Petrified Campus, By David Bersucan, Robert Bothwell, J L Ganatsein, Publishers- Random House of Canada.
6. Universities as Drivers of Regional and National Innovation, San Diago's Program for Hi- tech Entrepreneurship, By Julian R Betts and Carolyn W B Lee, pulished by Queens University Press.
7. Globalization, The Impact on our lives, By Rob Bowden, Rain tree Chicago Publication.
8. Globalization and the need for Higher Education Reform, By David E Bloom.
9. Innovation U-New Practices Enabling Cultures By Lous G Tornatzky.
10. Creating Knowledge- Strengthening Nations, The Challenging Role of Education Edited By Glen A Jones, Patricia L McCarney amd Michael L Skolinik, University of Toronto Press, 2002.

3

Gap Analysis between Indian Institutes and Their Counterparts Abroad

Synopsis

Where does India stand in the world list in higher education? Why thousands of students every year go abroad? Have we failed as a society to provide adequate opportunities to our youth to be educated in world class manner? Have we failed in creating a vibrant educational ecosystem that supports cutting edge research? How are their institutes different from Indian? What do they teach which we do not? Where do we go wrong? Teaching profession in India is a grim affair. Where as it is prestigious in foreign. We have too much of rote learning. They have more of innovation, creativity. All teachers abroad hold doctorate degree, where as in India very few. Why coaching industry in India is booming? Nalanda and Taxshila were the first universities of the world, where scholars in 6th century B C used to come from abroad. Now why a shift in culture has taken place and our scholar students going abroad? Is it due to inadequate value attached to discovery of new knowledge, new theories? It is essential at this juncture of time to make introspection and learn from the world experience in science and engineering education. The future of youths depends on knowledge, rather than resources. Status of India in world, in leadership, income level, and well being of people depends on its scientific and technological capability. India, to cope with challenges will have to enlarge the scope of institutions to cover research, innovation, creativity, generation of theories, technology creation, patent and IPR, creation of New Technology Based firms etc. What value we attach to above in budgeting? How can we bring back the past glory of Nalanda? Students studying today in universities are tomorrow's leaders, in politics, industry, academics etc. They sit in parliament, board room, write books, become creative thinkers, and drive the society to progress. For India to win in world economy they have to be competitive by world standards. To be able to have world class leaders tomorrow we have to have world class professors and world class institutes today. They have to learn not only known knowledge but learn to discover unknown. The article presents in brief, the gap analysis in respect of visions and missions; policies and practices; organization structures, systems and procedures in India and their counterpart institutions in developed countries. They are critical to the success. IITs were set up under foreign collaboration. Their visions missions, policies and practices are molded on foreign lines. Hence they could shine. The paper observes that rest of the Indian higher education is far too behind. India will have to capitalize on emerging technology to fulfill people's needs. Institutions will have to have wellsprings of new knowledge like in developed countries and not remain mere reflection centers. The gap analysis presented here makes an attempt to find answers to the questions raised above.

Institutes Abroad have built visions to create leaders for future. Have we?

Importance of academic institutions in today's volatile time is very high. It is the institutions which are furthering human civilization to greater heights. It is the academicians who provide new knowledge, new theories new technology and competent manpower to industry, leaders to government and leaders to the total economy. This in turn creates wealth and comforts. Industry, society and government in return ought to provide funds to academics to make it grow. India and for that matter any nation can be richer only by use of advanced knowledge. There is no other way. What kind of leaders our institutes produce matter.

This is a time characterized by change. The world under the forces of globalization is changing fast. Institutions would have also to change. Only those who change to innovate and again innovate tend to educate the youths on correct lines. Students now demand world class education. Institutions in India will have to be competitive by nothing less than world class so as to remain in service. Other wise foreign universities will come here and capture major share of education market, and our students like in the past will keep going abroad. Entry of Foreign universities is held back in parliament bill. One day it will come out.

People in India are as intelligent and hard working as else where in the world. However, today their efforts do not bring fruits as much as their counterparts. We work six days a week as against five days in foreign. Yet per capita income is around only 600 dollars where as that of USA is 30,000. It is 50 times more. They work less and earn more. 25 % people in India, live below the poverty line. It is mainly because of the lack of new visions of new world. It is due to lack of dedicated effort to realize the vision. We lack vision of research based education, relevant to the current needs.

The systems employed in India in education and all other walks of life are less efficient than those in developed countries.

Indians when they migrate abroad they are found to contribute far more. It is the systems efficiency which enables people to contribute more. We are spending resources and efforts on education but because of outdated systems output is less. Indian students study so much with less relevance. Foreign students study so little but with high relevance. This makes them more competitive. Our visions and missions, policies and practices, systems and procedures need examination in the light of world proven policies and practices. They need substantial improvement. Hence is the importance of gap analysis.

Identification of Gaps, and Their Analysis

The paper presents only critical gaps which demand immediate attention. They are presented with a constructive criticism.

Creativity, Discovery, innovativeness is the character of institutes abroad. Is it so in India?

I was reading an article written by an American author in the journal, "Fortune". The writer was addressing the question, "Can India ever compete with US in software business?" To answer the question he made an analysis of higher education in both countries, and recorded that Indian system is rote learning that is to say mechanical, stereo type based on memorization and not creative thinking. Students are taught sunset knowledge. Institutions in India do not produce new knowledge, new theories. Students are not learning innovation and hence they do not know how to discover unknown. They are reflection centers teaching that knowledge which comes to them from developed countries. It does not focus on creativity, discovery and innovation. He came to the conclusion that Indian institutions can produce at best followers in technology but not leaders. On the other hand, thrust of US universities is on producing leaders, discoverers, creators, who obtain patents and intellectual property. It is US which are pumping new technology most in the world market. 85% of IPR is held by Americans. He said student's education in universities and colleges is an enabler to competitiveness of software industry. A nation creating followers can never compete with a nation creating leaders, unless in future it improves. Universities in India need to incorporate creativity in syllabi and aim to produce leaders.

Another study from Duke University was examining if there is a threat from India to US competitiveness. It observed that today the quality of Indian engineering schools is by and large poor. The number of M Tech and PhDs who are crucial to technological innovation are too few and so India is far too behind in innovation. It concludes by saying that India on account of poor higher education does not pose a challenge to US competitiveness in near future.

Universities abroad have been upgraded as birth places, [maternity homes], of New Technology Based Firms. How many of our universities do this?

MIT Boston is giving birth to as many as 50 companies every year. Microsoft was born in Harvard. Apple computer was born in MIT. There are more than 3000 companies which owe their origin to MIT. Australian universities [Fang Zaho][1], each one is giving birth to 40 companies every year. Chinese universities of late are also doing the same. Why Indian universities can not? How many companies are born in Indian universities? They can do this. But they need to have this vision. Where do our institutes stand in comparison with their counterparts? In the recent past IIT Mumbai has set up a Technology incubator, Business incubator. It has started spinning off hi-tech enterprises. Employment and income generation depends on New Technology Based Firms. It is these companies which provide new life and blood to industries and keep them technologically up to date. This gap needs to be filled up with priority. Indian Universities need to take a drive to adopt new visions as their counterparts to install a mechanism for spinning off companies. It is reported that IISC Bangalore has recently made collaboration with MIT Boston in this respect.

Institutes Abroad Display Patents for Sale in Industrial Exhibitions

Do we do that? Patents are unknown to institutions in India. It is good to do research but it is essential to make commercial exploitation of the findings of research. This makes research financially more viable, and attracts more funds. Today, the economic returns obtained from research done in India are far too few. This has been our weakness, and so actual funding for research does not grow.

A few years back I happened to visit Hannover industrial exhibition. There was a pavilion meant for universities and colleges. It was most crowded by the visitors. Students were explaining the new researches, emerging technologies like, patents and IPR to visitors. Universities had come from world over to display. Visitors wanted to know the technologies of tomorrow. In India how many institutions have obtained patents and participated in industrial exhibition? Students do research for PhD, M Tech. Thesis remains in library. It is published in journals and is being harvested by foreigners for obtaining patents. We do not exploit research done commercially. Even the traditional knowledge like Haldi, Turmeric, Ayurvedic medicines, Wheat etc are converted in to patents by USA. We need to build this culture in our education. If the young students learn this they follow in future career. If they do not learn they do not practice. Attempts by Technology Information and assessment Council [TIFAC], New Delhi a government of India body, are being made to popularize patent, IPR. It has yet to reach universities and colleges. We need to protect our research findings before publication by patenting and convert it in money. Research is a wealth generating mechanism provided it is converted in to patents, IPR. When shall we realize this? [Naik[2] 2004]

Institutions in India today are distinctly a technology follower. They do not lead; do not give birth to new technology. They are by and large inward looking, restricting to class rooms and not going beyond. They lack the world vision. They are not enabled to think and act in this direction, the situation needs correction.

We need to install patent IPR centers in each institute and display patents in exhibitions. Industry is keen on knowing emerging technology. Institutes should aim at that. Visions of our institutions need to be enlarged, to go beyond to what their counterparts else where in the world are doing.

Institutions abroad are in driver's seat. Indian institutions are followers like bogies of a train

A friend of mine 25 years back went to USA. He studied MS, PhD and then started a company in Silicon Valley. He returned to India after a gap of 25 years, we received him on the airport at Mumbai. He was curious to know about the progress made by India. We were driving by car to Pune. He was happy to see the new high way, as good as in USA. When we came to Pune I was telling him now we have entered Pune. He was not able to see any signs of his time on roads. He would not believe that this is Pune. He said how Pune can change so much, beyond recognition. We came on Deccan Gymkhana, yet he was not ready to believe that this is Pune. Then we came on Laxmi road. He did not see a single bicycle, which at his time used to be crowded. Then we came on railway station. He did not see a single horse tanga. He refused to accept that it was Pune. Then we brought him to the college where he studied. Immediately he exclaimed, now I can not refuse. He said whole city has changed but his college has not. He said in USA Cities change because of institutions. In India, institutions are followers of change.

Institutions in India, instead of becoming an engine have become bogies. This he said is an unfortunate situation. Legitimately institutions should have to initiate changes in society. Institutions need to have attitude to shape the development. Only those cities are well developed where universities are having such visions.

Institutes abroad have Innovative Character. They produce far more captains and Generals [M Tech, PhDs]; we produce more soldiers, [B Es.] Teaching Assistantship and Research Assistantship in India are almost absent.

I have visited more than two dozen universities in Germany, China, UK, US. I found that they are in the pursuit of discovery, research and innovation.[3] Their center of gravity is on post graduation and Doctoral studies. They produce far more graduates of advanced degrees. They produce more captains and generals. We produce more of soldiers. They produce around 7720 PhDs [2006] where as in India around only 5000 are registered for PhD, many of them are in service lecturers from little known colleges. There are no schemes like Teaching assistantship and research assistantship in many universities, to attract the fresh scholars. This is a serious short coming of our education.

It is on account of advanced courses offered in the institute that the quality of UG becomes superior. They teach sunrise knowledge and sunrise technology. According to the report of G Bush Commission, namely "Science the Endless Frontier", research is the main function of university and teaching is a byproduct. Teaching with out research leads to irrelevance, and obsolescence. In India this is the status.

Many universities in India teach sunset technologies to students. Institutions are behind the time. According to Mckinsey report published recently only 30 % of the engineering graduates are employable. Government has now proposed, "Finishing schools" in IITs and NITs to educate half baked graduates coming out of universities. From NASSCOM to CII, every body is crying hoarse about the quality of our technical manpower.

Education to policy makers to make policies enabling institutes to become innovative like abroad is necessary. Policy makers should enable the professors to be innovative and produce more of M Tech and PhDs that is to say captains and generals. This is a major point of difference between Indian institutes and their counterparts abroad.

Size of Institutions Abroad is Large and Hence Economical. In India it is Pigmy, Uneconomical

National University Singapore has 350 acres of land but it has 1900 professors and 32000 students. MIT Boston has about 500 acres of land and 40000 students with 3000 professors. Georgia Tech University has 20000 students and 1000 professors. It offers 130 different courses. Karlsruhe University in Germany has 30,000 students and 2000 professors. Our universities by and large are pigmy in size. They have big land of the order of 1000 acres but students and professors are far too few. Pankaj Jalote[4] [2007] in one of his articles has advocated scaling up the strength of students in IITs from 4000 to 10000. Courses offered are stereotyped besides too low in number. Most of the universities like Pune Mumbai in their campuses have too few students and faculty. Aurangabad University for example has 500 acres of land, has 1000 students and has only 100 faculty strength. The size of our institutes is uneconomic. They are over capitalized in terms of land and buildings. Universities abroad open at 8 in the morning and remain open up to midnight. We open at 10 in the morning and close at 5 pm. There is a big difference in libraries. They are far too behind. Capacity utilization of installed facility in India is too small. Private colleges in engineering are like small "pan shops" with out PG and PhD education. There are no well springs of knowledge in the institutions. They depend on borrowed knowledge. The scope of our institutions needs improvement. They need to see what is happening elsewhere in the world and do benchmarking.

They have Built Visions for Patent IPR Culture for the Year 2015. Have we?

How many of our universities and colleges have patent culture? MIT Boston every year obtains around 100 patents. The institute has a Technological Licensing Office with 200 people working in it. There is a trend of commercialization of new technology in almost every university. It is a source of income to the professors, students and the institute. Many universities in Germany, UK have patent departments. In fact their performance is measured in terms of how many patents are obtained and the revenue earned. They have Technology Incubators, Business Incubators, research parks and Venture Capital Firms available in campus. Students develop skills of innovation and patenting in them. This is our serious weakness. This is one of the important reasons why Indian students go abroad. We need necessarily to learn from international experience abroad.

They give High Priority to Education in National Budget. What priority we give?

Professor's profession is very important, but the profession is not made attractive. Education is not accorded the priority it deserves in national budget. It does not get budget as their counterparts. India spends around 3% only where as developed countries spend around 10 % of GDP. Budget allocation to R&D in India is only 0.8% of GDP where as in China it is 1.5%. Papers published and patents obtained in China are ten times larger. Less number of people and that too poorly are therefore educated. This adversely affects the quality of leadership in all walks of life. Technological content in economy is far too low. It is to be realized that it is education which makes a man competitive. Without education man is less than an animal. It is like training a cook to prepare food. A trained cook uses less material yet prepares tasty food. Untrained man is unfit to live a worthy life. Nobel Laureate Dr Amartya Sen recommended increasing budget on education. The then finance minister Mr Yeshwant Sinha asked him what should be the first priority in budget. He replied Education. Then he asked what should be the second priority? He again replied, education. Then he asked, what should be the third priority? He replied again Education. Should the Government care for his advice?

Policy Makers in India are not Galvanized with New Ideas

Foreign universities galvanize their leaders from time to time with new ideas. Do we? Strategies employed in India are far too behind the world. The strategies have almost no strength to take the nation forward. Research subsidizes education and education subsidizes research. Research and education are complementary to each other. This world proven fundamental strategy is not adhered to. Strategies adopted in India are not strong enough in world comparison.

There is a storey of two armies which were fighting a battle with each other. One army had a lion as its captain, but the soldiers were sheep. The second army had a sheep as its captain and lions as soldiers. The lion captain employees bold strategies. The other captain, a sheep designs strategies like a coward and loses even though his soldiers are lions, because the soldiers have to follow the strategies drawn by captain. It is the strategies which enable the army to win.

Situation of India is something like sheep as captain. We have a strong base of intellectuals, and academicians but strategies which are drawn by leaders in bureaucracy and leaders in politics are weak. Academic leadership as a result at national/ state/ institution levels is crippled. Students of today are tomorrow's leaders. To have good leaders tomorrow we have to have good institutions today. Shivaji had much smaller army than Aurengzeb but still he could win, because he employed better and bold strategies like a lion.

There is a greater need to shed the mental weakness in academicians. They need to be enabled to grow at par with their counterparts abroad.

Brain Power is Nursed Abroad. It is Wasted in India

Brain power is said to be more powerful than any other power, like money power, political power, electrical power etc. Demand for knowledgeable people in globalize world is sky rocketing. SEZs and industrial development plans demand people with skills like research, innovation, entrepreneurship, patenting and IPR. Nations which understand the dynamics of world market and match it with institutions will win. Others may work hard, spend resources but will lag behind in brain race. Those who take strategies in favor of nursing brain power are only to win.

We have to recognize the importance and work with knowledge, IPR rather than muscle. Salaries of only a few in industry are sky rocketing. Many on the other hand are jobless. They have brains but under nourished. The dichotomy can be resolved only by upgrading the institutions.

Academic freedom is the legal right of students and professors abroad. In India professors are servants without any academic freedom. They have to teach what is given in university syllabus. They can not teach based on personal research. Students have no choice than to learn what is handed over to them. Yet we say, this is a student centred education. In fact it is teacher oriented, bureaucracy oriented.

Institutions also do not have academic freedom. This is proved from IIM-A case. They have become puppets in the hands of Government. Independent free thinking and decision making is not allowed. CAFETARIA approach courses are not run, although badly needed. Industries are varied in nature and so are their manpower needs. Courses ought to be unique. Standardized stereotyped courses are giving birth to mediocrity. Hence coaching classes industry is booming.

Academicians are being exploited by governing boards. The students and public at large are also being exploited. Academicians however, ought to work in only public interest. Some times the government, institute and industry are too selfish damaging interest of public at large. Academicians therefore ought not to work to further in the foul interest of institute, industry or government. They must behave fully in a professional manner. For this they have to be autonomous by law although they receive salary from institute, and from government or industry. World experience tells us that nations grow best only when academicians can function in autonomous manner.

Academicians Generate sunrise knowledge and educate people to use. They essentially should not have to go too close to education barons, industry or to government. They should have academic freedom to be able to play their legitimate professional role including that of a critic. Academicians have to work in larger public interest, for maintaining a healthy national economy. They should not have to bend before education barons, industry or government. They work in the pursuit of new knowledge.

Indian economy is a low income economy mainly because of lack of application of new knowledge. All institutions and professors should forth with be made autonomous. Parliament and State assembly should pass laws in national interest empowering professors for the cause of education.

Universities, institutions and private colleges have become the prisoners in the hands of Government. Non educational principles and strategies of government are guiding the people in universities and colleges. In fact it should be the other way round. Higher education institutes have become slaves of whims and fancies of government. They change every five years when new party comes to power.

The scheme of contract appointment of lecturers on fixed salary of Rs. 12000 is introduced in Maharashtra state. UGC and AICTE have objected. It has no backing of any academic body but only of bureaucracy. Mediocre are getting in. Although cheap, quality of education is deteriorated. Can the entry of professionals in teaching be protected? How can we produce globally competent leader engineers?

Government is not best qualified to govern education. Government should make only legislation for which it is meant. Long range policies and practices in education in India need be made by professionals considering the trends in world.

Research is Main Focus Abroad. In India it is Lacking

Research is given back seat in higher education. Professors have no research grant. Institutes and universities have become teaching shops. Professors and students have no budget for research. Professors teach sunset knowledge coming from abroad. They have no research skills. They learn parrot like that which was taught to them ten years before. Neither the teachers nor students are trained to learn to discover what is unknown. Unfortunately teaching and research have been segregated from each other. This leads to weakening of both. This is not the way to build a nation. They therefore remain followers. Research must become the core function of an institution.

Institutions are Governed in India by those who have Low value for Academics

Privatization of education is good provided it is governed by those who have value for academics. In most of the cases it is the politicians who do not understand it, and sit on the governing board. Today, education barons have usurped the powers of academicians. Professors have become humble servants.[5] They have no freedom to think and freedom to act. They have no budget for research. While money earned in colleges is siphoned for political purposes. This is too damaging for the future of children and grand children. That is one of the main reasons why brain drain from India is rampant.

Education barons have brought unethical commercial trends in education. Government is a party to it. Thinkers have no place in education. Nobler aims of education are thrown to winds. Bottoms 50% of population, because fees are high, do not have access to higher education. Upper 50% population is mediocre but wealthy and so gets access to higher education. India with such policies will stand to lose in brain race in long range.[6] The fabric of Indian culture is likely to be damaged. At a time when the level of education needed for productive employment is increasing, opportunity to go to college to bottom half population is decreasing. The common man is getting a feeling of betrayal, causing resentment which may lead to discontent, instability, even riots, which may be very costly. The present policies are an aid to Nexalite movement. Education institutes can not and should not be run on commercial lines like General Motors. Public interest is being sacrificed by both government and industry. When shall we realize this?

There is no affiliating system abroad. In India it is rampant. It has killed the innovation capacity of students. Chancellor of universities should not be Governor. He should be an academician. Policies are at fault.

Inbreeding in higher education is taking place. University Acts are obsolete. Governor of a state who is not an academician but a politician is at helm of affairs, as the chancellor of universities. Chairman of UGC, Chairman of AICTE are academicians. How come chancellor of universities is a politician? This is not so abroad.

The chancellor of universities is the appointing authority for vice chancellors. He does appointments mostly on political considerations. Most of the VCs are misfits. He inducts politics in universities. The situation perpetuates down below. This has resulted in politicization of higher education. Blame is wrongly passed on to professors. Policy makers and the chancellors are truly at fault. The situation demands immediate change. We need to adopt international visions to improve.

Unless the change is brought in chancellor's post as suggested above, the affiliating system may not go. There are no affiliated colleges in developed countries. Every college from its beginning is autonomous.

There is more number of technical universities abroad. India has very few.

Almost half of universities in US are technical. Germany has more than 84 technical universities.[7] So is the case in Japan.

It is observed that those nations which have more of technical universities have capitalized technology more effectively.[8] India has more multi faculty universities, which is an outdated model. In these universities Technical discipline does not get a deal it deserves. Hence it lags behind the world. AICTE has recommended establishment of exclusive technical universities. However in most of the states there is only one technical university and many colleges are affiliated to it. It creates monopoly, bureaucracy. Efforts, investment done by colleges, students as a result do not get fruits they deserve. Agriculture Universities which were set up in sixties developed new varieties of seeds, which have resulted in increased food production. Technical Universities should not be only examination bodies awarding degrees but should generate new technologies and improve industrial production.[9] They should become, "Light House" for industry. Future of children is linked up with creation of technical universities.

Conclusion

Good ideas are available not only in India but also abroad. We should not close our eyes and ears to them. We should not miss to benefit from them. Foreign collaborations are necessary. It is too costly not to interact with the counterparts elsewhere in the world. Mobility of professors to world best universities at any cost must be planned in a big way on priority. This is the only way to build good leaders and to take India on world map.[10]

We lack visions and not the resources. We lack interaction with our counterparts elsewhere in the world. We lack dedicated efforts. Institutions, universities need to show new visions of new world which inspire students to become leaders on global level. Institutions ought to shift their culture in favor of creativity, IPR and discovery. India's growth rate can be sustainable only if academic institutions adopt innovative character. Visions drive the national economies forward.[11]

In this time of knowledge society it is the intellectual capital that matters. People work with hands, but it is the brain behind which gives inspiration. Government should have to attach more value in national budget to create and use new knowledge.

The paper has identified only a few gaps, which are critical and need to be attended to forthwith. Without which higher education will not be up to the mark and fulfill the growing aspirations of people. Opportunities do not last longer. They do not wait. Achieving the declared dream of India to become a developed country by the year 2020 depends on how ably and urgently we initiate steps to make up the gaps.

We must not forget to recognize the importance of IPR. Creation of favorable environment for the same should be our top priority.

Rapid up gradation of higher education institutes and universities in the light of experiences in the world should urgently be taken up. There is nothing more urgent for India at this juncture of time than reviving higher education.

References

1. Fang Zaho, Academic Entrepreneurship, Case Study of Australian Universities, Published in International Journal of Entrepreneurship and innovation, pp. 91-97, IP Publishing Ltd. Vol 5 number 2 2nd May 2004.
2. B M Naik, Needed – Innovation and Entrepreneurship in Higher Education Institutes, published in Indian journal of Technical Education, January- March 2004 Vol 27, number 1, pp. 27-32.
3. Green paper of European Union on Innovation and technological transfer Enterprise Unit DG, EUFO, 2295-2920 Luxemburg.
4. Pankaj Jalote, An Opportunity To Scale Up the IITs, Economic Times, 26 April 2007.
5. B M Naik, Privatization of Technical Education, Identification of Risk factors, and their Management- making Education

affordable, Journal on Engineering and Technology, i-manager publications, volume 1, No. 2.

6. James J Duderstadt, "A university for twenty first century". The University of Michigan Press.
7. Derek Bok, Universities in the Market Place, The Commercialization of Higher Education, Princeton University Press Princeton New Jersey.
8. Clark Kerr and Marion L Gade, Association of College Boards of Universities of America." The Guardians, Boards of Trustees of American universities and Colleges", What They Do and How Well they Do It.
9. William G Bowen and Derek Bok, Princeton university press, "The Shape of The River, long Term consequences of Considering race in College and university admissions.
10. B M Naik Book, "New Vistas in Technical Education", Vivek publication, Aurangabad 1996
11. V Raghunathan, "India Needs More quality PhDs", published in economic Times.

Innovation theorists must learn to live with controversies. Innovators disturb the present equilibrium. Till next equilibrium is brought to order they may have to face rough weather.

4

Privatization of Technical Education Identification of Risk Factors and Their Management-Making Education Affordable

"We find today a time bomb ticking under India's social and economic foundations. At a time when the level of education needed for productive employment is increasing, opportunity to go to college for bottom half population is decreasing. The academic values in institutions are eroding. Sweeping changes to halt sharp increases in tuition fees and increase of public and other sources of revenue for higher education is the urgent need."

INTRODUCTION

In an age of knowledge economy in which educated people and their ideas have become the wealth of nations, the universities, higher and technical education institutes have become of critical importance. The education opportunities offered by institutions the knowledge they create and the services they provide are the key to economic competitiveness and well being of people. The impending revolution in the structure and function of higher education stems from the world wide shift to knowledge based society, that is to say more brain means more gain. The principal challenge now is how to discover new ways and means to respond vigorously to rapidly evolving world, and creating opportunities of quality education at affordable cost for vast masses. Privatization of higher education provides a means to achieve this. Private institutions must have to preserve the cherished aspects of the core values like academic freedom, autonomy so essential to ensure better future. Opportunities in private are always accompanied by risks. Which need to be assessed and guarded. Prime minister had appointed recently "knowledge Commission." This is a step in right direction. The report is now available.

STATEMENT OF THE PROBLEM

Privatization is presently a flash point of crisis, in whole of India and elsewhere in the world. This is the central issue of debate and discussion in parliament and assembly of various states. Turmoil is breeding every where, because of rising fees in self finance private colleges. Pretty strong signals, that something is not quite right, are being received in India and also in USA. Frequent agitations from poor and disadvantaged families for whom it is difficult to bear rising cost have become common. The policy makers and educators need to listen to their voice. It is feared that if majority of the bottom half population are not able to send their children to college, long term damage is likely to be caused to the fabric of Indian culture. The poor and disadvantaged people feel that the nation in its attempt of development will lose the talents of majority of population, and undoubtedly will miss the cherished goal of development. Poor and middle class people feel that programs in government are perceived and planned only for the rich, adversely affecting them. They have a feeling of betrayal causing resentment which may lead to discontent, instability, even riots, which may be very costly.

Private self finance institutes, in India, are mostly managed and maintained by political leaders, rather than those who understand it. They have little understanding of deeper purposes of education. In most of the cases they are self centered going to the extent of causing damage to the core function of academics and jeopardizing education. They put the students and public to disadvantage. Short term gains dominate the long term objectives, like raising people's intellectual capabilities. Concern for students, faculty and staff is likely to be lost, in favor of management whims and fancies.

Government, in the recent past has reduced investment in higher education and as a result privatization has spurred. Private institutions have become practically tools in the hands of politicians and businessmen who do not appreciate academics. Consequently, the deeper purposes of education are lost. Loyalty to the cause of education is reduced. Admissions are practically being made in spite of Supreme Court decision on capacity to pay for, rather than merit. Brainy students who are a national asset, from half the population are excluded from education.

Academics is getting back seat and money making has become prime. Professors have become employees having almost no say in governance. Professors are required to bend before politicians and industrialists. Respect for them in the eyes of students and management has gone down, adversely affecting creativity. Short term private gains are getting priority and long term nobler public interests are sacrificed. Professionalism is adversely affected. Governing boards, it is said have polluted the academic atmosphere.

These risks in privatization need to be understood, analyzed and accounted for. US government has appointed recently a commission to examine how privatization is undermining core academic values and its long term impact on national economy. Many people in India, also have fears that uncontrolled privatization, in the long run will shadow Indian intelligentsia.

Higher education leads to both public good and private good. With the increase in education, economy grows, so also the tax collection. An educated man benefits the whole society. This is the public good. The individuals also earn more, which is termed as private good. Both the beneficiaries should share the costs. This is the pattern accepted world over. Can we in India not accept it? Government today is gaining additional tax without paying for costs, cent per cent cost is borne by students, which is unethical. Government should have to pay its share. When other countries are spending up to 10% of GDP on education why India can not? Spending on education is wealth generating. Those who understand this will win.

The paper identifies the risk factors and delineates what universities, government, and academics at this juncture of time should do to limit damage and yet make most of privatization.

POSITIVE ASPECTS OF PRIVATIZATION

Wisdom to establish and run an institute of higher education is not the monopoly of government. It is available also in private. India can not forego imaginative ideas, funds available, organization and management capability so abundantly available in private, so as to win in global competition. From 1981, a wave of self finance private institutions has been initiated, and now proposal of private universities is being moved.

Private institutions being relatively thin and lean are quick to respond to opportunities in changing times. They enable people to learn that which is relevant and en cash income and employment chances in global market. Private institutions can afford to take more risks and thereby avail more opportunities. Their rules are flexible, and this is their strength. Privatization of higher education is found to accelerate industrial development, generate employment and income. Governing boards of private institutions are mostly consisting of professionals like lawyers, industrialists, doctors. They can better regulate higher education institutions than legislators in government, who hardly have any orientation, and priority so is the observation world over. Private institutes are nearer the free market, which facilitates them to adapt quickly to changing situations, which leads to effective governance. It is obviously wiser, to use money, energy, talent etc. of private for the public cause of higher education.

It is not a matter of only providing financial resources for higher education. More it is a matter of organization and management capability. If the same amount, for example, as invested by private institutions, was invested by government, for establishment of new institutions, they would certainly not have come up as fast and better as they have. The limiting factor for success, it is realized, is not funds alone but the expertise. India at this juncture of time needs to depend not only on government institutions but to exploit the dormant capacity available in private and without which its economic and social development plans will undoubtedly lag behind. Hence opening of private institutions and universities should whole heartedly be welcomed. This does not mean that all is well with them. Only private institutes do not suffice. Education should not be the monopoly of private. Equally important and essential for competition is the opening of new government institutions. A national policy favorable to both is the need of time.

The one time leading universities of Europe today are falling behind, mainly because they have not adopted privatization. American universities are leading. Nine out of ten world best are form USA. US were the first to adopt to adopt privatization, and hence are ahead. They created competition between public and private institutions and this gave a Phillip.

INVESTMENT IS REWARDING

Governing boards of private institutes are found to be active and more successful in raising funds from alumni and others. They also collect innovative ideas, to orient institutions to scientific management practices. They provide increased access to more number of students of all ages. They successfully raise intellectual capacity of the nation. They are found to give more and better leaders to government, industry and to various walks of life. They have in the past given many inventions and innovations, which have enriched the human civilization. They would now shake up not only the higher education sector but also the national economy. India, so as to fulfill its dream of becoming a global power needs to harvest capacities in private institutions most. The rate of return on investment in higher education is reported to be very high, of the order of 70 to 100%, which very few commercial projects can achieve. More investments India makes in education, more financial returns it can obtain. It is a case fit even for borrowing from international market.

Privatization of higher education in India, since 1981, has delivered good results. Private, self financed institutes have contributed remarkably well to economic and employment growth. For example, in IT sector it is observed to have made a mark on international plane. It has raised the image of India in the world market. In USA almost half the institutions are private.

RISK FACTORS TO BE GUARDED

Privatization is good provided it is planned and regulated well. But when uncontrolled it may harm the society. There are limits [Laxman Resha-in Marathi language] with in which if they remain privatization succeeds. If they go beyond they enter danger zone. The limits need to be borne in mind by all concerned and especially the governing boards, government and academic leaders. They have to guard against the risks at their respective institutions. This is so essential for their survival, and to make most of privatization.

Future of Higher Education At Stake - The Long Term Risk

The supreme court of India in its various rulings time and again, have stated that admissions be made on merit and not on the capacity to pay for. All merit students however may not have money enough to take admission in private institutions. True that education loans have now become available. Yet they are not that easily available. They need guarantors, land, buildings etc. for mortgage, and capacity to repay. Such merit students may be deprived of making a better career they are capable for, and ultimately the institutions will be without brains from poor, and hence the nation stands to lose to that extent. These colleges in turn may become institutes only for the rich, mostly mediocre. Instead of bridging the gap between the rich and poor they are perpetuating to widen. They themselves and the nation at large may in long term become socially unstable. The limits of privatization need to be understood and followed in spirit. Scholarships need be provided to poor meritorious students.

Fees in the self finance colleges in medical and engineering courses have sky rocketed. Institutions are found to admit students on the capacity to pay for, rather than merit. The standard of education in private colleges has been diluted. Private colleges have taken a hold on most of the universities, and have been bending rules to preserve their interests, resulting in dilution of standards. The board sometimes appoints only such professors who would be co-operative. The institutions have turned mediocre. Imagine the plight when students form such institutions get degrees and join professions, and thereby license to practice profession. Would you take your patient to a doctor passed from such an institution? They do not follow the ethics but exploit situations. Institutions would have to guard against this tendency.

NOBLER AIMS THROWN TO WINDS

The motives that inspire professors may be nobler, going far beyond those that animate political and business leaders.

Commerce is irrelevant to learning, discovery and acquisition of knowledge. Nothing from politics or corporate sector can measure the value of research output or determine reliably how valuable is the knowledge. Academic institutions should therefore be meticulous in following the norms and standards of faculty, staff, and infrastructure, laid down by academic authorities like UGC / AICTE. Professionalism should be maintained at all costs.

Management of college has a tendency to appoint experts from corporate sector to economize expenditure and yet improve performance. These experts who do not understand the pulse of academics may try to apply corporate methods. They may identify redundant positions in science departments but this may diminish quality of education and research. So as to really encourage innovation and creativity, you need to have a good deal of slack time. Ways of corporate sector are however neither consistently useful nor wholly irrelevant. This makes problem handling in academics more difficult. Educators must have to use their own judgments to decide how to pursue improvement, and economize. Simple cost benefit analysis will fail. Would you like to admit your son or daughter in an institution where there is no professionalism?

There is a growing influence of business on academics. Interaction between the two for exchange of ideas and experience is essential. Some observed that working of academics for business is beneficial and not at all harmful. While this is true, academics must remain academics and business must remain business. Separate identity of the two is essential. Companies provide funds for research and wish that for competitive reasons the result should not be published. This secrecy is not desirable for a public institution although desirable for company. Institutions should have to prepare the rules, legal frame work, and professional ethics without which they will yield to pressures from companies. Academics should not be required to bow down to business. This in long range is too damaging. Corporate money, it is said would try to subordinate the public aims of research and education to private ends. Governing boards ought to hold academic values even at the cost of lucrative opportunities to earn money, win public trust, and retain the interest of faculty and students. They should create an atmosphere favorable for truth to prevail. Academic institutes by virtue of research and innovation should show the way to industry. They should be like light house for industry. **It should not be the other way round**. Academics and institutes should remain in driver's seat, and not be driven.

ACADEMIC FREEDOM USURPED

Government is asking institutions to speed up innovation, inventions, job creation, and income growth by co-operating more closely with industry. There is a growing demand from society to benefit from academic works and draw rewards from market place. Academics should certainly put academic work to practical use by selling patents, scientific discoveries and earn money. While this is true the ties between the two should be open and follow sunshine laws. They should not be suspicious. Academic institutions private or public both work for the public cause. Academic sanctity should be maintained. Academicians should essentially have academic freedom to publish the findings of their research, so also conduct research they like. These limits should be observed by both the academics and business. Business should not impose a constraint on them.

Academics are expected to play their legitimate role of critic for both the government and industry. They essentially should remain autonomous, for maintaining a healthy national economy. Would good professors like to join as faculty in such on institution where there is no academic freedom?

The sanctity of professorate in private institutions is also likely to be adversely affected. The respect of professors in the eyes of governing board and students is going down. They are treated as simple employees available on payment and not as gurus. Their emotional involvement in education is not tapped. They are not permitted to possess academic freedom. This in ultimate analysis may damage the creativity so badly needed, for a nation to prosper.

It is further observed that government has reduced investment in education and hence students are forced to go to private self finance colleges. Some feel this is a plot of politicians who on one side sit in government, and on the other as chairman of private self finance colleges. Loyalty to education of governing boards in the eyes of public has become doubtful. This is the finding of a study conducted in Maharashtra state in the year 2003. 95% of the respondents from college professors said they have no confidence in the political leaders for the cause of education.

INSTITUTIONS AS BUSINESS CONCERNS LEAD TO CATASTROPHE

Governing boards should primarily be guardians of academic values. They should see to it that academic values are not compromised. Many are afraid that private universities if started will shadow in long run the intellectual and academic culture. Irreplaceable values may get permanently lost in relentless growth of privatization. These are the negative side effects which need to be guarded.

Linking academic research to business, only in a limited manner is good. Opening offices by institutions for commercial sale of patents and technology is good, but within limits. The limits need to be defined and identified in rules of the institutes. Nothing should be at the cost of education. It should only supplement. This however is not an easy job.

Institutions should not become tools in the hands of those who do not realize the value of academics. Academics should not be viewed as business but service to society. It is now time proper, in the face of globalization to revamp higher education. We must accept the challenge, in spite of difficulties and tap opportunities in world market. Academic professors and directors of the institutions should be appointed who bring scholarship to the institutions. Often professors and principals are appointed who are good in raising funds. This is the side effect to be guarded. Business effects are for short term while academic effects are for long term.

Privatization affects the behavior of professors, and officials. The element of social service is being driven out. This may change their character for worse. Self finance institutions are tending to become business concerns instead of moral and intellectual. Privatization leads to surge in money making activity in campus. It stems from the attitude of top management. Education values are likely to be sacrificed. A wrong message is likely to go to younger generation. Are teachers granted role in governance of the institutions?

The institutions in private sector also are accountable to public interest. University or an institution is a means to prepare a brave new India. It is a national asset of very high value. Therefore private colleges should be regulated well. Education has assumed a central role in national development. Are institutions accountable to public interest?

STATUS OF PROFESSOR, THE KEY PLAYER, IN DANGER

Business executives are being appointed on boards of institutions. They are appointed even as chairman. This is welcome with reservations. Many professors in all their humbleness do not appreciate the move. They feel institutions should not be run like General Motors. Principal purpose of institution is academic. They should be run by academicians who are specialized in them and not by administrators, politicians or businessmen. Success is measured in terms of research output and education quality. Cost saving in teaching and researching by those who do not understand the pulse of academics is hazardous, which can do more harm than good.

Long term damage to institution may take place. They may make a business of institutions and academics may be given back seat.

The time and energy of students may be diverted to commercialization and not education. Long term damage for generations is therefore possible and guarding against this happening is of vital importance. Non academic things like campus maintenance, food service etc. may however be better managed by persons from non academic fields. Governing boards may be oriented to changing academic needs in global environment. People at the time of elections have their votes in their hands. They should cast them in favor of those who attach high priority to education, and fund adequately, equal to if not more than defense. What is the value of that governing board which does not win confidence of faculty, staff and students?

Students from bottom half of the population is observed to be late developers, having greater enthusiasm and having a greater drive for higher education. Many of such persons after graduation have grown faster into successful professionals, and leaders in social and community activities. They are observed to become more productive and ease tensions in the society. It is these common students who often do uncommon. The governing boards ought to give consideration to these aspects, give poor and middle class students wider access to private institutions.

4. SUMMING UP

Risk factors involved in privatization of higher education demand a wide scale debate and discussion. This is essential so as to understand the gravity, and keep in check the negative side effects arising out of privatization. The paper has attempted to identify some of them.

Higher education institutions essentially should not go too close either to business or government. It has to have academic freedom to be able to play its legitimate role as critic. It should essentially therefore be autonomous.

The honor and respect of professor, which is the highest post in academics, should be by law, maintained at all cost. The authorities and responsibilities of professor should be written down in university act. This is essential in public interest. It is they and the students who make on institution. Others even chairman, governing board, etc. although important, are ancillary.

We need to appreciate that higher education is public good, besides private.

The two namely public and private beneficiaries must have to share costs in a proper mix. In USA fees paid by students is 31% of the cost of education. Central and state government contribution is 48% as public good; rest is contribution from donations and earnings from technology sale.

We have entered a period of significant change. We must ask two questions to ourselves, whom do we serve? How can we serve better? Certainly the need for higher education will be of increasing importance for masses in knowledge driven future. The current paradigms of teaching, research, and service to society, and of obtaining finances all must change. During change, interests of lower and middle class people should not be forgotten. Without increased access in higher education to down and out people undoubtedly India will remain poorer.

If institutions keep on increasing tuition fees and state does not support financially, as an obligation of public good, one day India will be socially unstable. Instead of becoming a power in the world it will then remain one of the poor most countries. If we stay on our present course, and do not change we are more likely to encounter disaster, in the years ahead.

New paradigms for providing and financing higher education are required for longer term. Shifting the financial burden from previous generation to next allowing the generation proper to bear the burden is one possible solution. Students should take loans today and pay back from their future income. It is like present system of housing loan or car loan. The debt on student will be too big. Assimilation of this will take time. Have the pervious generations paid for establishment of institutions for generation of today? They have paid when the country was poorer. Why now prosperous India can not?

The tuition should not be too low, to mean that tax payers are paying for the rich. We must reestablish our priority, to provide educational opportunity to all, who have the desire and ability to learn. We must sustain these institutions to serve our children and grand children, by abandoning the erosion of government support. Human competency Increases with education, and the government will only be richer if it does so. When other countries are spending 6% to 10% of GDP on education why India can not? **Roots of poverty lie in low level national funding for education.**

While most of our institutions are already trying to change and adapt to a changing world, they are yet far too behind the target. Actually due to privatization the standard is falling down, when the need of knowledge and skills in competitive environment is rising. They must, regardless whether they are private or public, maintain fundamental scholarly commitment and values required for a worthy democratic society. **The key persons should keep in mind the deeper purposes**. Those institutions which show visions, wisdom and courage will lead in years to come. Poor and middle class people are looking with hope to them.

It is hoped that the governing boards and academics that control the institutional performance, will show wisdom to recognize their obligation to community, region and even the world. They should take their duties and responsibilities as a moral vocation, show scholarship in public trust they govern, and provide public service in an exemplary way. They can certainly cover all the risks arising out of privatization, and make it a success.

"The solution of virtually all problems with which government is concerned like housing, poverty, health, education, environment, energy, urban development, international relationships, space, economic competitiveness, defense and national security, all depend on creating new knowledge, producing competent manpower, and hence upon the health of academic institutions."

References

1. A university for twenty first centuries, By James J Duderstadt, The University of Michigan press.
2. The Guardians, Boards of Trustees of American Colleges and Universities, What they do and How Well They Do It, By Clark Kerr And Marion L Gade, Association of college boards of universities and colleges of America.
3. Universities in the market place, the commercialization of Higher Education. By Derek Bok, Princeton University Press, Princeton, New Jersey.
4. The shape of the River, Long term consequences of considering race in college and university admissions, By William G Bowen. And Derek Bok, Princeton university press, Princeton, New Jersey.
5. Elite Colleges increase aid to woo poorest top recruits. By Marcella Bombardieri, published in Boston Globe of July 16 2005.
6. Out Of State Schools on the Move, Boston Globe, of August 28, 205 by Anand Vaishnav.
7. B. M Naik, New Vistas in Technical Education, Book by Vivek publication, 2001.
8. Commission appointed on 19.9.2005 by Secretary Spellings, on Higher Education for America to remain a global economic leader. Serious implications of the ability of millions of Americans to pay for college are to be examined. College affordability is the issue.

5

India Dreams to Build a Knowledge Society

"First we shape our institutions, then for generations they will shape us."

Technology is found from world experience to give winning edge to a nation. Pandit Nehru on the occasion of laying the foundation stone of IIT Mumbai on 10th March 1959 said,

"Technical Institutes are the centers of knowledge and new technology, where future of people is created. They are fountain heads of new technology. They are the places where scientists and engineers needed for the country are created."

The institutes play a crucial role in building India a technology oriented nation. What investment India makes today in education decides the fate of people tomorrow? So as to keep India progressing even in politically turbulent atmosphere, it is essential to redirect national effort and build a strong world class knowledge society, that is to say a technological society. Professors are the knowledge workers, who work in knowledge organizations. It is only they, who by innovative ability can create knowledge society. Professors are like navigators of ship who give direction to industry and human civilization. Their business is to see beyond the immediate and guide. It is expected that they play a leading role, without fear and favor, to build knowledge society, competent by world standard. The vision of India is ambitious. It intends to become a world technological power. Undoubtedly, we all share the dream and also the necessary effort. In this direction, the pertinent question is whether we can afford not to?

How long industry can be run on borrowed technology?

A new principle has emerged from experience in the world that industries can not progress and achieve peak performance all alone by themselves, in isolation from institutes. So also institutes can not. They have to be supportive to each other. Institutes must generate sunrise technologies and industry should use them in production. This combination helps the economy to achieve global competitiveness. It is relatively easy to start and run an industry. But it is more difficult to start and run an institute capable enough to generate, Sunrise Technology on continuing basis. Unless there are world class institutes there can not be world class industries. Time has come to realize that our industry today is faltering in global competitions mainly because it does not get supply of newer technology. We are using foreign brands, like Sony, Toyota. Indian industry, in order to derive "First Mover's Advantage" should involve more in research in partnership with institutes. Industry can not be competitive on borrowed technology, which often is pen-ultimate and costly. Indian academics like in developed countries will have now to propel the industrial development of the country. Do we the academic leaders see this challenge and accept? Does the Government provide favorable environment?

Mediocre Institutes are More Costly than the cost of their up gradation:

World class institutes are found to produce world class manpower and world class technologies. This in ultimate analysis works out cheaper. Mediocre institutes outwardly although look cheaper truly they are not. World Bank report of the year 1999 observed that due to superior technology wealth is flowing from developing countries to developed countries. It has expressed concern how this can be reversed? How brain drain can be converted into brain gain? It is the professors, their academic, competency which matters. India has a potential to become technology leader. However, systems are outmoded, rendering competent people ineffective. They need to be re-engineered in the light of work experience. Due to weak systems the huge Indian market and abundant raw materials so also brains are being utilized by foreign countries.

What are the New Features of Modern Institutes? Shall Institutes Adopt Forward Policies?

The new model proposed here is given in figure below. It will be seen from the figure that the institute is not just for doing routine teaching and irrelevant research. The essential feature is that it conducts multifarious activities in partnership with industry. The institutes have to be innovation and research oriented. They have to generate newer technologies, products and processes by making use of the expertise of professors and brilliant scholar students, The activities are performed by various centers of excellence like (i) Research park, (ii) Product / process innovation center, (iii) Incubator, (iv) Corporate Education Center, (v) Patent and IPR center, (vi) Innovation Relay center, (vii) Entrepreneurship center, (viii) Alumni Foundation, (ix) New technology based firms, (x) Venture capital companies, (xi) Industrial service center / clinic for sick industry, (xii) Test house, (xiii) Technology park, etc. The institutes using this; model does not remain teaching shops. They become "Light Houses."

They attract industries and inject in them new knowledge and new technologies. This brings down the cost of education substantially, and makes it more relevant and purposeful. The

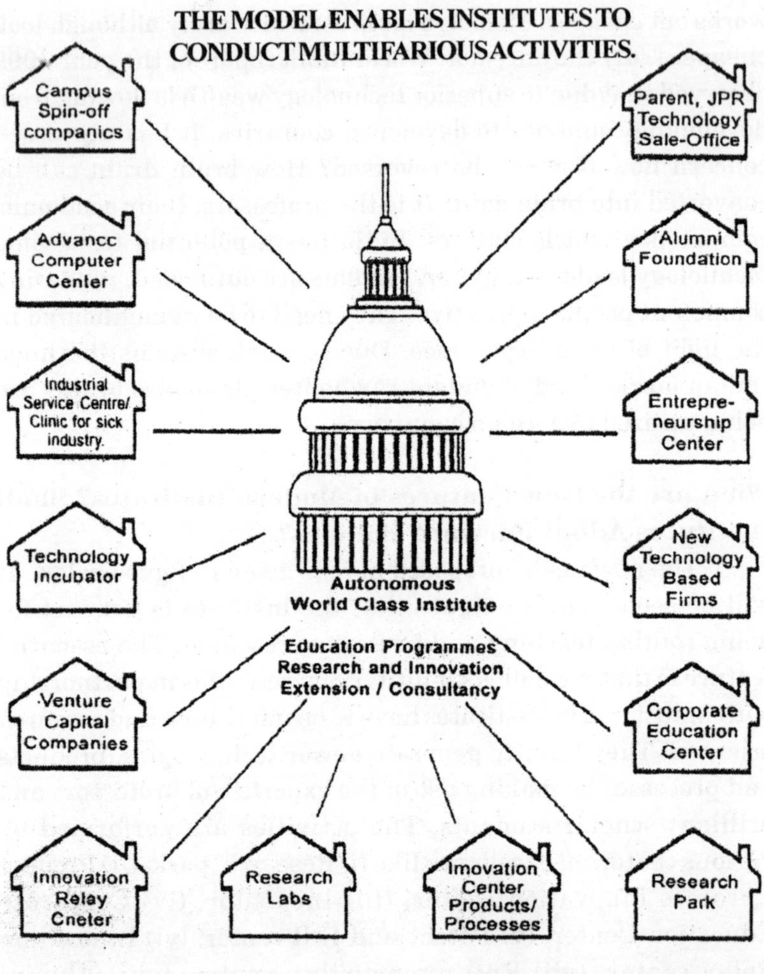

The model makes education more relevant and brings down cost

MODEL OF A MODERN INSTITUTE

counter part institutes in developed countries have been using this model from the last more than 25 years. It is on account of this that they have become more prosperous. The model deserves to be adopted by both the private and Govt. Institutions. Availability of resources for institution building is certainly necessary but having only resources is not enough. They need long range world class visions. The pertinent questions which need to be addressed by the institutes are.

(i) How many patents the institutes obtain every year?

(ii) How many New Technology Based Firms (NTBF), are spin - off every year?

(iii) What is the research out put of a professor every year?

If the research output is nil, it means the professor has been teaching dead, irrelevant, yesterdays' knowledge today.

How many in service engineers are trained by an institute? This is vital for continuous up dating of the economy.

Do the institutes have magnet like force of knowledge to attract companies etc.?

Agenda for Modern Institutes:

They should have both a long range and short range focus. There is wide scale feeling that the scientists in the west should do research, do innovation and when it is tested and proven Indian industry should import. The modern institutes have to work to wipe out this feeling and create confidence that the research and innovation equal to foreigners could be done also in our institutes.

Following are some of the items:

(a) Elevating the quality of education to world class level.

(b) Institutes should produce "Technology Leaders" and not just followers.

(c) An institute should become a "Light House" for industry.

(d) Institutes should generate newer technologies, obtain patents and guide industry for modernization.

(e) They should help industry to increase productivity and make them globally competitive.

(f) They should serve as "Industrial Clinks" to remove sickness.

(g) Help to increase "Technology Absorption."

(h) Uplift the skills of ageing work force.

(i) Install Research Park, Innovation centers, Test house, etc.

Organization Structure for Modern Institutes

Autonomous Institutes or Deemed to be universities alone can facilitate to implement agenda given above. Institutes in developed countries are born autonomous and remain autonomous throughout. There in no affiliated college system with centralized examination, common syllabus; etc. Autonomous system rightfully empowers the professors. Affiliating system is the root cause of trouble promoting coaching class culture in India.

Affiliated college / Polytechnic to a University / Board are like a child born handicapped, who is life long, a source of problem instead of providing solution. Govt. should permit only those colleges to start, which can become autonomous from beginning.

Polytechnics and colleges should attempt to be self reliant instead of becoming puppets in the hands of boards or universities. Unless they do so their energies and capacities will remain imprisoned. They will not be able to become innovative, creating patents, IPR, innovation relay center, etc. The old structure of affiliating type is over centralized, outdated. It needs to be thrown out forthwith. Systems Matter - the poor systems have rendered our competent people ineffective, and opportunities missed. "Autonomous system" increases "Adaptive efficiency", response ability and facilitates creation of knowledge society to harness opportunities in world market.

CONCLUSION

India in this period should focus its attention on building world class knowledge society, that is to say technological society. Universities, colleges and polytechnics matter most in this cause.

They need to re-engineer their visions and missions to carry out multifarious activities. Autonomous institutes / Deemed to be universities enable them to be enterprising. It is the need of the hour to say good bye to old affiliating model and welcome to new autonomous model carrying out multifarious activities, as detailed in this article. This makes education institutes more viable, and competitive, bringing down the cost of education within the reach of masses. This is the only way to empower vast masses with technical skills, knowledge and attitude for employment in modern world. Investment by Government in such projects will pay back 100 times more. Today less viable projects are being funded which for want of competent men become sick. Government, industry and institutes would have to come together and synergies efforts.

6

Continuing Engineering Education (CEE)

"So as to win in competitive world,
It is now necessary to build a
Learning society consisting of learning
Organizations and learning individuals"

UNESCO in its policy paper on "Continuing Engineering Education" has projected high demand on educating engineers not once but again and again in 21st Century requiring the institutions to undertake this activity in all the countries. This has become very essential especially because of the knowledge and technology revolution. Application of new technology in professions and vocations so as to remain competitive globally has become essential. With the increase in population and their rising aspirations "Science and Technology" need to be respected, developed and applied on increasing scale in various walks of life. Innovations in science and technology have to be encouraged and incentives provided to science and technology personnel for their outstanding contributions.

The potential of personnel qualified in science and technology, regardless of the boundaries of the nations, need to be fully explored. Continuing Engineering Education plays an important role in this. Some of the important objectives of C.E.E. as outlined in its policies are -

1. To increase National and World productivity.
2. To use latest science and technology.
3. To avoid sickness of Industries.
4. To respond to international competition.
5. To improve competence of working engineers.
6. To accept challenges and make best use of available opportunities.
7. To keep engineering talent up to date.
8. To promote innovation capacity of engineers.
9. To maintain lifelong competence.
10. Preparing engineers to shoulder responsibilities more ably.
11. Greater job satisfaction.
12. Change of job for betterment.
13. Learning new technologies.
14. Job growth and promotion.
15. Filling gap between formal education and practical industrial needs.
16. To avoid obsolescence – ensuring employability.

Not only machines become obsolete but men also. With this logic budget is being earmarked by UNESCO for undertaking C.E.E. Programs all over the World. Project proposals are invited time and again from various countries, which are scrutinized and funded. An International Association of C.E.E. with the objective of providing Continuing Engineering Education World over has been constituted with the head quarter in Helsinki (Finland). Activity of CEE is highest in Finland. On line education using internet is very popular. MIT has developed soft ware and being offered free of cost all over the world. One can obtain a degree by distance mode without visiting university. Almost everybody every year undergoes retraining. The situation in various countries is as under.

UNITED STATES OF AMERICA (U.S.A.)

In U.S.A. "Continuing Engineering Education" is quite an old hat. It is offered by many professional societies. It is also offered by universities, most of whom have opened special departments exclusively for C.E.E. About 30% students in universities are C.E.E. students. C.E.E. is being further strengthened to maintain and develop superiority and competitiveness of United State Industry in the world.

The need of Continuing Engineering Education is perceived by the engineers for their own growth, so also for the growth of their employing organizations. Universities find it a rewarding experience to run C.E.E. courses for they generate income besides obtaining interaction with industry.

There is a committee appointed by Government to look into lifelong education. On its recommendation Government have established accreditation Board to control quality of C.E.E... It is realized that the C.E.E. is very useful to increase National Productivity and develop intellectual resources. This ensures better prospects and keeps the people happy on jobs.

University of Texas, Madison and several others have setup, CC TV Uplink Antenna, Networking, Interactive video disks, PCs, Computer Aided instruction etc. Cable Television, Microwave transmissions for C.E.E. is very important. Engineering schools are widening their scope and working for professions besides teaching to students. They are now aiming at developing learning individuals and a continuously learning society, which is believed to be crucial for welfare of human kind.

CHINA

In China the concept of "Continuing Engineering Education" was introduced from abroad around 1970. So far C.E.E. has played an important role in improving the performance of industries, as well as adaptation of imported technologies. Experience demonstrates that C.E.E. in China has played a key role in economic development.

It has been the policy of Government to promote C.E.E and have established many Institutes exclusively for the purpose. Every Ministry has formulated plans and programs to train engineers. At the enterprise and institute level, plans have also been made for identification of objectives, contents, requirements, and adopting scientific measures for Continuing Engineering Education.

In 1981, Government made it a rule that each Science and Technology person must receive minimum one month training in 12 months period. It has now become a pre-requisite for promotion of professionals. C.E.E. in China is both a right and obligation of Science and Technology personnel. It is a constituent part of development plan of the department, and expenses incurred are regarded as production cost.

Various professional associations have also played important promotional role for ex. China Association of Science and Technology (CAST), China Association of C.E.E. (CACEE). It arranged International level Continuing Engineering Education programs for top executives, especially in Collaboration with UNESCO.

They have prepared a grand master plan using satellite TV, Audio, Video, PCs, etc. for Continuing Engineering Education.

The two major difficulties they experience are –

(a) Shortage of good Professors having state of the art knowledge,

(b) Education material.

Professors are invited from abroad, so also the education material to make up the shortages.

China is considering making a law on Continuing Engineering Education so that the large organizations pay for themselves and Government to pay for small organizations.

Quality teaching material constitutes the basic guarantee for the success of C.E.E. is their experience.

WEST INDIES

They lay more emphasis on use of satellite of Continuing Engineering Education. University of West Indies is using satellite from 1978 to cater to 14 territories. They regularly arrange interactive video conferences, symposia via satellite. Faculty of engineering of the University has played a pivotal role in establishing the centre.

Traditional methods of C.E.E. have many limitations. The same are overcome in this method. However, there is a inherent danger in this method viz. of lack of quality control on education. By careful planning errors can be kept to minimum if not eliminated. These methods are more cost effective. It requires a sound organization and good faculty to prepare lessons.

Satellite has a large impact on education, with satellite telecommunications; one will be able to attend international conferences at one's own place. It is very inexpensive method, and is making a beginning of a new era in education. Potential is being exploited on priority basis to extend it to wider areas.

In Japan, "Continuing Engineering Education" enjoys not only support from top management but also leadership and active participation in the conduct of programs. They believe that employing people without education and training is a mistake on the part of management. Employee Education starts with the start of an organization. They consciously attempt to develop self supporting and challenging individuals with the ability to cope with the changing environment by self initiative and self learning. In many companies the basic philosophy is, "company is only as good as its people." The foundation for company development lies in development of its people, such that they work with joy and pride.

The training consists of modules such as Administrative, Economic Political and Technological systems. Emphasis is laid on hi-tech as Computers, Microprocessors, and robotics. Universities and associations of industries take a leading role in imparting Continuing Engineering Education.

It is a firm contention that Continuing Engineering Education ought to be connected with technological innovation and research. A University or Engineering School can be effective in C.E.E., if it has a faculty group that keeps pace with the rate of technological development. Continuing Engineering Education is not an additional burden on colleges. It is instead an important factor to bring about self development and reform in education. The interaction opens up new areas for research and raises the level of teaching and scientific research. Continuing Engineering Education helps teachers to convert their knowledge into productive force, and raise their influence over the profession. From the society and nation point of view it provides a chance to theory to influence practice, which is so essential to advance the professional practices. CEE is found to be a enriching experience.

The most vital task in this is the development of R&D manpower. After development with so much effort it is likely to be underutilized, which is a serious concern.

An observation in Korea is that 83% of PhDs work in Universities having access to only 10% of resources and 10% of PhDs in industry having access to 80% resources. Academic and R&D manpower is grossly underutilized in Korea. Continuing Engineering Education has resulted in Korea to form ambitious plans for industrialization, and continuous dialogue between industry and institutes. Furthering of C.E.E. demands a passion on the part of teachers to teach and rewards to those who received C.E.E Without incentives C.E.E. becomes difficult.

In many Countries like China, USA etc. satellite is found to have a large impact on education. Automation in education is the new trend in which Computer Aided Teaching (CAT) occupies a prominent place. The new technological development requires new advanced methods of transferring education.

In many socialistic countries like USSR, Poland C.E.E. is considered both an obligation and right of an employee. An employee must undergo C.E.E. when deputed. When not deputed he can as a matter of right ask for opportunities for education.

In Germany, "Continuing Engineering Education" is considered to be an investment and insurance for better future. It is believed that the College or University Education can only react to fundamental new developments with a time lag. Usually several years elapse between introduction of new technologies and their inclusion in curriculum of teaching institutes. The aim of engineering course is to produce graduates fit for employment not that they are necessarily fully trained. Introduction of advanced technologies in industry demand C.E.E. for qualified employees. It is the contention that, at present the greatest barrier to the implementation of technological innovations is the lack of qualified employees. In other words, organizations do not find suitably qualified personnel on the labor market and pressure of time hardly allows them to train. In future, the updating of qualifications must be one of the factors taken into consideration when planning the introduction of new technologies.

Big Companies in Germany spend on education of their employees. While with the small companies such measures go unrecognized or are undervalued. Their experience is that company run courses are more effective. They have high standard, and are practice oriented. New technologies create new needs of C.E.E. is well recognized in Germany. It is possible to learn in a course new things which would take perhaps years to learn on the job. They teach to forget the traditional ways of thinking and promote new ways which are untried as yet.

Continuing Engineering Education of Engineering Teachers stands as foremost in developing Countries like India and that international exchange of professors and support from UNESCO in the form of fellowship needs to be increased. In the absence of well competent Professors in Engineering Colleges, not only the students remain inadequately educated but the whole engineering society tends to remain less competitive by global standard C.E.E. tends to remain less effective. The efforts being made to train teachers under ISTE and QIP programs are very well appreciated. In conclusion, in India it is necessary to build partnership between Institutes of Technical education and Industry for the overall growth of both of them. Technologies employed in PWD, MSEB, State Transport Corporation and other State and Private Industries is requiring modernization urgently. A scheme must therefore specially be drawn out to open C.E.E. Departments in every Engineering College. A seminar or meeting of key persons of our department and industries may be organized to welcome the innovative ideas for implementation of C.E.E. Success depends upon how eager industries are to depute people for training and secondly on how competent professors are to impart training.

The New Education Policy of the Government of India (1986) and NKC 2006 have also emphasized the need of starting "Continuing Engineering Education" centers to begin with in selected colleges. They have recommended establishment of Regional Resource Development Centers for "Continuing Engineering Education" to develop learning resources, which would keep linkages with Indira Gandhi Open University, New Delhi. Advisory Committees for each cluster or sector of Industry are also proposed.

KEY TO COMPETITIVENESS

After globalization and WTO, there is an influx of goods, in India from east west countries especially China. Foreign goods are being sold at almost half the price. This has puzzled Indian industry, which now is questioning, how can they afford?

Indian Industry captains are re-engineering their industries to improve competitiveness. They are engaged in SWOT analysis, and keen on using modern management practices to improve productivity. They are doing Benchmarking with the best in the world to find out how their productivity has become high and why our productivity is low? Indian labour is intelligent, skilful and as cheap as anywhere. Then how come they cannot produce and sell as cheap as others?

SOLUTIONS TO COMPETITIVENESS PROBLEM

Lifelong education-Non stop

If we make a search for answers to the above questions, we come to a conclusion that there are many reasons. But the important one is that in those countries the employers are giving not only good salaries to engineers but over and above they are giving best professional training on continuing basis and facilitating them to grow and remain competent lifelong. They now do not guarantee jobs, but **they guarantee opportunities for learning and growing to the level they are capable for. This indirectly ensures not only jobs but also further rise and keeps industry productive and progressive.**

Joy of work

They have designed the organizations and jobs scientifically such that employees get joy in working and joy in learning. It is mainly on account of joyful lifelong learning that their industry is more competitive. Around 5% of their budget is earmarked for training of in service personnel. On the other hand how many of Indian employers care for training of their engineers? How many industries big and small earmark budget for training? How many of the engineers receive training every year? Only 5% Indian engineers get training as against 100% in those countries. We have almost no culture of learning lifelong. Our employers are still in old mental setup that **engineers are paid for working and not for learning**. Industry should realize now that although imparting training to employees is costly, time consuming, taking them away from jobs, but not imparting training leads to loss of competitiveness, sickness, and even closure. Days are such that giving only salaries to engineers, is not enough? It is essential to impart training to do the jobs productively today and also tomorrow. Employees appreciate the employers who help them to grow on jobs. If companies look to the interests of employees, look beyond and enable them to become fit for tomorrow, industries will not find sorrow at hand. The invisible loss due to not training is very large. It is reported that Rate of Return on investment in CEE is one of the highest. Unless we change our mind set for training, our industry is less likely to become competitive.

There is a story of a woodcutter who was cutting the branch of a tree with an axe from morning to evening, for several days. One day, a person passing by asked the woodcutter to show the axe. The axe was blunt. He advised the woodcutter to go in town and get the axe sharpened. The woodcutter said, I understand this, but my master says, if I go for sharpening the axe who will do wood cutting?" The situation is something like this in the industry. People are busy in work and have no time to learn. Consequently, they are working with outdated less-productive knowledge and skills. The tremendous loss of competitiveness due to absence of CEE is not realized by key people.

Case Examples

Motorola Company observed that one - dollar investment in training produces 30 dollars in three years. 60% of productivity gains are realized from the training. Bill Gates in his book "Business at the speed of thought" wrote that 60% assets in developing countries are underutilized because of lack of training. People need to sharpen job skills, knowledge and attitude. New projects are created on one hand at high cost and on the other hand they remain underutilized, after commissioning in both private and public sectors, due to lack of training. The capacity utilization is only 60%. If 40% idle capacity is brought to use it is as good as 40% capacity created. Is this not a colossal wastage? This is due to lack of training. It is much cheaper to train people to use installed capacities of projects than to build new projects. Industry ought now to realize the value of training for their survival and growth. The following figure further explains the point.

CONCLUSIONS

1. India's ability to compete in competitive environment will depend on the competence of the work force.
2. Many jobs will change or go out of market requiring employees to relearn new skills, acquire new knowledge and even change attitude. CEE keeps them competent for changing situations.
3. Governments have to realize that they must provide the resources for lifelong learning. If this is left to industry, short-term profit considerations will dominate and preparation for the future will remain inadequate. Hence Government role in CEE is important.
4. Companies in India have realized that the current training facilities are not sufficient to maintain core competencies and increase competitiveness. They are seeking new approaches. But they do not find institutes to help them.
5. University education today does not meet the needs of industry. They will have to build contacts with industry, and become customer focused. They would have to start "Corporate Education enters is partnership with industry."
6. The knowledge explosion and the low rank of India in competitiveness are adversely affecting, the job prospects of youths. CEE enlarges job generation and prepares people to discharge their duties and responsibilities ably.
7. Engineers do seek continuing education in self-interest at their own cost, time and energy. Mid-career education and mid-career changes in jobs have become common. They need recognized degree in world employment market. Is it available?
8. Industry and education institutes would have to come together to maximize performance. They should have common programs and common goals. CEE is good in institutes where the professors pursue research and consultancy. Industry persons attend courses of such innovative persons to learn new things they might have discovered.

9. Changes in education technology to increase productivity must be implemented.
10. There can be a tremendous possible gain in competitiveness in India, if CEE is given the required boost. The key people are yet insufficiently aware of the need and importance. As and when they wake up, to the national call for continuing engineering education the economy will improve. It is high time that CEE centres are installed to educate 100% of the work force every year. The costs are much less than the gains. If CEE is efficiently conducted and made obligatory to employers and employees, like in china everyone will become an asset. There will be no surplus labour and the pains of retrenchment or VRS can be avoided.
11. Countries like Finland, USA, France, china, etc. through CEE have created a knowledge society and are winning in the world. This is the only way for India to succeed.
12. Govt. of India should make it a national agenda to educate every one-life long-nonstop-for better future and earmark sumptuous budget for the same.

"They know enough-Who know How to learn"

Education before employment and education after employment should be the routine practice

7

Management Education for Inservice Engineers

Countries are Underdeveloped Because They are Undermanaged

This article outlines in brief the objectives of management education for in service engineers, especially in the context of dynamic economy, fast changing technology and high degree of political interference. It analyses the existing system of management education in India and points out its inadequacies. Reforms are suggested to be able to achieve the desired objective

Science and technology is advancing at a much faster rate than at any previous time. There has been a mushrooming of scientific findings in the last two decades, and new dimensions to professional and management skills have become open. As a consequence, demands made on engineering personnel, especially because of the launching of five-year plans, have greatly changed. The development plans, programs and projects are characterized by super size, complexity, uncertainties, new technology, and involvement of multiple agencies, besides, frequent political interference in their implementation. However, the engineering personnel in charge of these are often not equipped in terms of the necessary managerial skills. As a result, the physical and financial resources are not optimally utilized and hence full value of their potential benefits does not become available for human welfare.

The existing system of management education is inadequate in terms of both quality and quantity. Management education is a decisive factor for economic, social and technological development of a country. It is therefore of vital importance to review the existing system and tailor it to suit the requirements of today and possibly those of tomorrow.

OBJECTIVES OF ENGINEERING PROFESSION

Engineering profession has certain obligations to the society-continuing services to improve the living and working conditions devising ways and means to effect savings in efforts and materials, safety to society, etc. The forefronts of basic sciences are continually advancing and opening new areas for engineering endeavor. An engineer has to be alert to assimilate and translate advances in science into engineering practice. Thus, engineering is far from static and is essentially a creative profession.

However, accomplishing this with only technological capability without possessing necessary management skills is a difficult task. There are a large number of obstacles of social, cultural and political nature which present serious problems. These are experienced right from policy level up to day-to-day working. An engineer, therefore, has to have capability to negotiate and get along well with them, use them in favor if possible, avoid if not, and find way through a hurdle race. Rising, capabilities of engineering personnel to tackle the situations, and to make most of the national resources for the welfare of the people, is the present need. Management education for in service engineers has therefore to prepare men to be fully competent to do the professional practice without fear, frustration and failure. Further, engineering and management education should inspire every engineer with necessary spirit to enable him to deal with new situations on his own initiative and confidence. He should develop a desire and sense of involvement for taking an active part in changing things in the profession. In India, organizations are undergoing drastic changes. New organization structures, relationships, delegation of authority, responsibility, in view of ambitious development plans are being formed. This can take a proper shape only if engineering executives are thinking in terms of shaping them rightly rather than merely accepting what is offered. An in service engineer has, therefore, to be able to identify himself in the context of changing society, organization, economy, technology and play an active role. Further, he should be able to think of a right approach to attack, evaluate and test the results at each stage.

WHY MANAGEMENT EDUCATION?

It is said, 'India is a rich country, but inhabitated by poor people'. India is rich in terms of natural resources like land, water, minerals, etc. but their utilization is poor. Although India has the third largest technical manpower, because of the fact of the management capability it remains one of the less developed countries. We have been spending large sums of money on establishing projects like irrigation, power, dairy, etc. However, largely due to inefficient management they are not coming up as they should. They suffer from delays and cost overruns. The break-even point gets prolonged so much so that at times it becomes out of sight and goes beyond the maximum production capacity. As a result even before the project is commissioned, it becomes 'non-starter' and sick. In India, about 20% of the sick industries are reported to be in this category.

Often the payback period gets prolonged. Before a project has paid back its capital investment due to fast changing technology, it becomes obsolete and is rendered sick. About 20% of sick industries are reported to belong to this category. Poor management is seen also in production and operation stages. As a result utilization of the already installed capacity in industries, land and water of irrigation projects, etc. is very low. Due to variety of reasons in manufacturing industry, capacity utilization is reported to be only 74.4%, whereas in agro based industries it is hardly 42%. In the other hand, capacity utilization of the multinational organizations operating in India, in the same environment, is more than 100%. The only point of difference between the multinationals and the Indian companies is management competency. On account of management deficiencies, Indian industries have been working with almost outdated machinery, retaining large inventories, inefficient manpower and adopting inefficient systems and procedures. Most of the technical personnel, who are holding managerial positions today, have picked up management knowledge only by observation. Very few of them had a systematic education in management science. As a result, no wonder they operate at less efficiency than what they are capable of. The loss due to not educating engineering personnel in management, therefore, is very high. If it is done properly it is found to increase the effectiveness of the application of technology facilitating rapid spread of the research findings to the remote rural areas. If the benefits of technology are to be carried to common man swiftly, an engineer needs to be trained properly to manage the same. Above all management education is essential to enable an engineer to make most of his potential abilities.

EXISTING SYSTEM AND ITS DEFICIENCIES

Management education in India is of relatively recent origin. It received impetus in the sixties when the management institutes at Calcutta and Ahmedabad were set up. When the products of these institutes were well received, many universities followed by opening management departments, offering courses in business administration. Because of popular demand, some of them have started part-time courses for serving people. One interesting feature is that most of the students studying management are having engineering background.

The Government of India has also been conducting since 1976, a large number of management development programs for officers in Government and public sector corporations. This is with a view to induct new management knowledge for improvement of performance of public sector. National Productivity Council has been conducting similar courses for private sectors. Besides, many organizations have their own in company training programs.

In spite of all these ongoing efforts it is found that the training facility, both quality wise and quantity wise, is very inadequate. The national level seminars and symposia held recently have recommended that there is an urgent need for upgrading the training effort.

One common deficiency observed in the MBA programs of universities and management institutes is that the courses represent borrowed models from the developed countries and as a result, there is a lack of fit. They are oriented more to industrial enterprises and profit making organizations whereas, in a developing country like India, these courses ought, in addition, cater to agricultural and rural developments. The social, cultural, economic and political factors are the crucial variables to be attended to by the development and managers and administrators. The management courses are highly deficient in these subjects. Therefore, although large sums of money and effort are spent, yet there is much scope to improve. The various elements of the system such as training institutes, faculty, physical facilities, training material, training needs and above all organizational environment need examination.

Sometimes short term training programs are cancelled for want of participants. Sometimes irrelevant courses are offered. Faculty of required subject and level is not available because the pay structure is poor. Some feel that receiving training is of no use, because what is taught is too theoretical and due to political vested interests it cannot be practiced. As as result, organizations consider it a waste of time and do not depute their people for training. Some programs are held in five star hotels, and the universities, the seats of learning, sit silent.

REFORMS NEEDED

Employers and employees in India by and large are not yet sold to the idea of lifelong education. The walls between learning and working still hold tight. Therefore, more effort and incentives are needed in both private and public sectors to make the concept of continuing education more popular and acceptable. Since developing management capabilities of engineering personnel is important from national point of view, it should be made obligatory to the employers to provide enough of the opportunities to their employees especially in young age, to continue education and to develop to the level they can. This means that employers should draw out a plan for the development of personnel. Persons need to be deputed liberally at national and international levels to attend the programs which may be offered in modules, such as, finance, personnel, operations research, material, marketing, etc. Government should encourage this by providing some financial incentives like rebate in income tax, etc. Employers in turn should grant special benefits to those who attend and acquire proficiency, pass examinations and publish articles. Maharashtra State Electricity Board, a public sector undertaking with a view to develop professional culture, grants advanced increments to those who pass MBA examinations. This trend should, however, multiply. Simultaneously, need is felt to improve the quality of management education suited to the needs of the country. In developing countries like India, MBA programs and other short-term management courses, unlike the similar courses in developed countries, should lay emphasis apart from profitability, on social and economic developments. The focus of management courses ought to shift from maximization of profit to maximization of human welfare. In the pursuit of profit, unscrupulous entrepreneurs otherwise do harm to the society by rendering the industries sick.

Participation of political and social leaders in the organization of the programs is likely to improve the position. Since, political interference in developing countries is increasing, introducing this new trend could be given a fair trial. Improvement in the working of institutions offering such courses naturally follows. Then only they will be able to attract the professionals for training and continue to do so. Good faculty members are the first prerequisite. In the absence of proper scales, however, it becomes very difficult to retain them. Facilities for faculty development by way of exchange programs between the countries are found to be rewarding. It is practiced in some institutions. There is, however, a greater need to enlarge these.

Engineering colleges, professional institutes like the Institution of Engineers (India) and universities need to equip themselves to open continuing education centers and extend to professionals their physical and academic base. A look at the structural formulation and functioning of universities and colleges is, it is felt, urgently necessary. The University of Roorkee and a few Institutes of technology have set up such centers and their experience is encouraging. A determined effort on the part of the Government is necessary to transplant this culture of continuing education in rest of the institutes.

CONCLUSION

In this era of dynamic economy, fast changing technology and high degree of political interference. Management education for in service engineers should be taken up on a large scale and it should reach the level of intellectual self-reliance to enable them to face bravely and resourcefully all kinds of professional situations without fear, frustration and failure. To be able to achieve this goal, management education has to be on a continuing basis. Government and other organizations must provide for and other organizations must provide for and create a climate favorable for lifelong learning to take place. Universities and engineering colleges must open continuing education centers, laying emphasis on rural development. Maximization of human welfare and not profit should become the goal of management education.

Take Away My Factories, Take Away My Equipment And Money, But Leave Me With My Men And I Wil Have All That Back In No Time

8

Training and Development of Professors New Approaches

Real Assets of A College Go Home Every Day At Night

The article makes an introspection of training and development effort for professors in India, and brings out the shortcomings therein. It is argued that the conventional objectives and methodologies of training and development because of the present day high velocity and competitive environment do not suffice and they need to be urgently revised. Besides teaching, professor is required now to initiate a change in industry by application of newer technologies.

The legitimate demand of engineering professors, like in any other country, is therefore to lead in technology and not merely to follow. Questions are therefore raised, whether our professors, by and large are capable of doing that? Do they have technological capability at par with their counterparts in developed countries like U.S.A., U.K. etc.? If not, should it be attempted? Can the economy and industry of India ever go with the developed world as is eagerly desired, without comparable standards of professors? Suggestions are made so as to rectify the deficiencies.

The potentials of engineering teachers / professors are said to be high, which for want of proper training and exposure to global competition remain untapped and even underutilized. Consequently, the technical education imparted to students in spite of huge effort, time and money spent is not only inadequate, but is also misdirected. No wonder, if the promise from Indian engineers and industry is also not fulfilled and available opportunities in international and domestic market missed.

A professor assumes the role of a kingpin in the process of techno-economic development. If he falls short of the requirements, the whole system of education and economy get damaged. The productivity of engineering education, returns from physical and financial resources allotted to laboratories, buildings, library, industry etc. for want of proper opportunities of development of professors remain low. Countries like Hongkong, China, Japan which have achieved high economic growth have invested in education and educators greatly.

The input required for training of educators as compared to capital investment in buildings, equipments etc. is far too low while the value addition because of high multiplying factor is too great. It is therefore argued that we have to learn to invest more in development of our educators.

Training and development of a professor is not only the training of an individual to teach technical subject in a narrow sense but it is much beyond that. It is more helping him to develop professional practices to raise them successively newer heights. An engineering professor has rightfully to be a leader in technology and not merely a follower. Engineering professors in our institutes therefore, be allowed, encouraged and helped to enable them to grow to the level of their counterparts in developed world. This has to be the revised target of training and development of our present day professors. What is the role of Government, Institutions and professors themselves is analyzed in the following.

ESSENTIALS OF A PROFESSOR

A professor is an engineering college/university worthy of the post is expected to lay an impact on the practicing professionals. He ought to be involved in teaching and research. Indian universities so far have neglected and have become only teaching bodies, which is damaging so remarked Prof.S. Chandrashekar Nobel Laureate during his visit to India in 1984. He said professor should also be able to connect his research with industry and to market it.

Technical knowledge is now the real capital, and latest of it ought to be possessed by a professor. He must also have attitude and ability to apply his knowledge for regional development and welfare of the community.

Previously, the technical institutes were on the periphery of the process of development. Now they have come to its centre. They are the major source of technical knowledge to improve productivity, 85% of National economic growth of U.S.A. and 88% of the employment generation is attributed to technological innovation. As and when waves of technology like steam engine, diesel engine, computer, and internet came up economy and employment generation grew fast. The worthy professors are now termed as engines of growth. They are the generators for innovative ideas. The demands on the engineering professors are

(a) To impart professional education to vast masses, economically and effectively.

(b) To be a leader in emerging technologies. About 40% of the students in U.S.A. are mid career students while with us they are only 0.05%.

(c) To provide new commercial ideas and technical talent to industry.

(d) To help to develop new industries and generate new jobs which are badly needed.

(e) To provide techno-economic information and advice to various development agencies.

(f) To participate actively in modernization of industry and import/export of technology.

(g) To obtain patents and IPR

(h) To love students like sons and daughters

He should sign a **Socratic Oath**; draft could be as under [From a university in USA]

I hereby devote myself to the advancement and extension of knowledge, recognizing that I have an obligation to my students, to my discipline, to my professional colleagues, to my university, and to the public.

I embark on teaching as a moral vocation. I recognize research and scholarship as a public trust and accept professional service as a social obligation. In pursuing my responsibilities, I will devote to both teaching and research the same sustained, imaginative, and rigorous attention. I will pursue new knowledge and creative activities in a scrupulous manner that befits the highest professional standard in my field. And I will play my full part in service to the larger community. In undertaking these tasks I recognize that teaching, research and public service are the fundamental responsibilities of every faculty member of the university, that they are responsibilities that must be continuously balanced, and that while they are responsibilities of comparable importance, teaching lies at the heart of the mission of the university. Towards this end, I will accept the trust that the transmission of knowledge implies so that accuracy, fairness, balance and integrity are exemplified in the way my subject is presented and arguments are handled. I will present my subject, whatever it may be, with rigor, but also in a liberal spirit, "illustrating the general within the particular" with a breadth of outlook and a humane concern for its foundations, contexts, relationships and implications.

I will respect the relationship between professor and student, in both personal and intellectual terms, so that hucksterism or improper advocacy is as unthinkable as abuse or harassment. I will be scrupulous in preparation for class, laboratory discussion, or other exercises and supervise the same scrupulous preparation, any student teaching assistants who might assist me. I will be objective, rigorous, and fair in student evaluation, and I will be available for student conferences, office hours, laboratory sessions, and other formal contacts outside the lecture room.

Finally I will participate in the life of the university community, cooperating with my colleagues in educational endeavors and participating in campus wide activities. And, as I develop in my own career, I will encourage, help and mentor my colleagues, especially those newly appointed, to become effective teachers and successful scholars.

This vow, which I freely take, I will keep, recognizing that the privilege of academic freedom that is entrusted to me carries with it the obligation of professional responsibility to honor and serve my students, my discipline, my profession my colleagues, my university and the larger society.

The administration of oath should be a public ceremony, a formal inaugural event held at the beginning of semester. All those who are already professors, the rest of the faculty should recommit themselves to this pledge. This will elevate teaching standards. It will rekindle community.

Essentials of a Principal

The Principal has to be a good professor, leader, a magnificent speaker, a good writer, a good public relations officer, a man of iron health and stamina, married to a virtuous wife. He should have spiritual qualities. He should be good in administration delegating adequately to others. He should be a great scholar, a social philosopher mobilizing public opinion. He should be a friend of a common man. He should bear in mind that future leaders of the world are sitting in class rooms, and then make human decisions. He has to frame the institution mission, goals. Everything else will depend on mission and goals. He should not think in smaller terms but make great dreams. He should remember that there can be no great creations without a great dream. He should be able to articulate the visions. He should be successful in creating the campus climate, recruiting the team, and providing resources to achieve the set goals. He should set an atmosphere of trust and confidence, take initiative, and build partnerships. He should reward achievement and reward success. At times he should take risk to break rules, if not in tune with time. He should meet students, faculty, alumni, and everyone in campus He creates leaders who will carry human civilization to greater heights. He should have high level commitment. He should be able to charge the people working with him with mental energy, ideas and give winning strategies. He should be fund raising and friend rising. He has to lead every activity in the campus.

ROLE OF GOVERNMENT AND PRESENT STATUS OF TRAINING AND DEVELOPMENT

Government pervades modern society. It has always been central to the process of development in general and industrialization in particular. Preparation of infrastructure for technical manpower is crucial amongst its responsibilities. It has obligations to develop the engineering educators matching with its industrialization plans. A balanced investment has to be made in technological education and physical assets of industry. Recognizing the importance of faculty development Government is running following schemes.

(i) Quality Improvement Programs (QIP)

These are in service programs formulated for upgrading the quality of personnel in engineering colleges. The programs are covering regular M.Tech. & Ph.D. courses. Institutes like I.I.T.'s N.I.T.'s and some well performing engineering colleges are offering courses under QIP programs.

(ii) Indian Society of Technical Education (ISTE) Programs

With an objective of advancing the cause of technical education of various levels (namely degree, diploma etc.) the ISTE sponsors short term courses, conferences, seminars and symposia in the area of engineering education, methodology, subjects, curricula and management of technical education. This is a major activity for up gradation of teaching skills.

(iii) Programs Sponsored by Professional Societies

There are a large number of professional societies in various disciplines of engineering and technologies. Institution of Engineers (INDIA), National Productivity Council, and Computer Society of India are leading amongst them.

(iv) Short Comings

The major short comings are as under

(a) Exposure to International Scenario

The various courses conducted by ISTE and other professional organizations are good. But they do not expose professors to training in developed countries like U.K., U.S.A., Japan, etc. As a result the professor in our country does not know the role played by his counterpart in other countries. They lack international perspectives.

Any amount of lecturing in this respect is not a substitute for going abroad. They would be much more motivated, if they are exposed to global scenario.

Professors are best developed, if they are allowed to rub shoulders with collaborators from foreign countries. There are thousands of foreign collaborators in India. Most of the deals are signed by administrators. There is hardly any transfer of technology through these deals. Only import of equipment takes place. The training component in these deals is not utilized to the full extent. The Indian companies are reported to be interested, by and large in only profit, production and not in technology. Conscious efforts need therefore be made by Government to involve professors in the import of technology. This will provide them an opportunity to develop to world standards.

(b) Lack of research grants and marketing orientation:

Experience in the world tells us that, researching is the best method of learning, which unfortunately due to lack of research grants from Government is not available to most of the teachers in engineering colleges. As a result the professor's growth is stifled and crippled.

Most of the research grants are presently given by Government to CSIR labs, where the research is done mostly by Science graduates.

Some professors who do research, often it remains in laboratories and journals. It takes a long lead time, if at all, to reach to industry. Structural organizations of marketing are absent.

The budget of the year 2010-11 has prescribed 175% of R&D expenditure as expenditure exempt from income tax. This is welcome step. It is now hoped that many companies will resort to increased funding for R&D.

(c) Lack of programs to promote skills for Book writing and video film making:

Most of the books in engineering subjects are imported. Very few books are written by Indian authors. It is a high time that our professors are provided facilities to develop skills of book writing, video film making. It is not only for saving foreign exchange, but it is more for need based books and developing capability.

There is a beautiful scope to export books to less developed countries, and these opportunities are also lost for want of in ability of our professors. If they cannot write books, cannot publish articles, it means that by world standard they are small and need to be developed. Our publications are one tenth of China and one hundredth of USA.

(d) Lack of Seminars

The training courses are effective for Junior Teachers but for senior teachers seminars are found to be more effective. Such research seminars be specially arranged in every branch of engineering so that competition and excellence could be promoted. However, the grants required for organization/ seminars are not available, as a result development of professors is not proper.

(e) Leadership Courses:

There are no schemes to prepare good principals, directors, and world class leader administrators. Academic leadership at state, centre and university levels is too week.

CONCLUSION

Government is ambitious to build India a technology oriented nation. Professors, who are the legitimate agents to carry the torch of Science & Technology, have a crucial role to play. They have to show the path of livelihood and prosperity to younger generation. Development of professors such that they become world class leaders in technology and not remain followers is the crying need of the hour. Internationalism and global competitiveness have therefore to be the new aims on agenda.

A long range plan for orientation of professors to hi-tech and deputation to developed countries would have to be urgently prepared and necessary budget allocated by both state and central government on priority basis.

Research projects and funds there-off need to be granted by Government on much larger scale. They ought to be involved in selection, adoption and transfer of technology from foreign countries. Technology parks like in U.K./U.S.A. be established to harness and develop their innovative capacities. Professors must further be oriented to market their research. Deliberate attempts by Government would have to be made to appoint them on Board of Directors and as advisors to industry. Mobility of professors to various laboratories, industrial organizations and to newer colleges in the larger interest be promoted and service rules regulations modified by Government to accommodate such changes.

The engineering professors have not been involved in the process of research. They are not involved in national and state development plans as they ought to be. They are thereby deprived of a legitimate role, by administrators in Government. Lack of opportunities for development has crippled their power of innovation. This however, is ultimately at the cost of public good.

Development of professors up to international standard is the need of the hour. They can help to make our human resources and industry efficient and competitive. Faculty development deserves much greater attention from Government. Of course, they themselves have to exercise to grow; at best Government can provide them facilities.

9

Science and Technology - 'Guru Killy' For The Development of Any Backward Region Like Say Marathwada

Institutes ought to set a tone of discovery, innovation, creativity, patent and IPR, spin-off New Technology Based Firms, create leaders [not followers] and technology pioneers. If they cultivate and acquire innovative character then only they tend to teach relevant.

Marathwada region and its people differ from the rest of Maharashtra not only in fewer resources, poor infrastructure and less capital but in general they have less access to knowledge of Science and Technology. This is true for not only Marathwada but true for many backward regions.

The content of S & T in various vocations and professions is too less. It is largely on account of the lack of access to scientific and technological facilities that the region and its people although intelligent and deserving are lagging behind.

The region does not have any CSIR Lab. There are no R & D Centers. Universities and Colleges are inadequately equipped in S & T consequently the Technology gap is too big. The region therefore remains industrially a back ward region.

There is almost no export of software from this whole region of eight districts, although the business is booming even in lanes of Mumbai, Pune. The engineering graduates coming out of colleges every year, most of them for jobs are migrating to other parts.

The region remains poor with 40% people living below the poverty line. There is rampant unemployment amongst the youth on one hand, and unlimited employment opportunities available in global market in sunrise technologies like information technology, electronics etc. on the other hand.

Aurangabad has rightly shown concern about present status of higher education and its future.

Investment in S & T is most productive:
Mediocre institutes are more costly than the cost of their up gradation.

Investment in S & T projects like science city, technical university, research parks, Technology Incubators, internet services, innovation centers, Technology Parks, is most rewarding. The rate of return on public investment in S & T projects especially in developing regions is highest more than 100%, which no project can every give so remarked World Development Report 1999. Imagine for a moment, all the institutes are suddenly closed. What saving or damage it will do to the society?

Projects like roads, bridges, irrigation, and industry become more feasible more economical when latest S & T is used in them, the investment being done in other kinds of development projects need a matching investment in S & T. Abundant opportunities, in globalization, are being created world over. Without the skills and knowledge they are simply not available.

So many new industries have come in Aurangabad like Bajaj, Garware, and Videocon etc. So much money is invested in them by both the industry and financial agencies like SEZ, SICOM, and IDBI. But almost no additional investment, no R & D projects have come in S & T in Universities and colleges. They remain go downs of old outdated knowledge.

For want of world class S & T base many industries are becoming less competitive and being merged or amalgamated with multinationals. The situation needs to be urgently corrected. For sustainable development of industries a strong S & T knowledge base is essential. The paper therefore advocates that the region should invest greatly in S & T. **Advanced scientific and technological research base is a pre-requisite for development. Only those who realize this will win.** Others may work hard, may have access to all kinds of resources, yet they will lag behind.

Proportionate Investment in S & T Needed:

Industrial estates are being set up in large and small towns. Lot of investment is being made in land, water etc. But many units almost (50%) are either sick or performing far below the norms. This is due to many reasons.

However, the main reason remains that there is almost a complete lack of front line technologies. New technology in Industry due to absence of research is almost absent. Industries can not be run on sun set technologies.

Elsewhere in developed regions there is a boom for establishment of Internet services, technology parks, Innovation Centers, Technology Incubators. But it is conspicuously absent in the region.

If the region remains slow in this respect is less likely to bridge the technology gap, economic gap and the future of people will remain bleak. The unemployment which is rising may continue.

Putting S & T at the centre of Marathwada Development is the need of the hour. It is very nice on the part of organizers of this conference that they have identified the need to promote S & T for economic and social development of the region, and have sponsored this program.

Peter Drucker said it is good to do things in a right way but in itself is not enough. It is essential to do right things in a right way, so as to achieve progress as desired. Marathwada needs to give thrust to S & T for its proper development.

World Class S & T Policies:

Compatibility in policy for industrial development and policy for higher education must be maintained.

Leaders in industry and leaders in academics ought to come together, remain together to convert intellectual capability of people in to usable goods and services.

Can and should we have to choose world class S & T policies in Marathwada? What are they? Where do you find them? Who does not want high pay, high tech, high quality jobs? How are they generated? Silicon Valley model of USA is adopted by Japan, Korea and many other countries.

We in Marathwada need to adopt this model to makeup the backlog in development. **People are hungry for good education in Science and Technology**. But University and colleges are not able to give. Best brains after 12th examination are opting to go to VJTI, Pune, NIT Nagpur, because such well established S & T facilities are simply not available in Marathwada.

If we do not do this right now the current poor performance of industry, employment and the economy will worsen and Marathwada will remain permanently behind.

Science and Technology and Economic Development:

Recognizing the need and importance of S & T our Prime Minister has long before rightly given a slogan Jai Vigyan'. He has given a call for creating a mass movement for innovation in S & T.

The future of people now is governed not so much by availability of physical resources, raw materials financial and markets. It depends more on people's Scientific and Technological Capability. This is obvious from the example of Japan, which has very less minerals and iron ore yet it is a major exporter of steel.

Dr. Bob Solow a Nobel laureate from MIT Boston found out that the industrial production of US doubled between 1909 and 1949 and that 85% credit is attributable to technology change.

He further advocated US Government to increase allocation of financial resources to S & T education and research. Now the Academy of Sciences of US have written a book, **"Rising Above the Gathering Storm"**, which recommended to the government to invest further more, if it has to retain leadership in world.

Taking a cue from this in 1945 US Government published a report Science - The Endless Frontier'. The Bush Commission vide this report advised US Government to create research Universities.

The main Product of these Universities is research, new technologies, patents and higher education is a by-product. Students learn best by researching, by innovation and hence it is relevant, up to date.

Two thirds of the budget of Universities is on research and extension while one third is on education. It is this policy in 1945 of promoting S & T in research Universities that made US today a forerunner in the world. The report of 1945 is reprinted by National Science Foundation in 1990 because of its utility even today.

The report further said that those nations, organizations and individuals exploiting the latest Science and Technology are likely to win; others may work hard, may have essential resources to draw on, but will lag behind without technological capability and adaptability. It is an urgent need to convert our Universities in to research Universities like Agriculture University at Parbhani.

Status of India in S & T Although Improving is far too Behind

India as a whole in S & T is too weak. We have never been a technology leader except in space technology. We are importing technologies and they are selling. Technology Upgradation continues to depend on imported technology. Technology transfer is often costly and ineffective.

The buyer's often lack the professional skills and technological competence to select technology that is appropriate to their needs. It tends to be expensive because of aggressive marketing by foreign companies, and agencies. So as to improve the situation; regions like Marathwada have to step up S & T activities. This will go a long way to elevate performance of India, to raise its head high in the world.

Research and Development: The energy giver:

R & D support is essential for sustainable development of Marathwada. The key to industrial development lies in using front line technologies.

Balanced development in R & D is essential to cope with ambitions plans of industrial development. R & D gives energy to economic development. It is a profit giving activity to the area. R & D produces much more wealth than in consumes.

It is an account of thrust to R & D that USA and Japan are leading. In 1950 Prof. Terman of Stanford University in USA observed that industry needs access to first class research in Universities and first class research in Universities need commercial application. These observations are very pertinent to Marathwada.

We have to have centers of excellence in Computer, Electronics, and Biotechnology etc. Ashok Desai, formerly advisor to Prime Minister has in his book on technology absorption prescribed that unless research is stepped up in India, technology absorption from foreign is going to remain too low.

Can Marathwada S & T Institutes Propel Industrial Growth? How?

Every where in the world it is the university research which is the engine of growth. Universities abroad are performing beyond education. They are bringing about regional development also. Our universities today are not able to shoulder this challenge. They are not stable.

There is lot of turmoil. They need to be restructured by giving autonomy to colleges and departments. They would have to take a lead in R & D, so badly needed for industrial growth of Marathwada region. Academics in Marathwada are brilliant, competent and capable.

But today, they do not have access to advanced S & T institutes in the world. They do not have mobility across the world. There are no innovation centre, technology parks, incubators on account of their absence we are lagging behind in industry and productivity in economy is low. We need a swimming pool to learn swimming. **So also we need S & T labs to learn and develop technical capability.**

India stands 43rd position in productivity, so is reported by a study Innovation - An agenda for Indian Corporate'. - Conducted by confederation of Industry (1999). The study has recommended building a structure of organization for innovation by establishing ties with foreign Universities.

It has highlighted the need to tap emerging opportunities in a global environment. In Marathwada we need to do this all the more and integrate themselves with global markets, by tapping international technologies and know how.

CONCLUSION

Experience throughout the world tells us that use of globally competitive superior technology, is the most important ingredient of economic success. It is principally the new technology which provides industrial management with means to compete.

Marathwada region, should certainly therefore worry about status of S & T. Government, Industry, Higher Education Institutes social reformers should come together to interact closely with each other so as to evolve a strategy of S & T, and help globalizing Marathwada. The regional economy can flourish only if there is a culture favorable for innovation. The priority being given to S & T budget in national and State Budget although increasing is far from adequate.

So as to build scientific culture it is essential to build a network of Science and Technology institutes doing not only education but also research and extension. Our Bench Marks', that is to say reference points, should be the **first best in the world.**

Marathwada Development Board in collaboration with university and colleges, Polytechnics, must set up technology diffusion centers in at least big industrial estates like Koh' in Japan.

It should build strong R & D base in engineering colleges, Universities, Technology Transfer Centers, Incubators, Patent and Licensing departments. Innovation based industrial growth is always sustainable.

Education does not grow where research, innovation, and infrastructure for patent, technology transfer is absent. Institutes should generate "well springs" of new knowledge, and not repeat what for generations is taught.

New technology based firms, venture capital companies need to be promoted, and they are the ones which have triggered the growth of USA and Japan. Can we not have mini Silicon Valley? Generation of new knowledge, new theories, new Technology, patents & IPR needs to be given fillip. This is the only way for prosperity. It is cheaper, appropriate and better, Borrowed, technology does not help much.

Marathwada for its development has two options. It can choose fast growth rate or alternatively slow growth rate. If it keeps S & T in centre, invests more in S & T, growth will be faster than if it invest elsewhere.

It should choose to promote S & T research, innovation centers, and adopt world best policies. Then the investment made in industries will become fruitful. We must have to boost research in Universities, comparable to those best in the world.

It is hoped that this seminar marks a beginning of progressive era in the life of people of Marathwada.

Aurangabad College has done a wonderful job in organizing this seminar which will go a long way to achieve sustained development of this region.

SOME SUGGESTIONS -

1. Appoint a committee of experts to frame policies and practices in S & T for Marathwada Development.
2. Establish Technology Park - Innovation Centre, Incubators, Technology Transfer Centers and Patent and IPR sale offices. Without them employment does not grow.
3. Establish Technical University in Marathwada in collaboration with best Universities in the world.
4. Science Centre in every District to nurse scientific temper.
5. Strengthen R & D in Universities - give many more scholarships to young researchers.

Professors who are involved in research teach valid knowledge, others teach yesterday's irrelevant knowledge today, resulting in educated unemployment. No institute can be bigger than the level of professors.

* * *

10

Needed - Innovation and Entrepreneurship in Higher and Technical Education Institutes for Employment Generation

What drives employment is the research and innovation. Resources in research, innovation and education are the most important growth stimulating instruments today.

ABSTRACT

The conventional wisdom in higher education which once served well is not fit for today and tomorrow. The time demands revolutionary changes to promote innovation and entrepreneurship. Institutions must act fast to reform; otherwise foreign universities are likely to take away the Indian education market.

Higher education institutions, without centers on campus for technological innovation, entrepreneurship development, patent and technology transfer, venture capital, hi-tech start ups, spin-off of companies and spin-off of technologies are incomplete, irrelevant and nonviable in modern sense. If India dreams to be a developed nation by the year 2020 the present higher education system needs to be strengthened urgently in respect of above stated centers. They have to be able to provide "Technology Push" matching with "Market Pull" and turn out graduates as leaders who are in short supply. They have to redesign their systems to generate new knowledge and new technologies ahead of others. The present departmental store approach, distributing knowledge generated elsewhere in the world only is unfit for the purpose. They will have to install systems as WELL SPRINGS of new knowledge.

Institutions have to establish above stated centers afresh in their campuses, essentially in partnership or in association with industry. Restructuring in the context of global changes has to be the main item on national agenda, without which the intellectual resource will continue to be wasted and opportunities missed. AICTE and UGC should have to do bench marking with the best in the world and make gap analysis. This is urgent because, our institutions follow only that which these apex bodies prescribe.

The key factor behind unemployment is insufficient innovation. Shortage of people with innovation skills is a major barrier in employment generation. Universities, colleges and polytechnics which have a major influence on nation's capacity for innovation should have to resort to new strategies. They would have to install systems to generate new ideas and new technology for industry and help them to win. Indian higher education institutes must recognize the full scope of the innovation phenomenon. They should produce leaders, and captains for industry of world standards.

STATEMENT OF THE PROBLEM

On one hand there is so much of unemployment amongst educated youths and on the other hand there is a shortage of entrepreneurs to develop innovative enterprises. There is abundance of natural resources on one hand and shortage of finished goods and services on the other hand. Lucrative opportunities due to lack of entrepreneurs are either dying or being taken away by foreigners. There is an influx of goods from east and west countries in Indian market. Indian industry unfortunately is far too behind the world. India ranks as low as 42nd in industrial competitiveness, and 127th in Human Development Index Government has set a goal to build India a developed nation by the year 2020. So as to accomplish this, young engineers urgently need to depart from their conventional approach and focus their attention on innovation and entrepreneurship. Higher Education Institutions in partnership with industry, in this cause, have a key role to play. They ought to become business oriented, with focus on spin-off of hi-tech start-ups. They ought to capitalize on emerging technology. Can they provide "Technology Push" matching with "Market Pull" on sustainable basis? The present frame of universities and colleges without innovation and entrepreneurship centers is not competitive enough to produce leaders of world class standard. They are producing good soldiers, which is necessary but not enough. They need to produce competent captains to lead in industry and economy. To be able to become so they are going abroad every year, in increasing numbers.

Universities need to be enlarged forthwith to cover centers like, Technology Innovation Relay Center, Entrepreneurship Development Center, Technology, Incubator, Business Incubator, Research Park, Venture Capital Foundation, Technology Park, Patent and IPR Center, Industrial Services Center, Technology Transfer and Marketing Center, Corporate Education Center, which are existing from last more than 50 years in counterpart institutions in developed countries. It is on account of this that those nations have prospered. IITs, IISc have recently started such centers in their campuses.

Institutions should have to initiate a movement for creation of New Technology Based Firms [NTBF] and venture capital foundations. It is a new dimension to be added to our present university and college campuses. They function as profit centers. They are not a liability on university finances, but generate wealth, which subsidizes cost of education and makes education relevant to market needs.

Prof Terman in 1950 observed that,

"Industry so as to remain competitive globally needs access to first class research in universities. So also the first class researchers in universities need access to industry so as to commercialize their research findings."

There is a greater need of University Related Research Parks (URRP), in India. Parks, in isolation from academic institutions being set up are good but can not substitute URRP. These centers have to be the key players. They have to be the drivers of technological revolution.

A formal policy of technological innovation in higher education is urgently needed to drive the spirit of innovation and entrepreneurship as a far reaching change in society, and not just to target potential entrepreneurs.

Need to Produce Leaders in Technology and Leaders in Industry

It was presumed in good old days that new technology could be discovered only abroad. Our colleges, universities and companies used to be happy to become best followers. We have been as a result constantly buying the technologies and they are selling. But now Indian talent has become conscious of its capabilities. It has become ambitious to discover new technologies ahead of others. Indians in Silicon Valley have made a mark. It is observed that students, who learn to innovate in college days, are better suited to discover unknown in service career. They are fit to lead in world market. Students who aspire to become leaders in technology and leaders in industry should have necessarily to acquire skills to generate new technologies, new products and new processes and obtain patents. It is realized that :

The key factor behind unemployment is insufficient technological innovation and entrepreneurship.

Do the institutes possess visions and missions to generate new knowledge? Have they nurtured culture to produce new technologies? Visions are in short supply and not the capabilities or the resources. We need to acquire them from world class institutions. Low aim is a crime.

Why do thousands of students go abroad for higher education? They have been going from pre-independence period. How many more years they may have to go? Can all those who desire go? What are the things which foreign universities teach, but we do not? Unless we teach students skills of innovation, skills for generation of new technologies, skills for discovery of new knowledge, patent and IPR, our institutes will remain behind the time and the outflow of talent will continue. Their institutions are innovative in character, our institutions are conservative. Foreign universities live today as if future has arrived, we exist today as we existed in past. They teach sunrise technologies we teach sunset technologies. They produce leaders we produce followers. They lead a change we follow the change. They are engines of growth we remain bogies. They are not afraid of change we are. They practice creative destruction.

The challenge now is to create a knowledge based society. It is that society in which new knowledge is not only used but also generated. The mindset of key people in UGC and AICTE needs to be reframed in favor of creating hi-tech entrepreneurship rather than to prepare youths with knowledge for employment in Multi National Corporations. Equipping universities in respect of innovation infrastructure is a crying need to achieve the desired goal.

Technological Innovation is an essential precondition for growth, maintaining employment and competitiveness. An innovative person never remains unemployed on the contrary he is more in demand. He has a mission in his life, which gives him extra energy and purpose. An innovative person constantly strives to improve. He is always dissatisfied with the prevalent. He wants to create new and again new. The innovation is progressing constantly on the strengths of new ideas of such scholar persons. Can the institutions produce such innovative persons more in number? If they do so institutions will be more in demand like Oxford and Cambridge.

Innovation is Indispensable

Ideas are the real capital. Ideas are needed to succeed. They come from innovation. Idea generated is opportunity generated. Idea killed is opportunity killed.

Knowledge memorized and stored in brains is important, but more important is the ability to discover new knowledge, new theories and new ideas.

Institutions are the legitimate places, the crucibles of experimentation, for the manufacture of ideas. It is their prime function. They have no reason to exist if they do not do so.

The importance of innovation to the country's economic future should be realized and infrastructure as stated above provided forthwith in higher education institutions. This will avoid the shortage of suitable persons for innovation and entrepreneurship, which is found to be a major barrier in employment generation.

Most of the students in colleges and polytechnics learn in a passive way. Students learn quietly what is handed over to them. They learn through transmission and are not guided to take active hand in creation of technologies. What did the famous philosopher Socrates teach his students? He taught how to raise questions. That means institutes have necessarily to ignite the creative minds of students.

The competency of work force today is measured in terms of its ability to innovate. People have to be innovative to see ahead of others the incoming opportunities.

India possesses the largest pool of youthful work force and high quality human capital. This is our competitive advantage. We ought to prepare youths for global needs.

Commercial Exploitation of Brand New Technology

Invention when exploited commercially is known as innovation. Research conducted in universities colleges and polytechnics often results in publication of wonderful papers, but rarely results in commercial exploitation. Thesis written mostly remains on shelf. No conscious effort is made to obtain economic value from them, mainly because teaching in this direction is lacking. Students do not get opportunity to learn to convert inventions into usable goods and services. To that extent skill set of students, in spite of potential, remains deficient. This in addition reduces utility of research done and reduces the rate of return on investment.

It is a good sign that higher education in India is growing. But acquisition of skills for commercial exploitation, which is the demand of time, is lagging.

Multifaceted units in partnership with industry, like Research Park, Innovation Center, Patent and Technology, Transfer Center, Entrepreneurship Development Center, Incubator, Venture Capital Foundation, IPR center etc. which constitute innovation infrastructure, is found to lead to creation on enterprising atmosphere enabling students to acquire innovation skills More the commercialization of technology more is the wealth generation. In developed countries innovation in academic institutes is a usual practice. This has generated a wave of entrepreneurship facilitating students and the whole community to be creative, tapping the market in the whole world. USA produces leaders who employ followers from countries like India. Unfortunately this wave of creativity, leadership and outward looking culture is yet to reach the Indian shores.

A New Vision of New World

How long students should keep learning knowledge generated by others elsewhere in the world? How long they should join the army of foreign companies, serve in supporting roles and be content with that? If the necessary infrastructure is provided some of the students, if not all, would certainly become **"First Movers"** the institutes and students need to dream high, in tune with global competitiveness. Learning innovation enables students to consolidate their knowledge of basics. Innovation Center is more than a learning place. It gives an inspiration to students besides generating economic surplus. The role of institutions in vision development should not be under estimated.

Innovation in education institutes in India is conspicuously absent.

Students do not get global perspectives. This is a serious lacuna. The institutes without innovation are truly incomplete in modern sense. They still follow an old outdated model whose, educational and financial efficiency is too less. They live in past, while their counterparts abroad are ahead of time.

Quality of technical education and research can substantially be enhanced and returns on investment increased if innovation policy in universities colleges and polytechnics is introduced.

Joblessness and industrial slow down is a result of lack of innovation. When shall we realize this? The situation is to innovate or die. Hence Government of India has launched the following program.

Quality Improvement Program

For reformation of higher and technical education Government of India has recently launched a massive program, termed as Technical Education Quality Improvement Program {TEQIP}. The objectives are, to impart world class education, to enable students to grow to the level they are capable for, so also reduce dependence on foreign technology.

From what is reported it is observed that the scheme is good, well formulated in many respects but in competitive environment it lacks a step towards "Technological Innovation".

Modernization of laboratories, library, class rooms, faculty development as usual are essential but not sufficient it is necessary to think differently, think great going beyond current practice. It is necessary to design new organization structure oriented towards innovation, and enable students to acquire enterprising skills equal to, if not more than their counterparts abroad, which is the need of the hour. This is to say that institutions must provide a portal through which all the students compulsorily should have to pass through, for practice of commercial exploitation of the new knowledge that is to say new technology. They should target their efforts towards production of marketable technologies, patents etc. The students should have to do some field surveys to identify level of technology used, productivity, and difficulties in using the latest technology.

Can Higher Education Institutes give new ideas, leadership to Help Industry to Win?

Surveys conducted elsewhere in the world indicate that NTBF started by young entrepreneurs with origin in academic institutions are far more successful than those started by persons with experience in industry Academic institutions provide a powerful engine to launch the new technology based enterprises and thereby generate employment.

According to a new item published recently. "India slipped to 21st rank from 13th in number of scientific output." The PhDs produced in engineering are only 293 [1998] as against China 2900 and 5930 in USA. The number of graduates produced in USA are almost double than in India. Yet all get jobs or become self employed. Still they have a shortfall. To meet the same they invite engineers from abroad. This is mainly because they produce larger number of PhDs. Who constantly explore new opportunities, everywhere and anywhere in the world.

A critical examination of the schemes of technical education in the light of global winds of change, so as to avoid mistakes is essential. If the infrastructures like Entrepreneurs Center, Research Park, Incubator, Innovation Centre Venture Capital Fund, Patent and Technolgy Transfer Center etc. in partnership with industry are not incorporated, it is feared that the whole effort of reformation will remain on traditional lines, preventing change. Massive investment being made will not yield expected results. The education policies and practices should have to come out of old ruts. They are less efficient, unproductive and outdated. You need new ideas to win in new world.

It should be remembered that any investment in present structure, present systems and procedures without introducing autonomy and improving academic culture is like investment to perpetuate and subsidize incompetence, inefficiency leading to failure.

Change is most wanted to replace worn out ideas. The resources should not be frittered away on trodden paths but should be used creatively on to proceed off the beaten paths, essentially importing academic culture and output. Developing countries in general, are hopelessly conservative, inward looking and hostile to change. Innovative societies are essentially outward looking. Individually, Indians are forward looking but society wise not. Unless we change our mind set and work to accelerate reformation process we can not progress.

Academic Culture and Infrastructure

Unless innovative measures like academic autonomy, administrative autonomy, are introduced in higher education the additional investment in infrastructure will not pay dividends. Our own people in college, university and government unknowingly, out of inertia become obstruction to reformation. The authorities who are used to older style of working and for personal benefits do not take initiative to change. However, this should be guarded to avoid failure.

The experience of India - Canada project and World Bank project in the recent past, has taught us many lessons. Financial Aid from World Bank to countries like Congo, Zambia indicates that the aid turned out to be counter productive. The men in charge of governance were accustomed to benefits from the present system. So they did not take any initiative to change. It went towards subsidizing inefficiency, bad policies, corruption, discouraging reformation etc.

The present case of universities and colleges, which are offering resistance to change, is a capability failure. Raising the organizational capability, making them competent and amenable to change is the key aspect which must be attended to with utmost care by aid receiving institutions. Without which they may not be able to make most of the aid. Development of an institute can not be forced from outside. It comes only from within. It is an endogenous growth. Organizational capability need to be developed so as to bring about change. Exposure to developed world needs to be made, time and again, to accelerate arrival of change.

Benchmarking with the Best in the World

What we observe differently in higher education institutes abroad is that they have on their campuses centers like Research Park, Patent and Technology Transfer Center, Entrepreneurship Development Center, Incubator, Innovation Relay Center, Industrial services center, etc. Venture Capital companies have opened offices in the campuses for early commercialization of technologies. Institutes have become sources of new ideas enabling companies to win. An institute functions like a light house for industry. It is these things which have increased productivity and added value to growing economy. Such institutes are functioning like a magnet attracting best of brains from anywhere and everywhere. In the world Benchmarking is considered to be a big driver for improvement.

Systems in World have Changed - Where are we? Can we Afford to be Stationary?

All these multifaceted centers provide an opportunity to students to learn beyond curriculum, as per their intrinsic motivations. They have been established especially after 1980, in 84 technical universities of Germany, in 125 research universities of USA, and in many universities abroad MIT Boston has a technology licensing office [TLO] in which about 200 people work. The author has personally visited this office. The institute earns about one hundred patents every year and earns as much as 20% of its budget from the sale of technology.

Quality and relevance of education in developed countries is reported to have improved mainly because of the presence of centers in the campus. Enterprising culture is imbibed in students, which leads to spin-off of companies. Around ten companies are born every year in MIT. Institutes have become the maternity homes, where good baby care is taken and companies are consequently born without any congenital defects. This is found to be a good help to budding entrepreneurs. Our institutions are lacking in all such ideas. Can we not adopt these strategies? True that is a long journey. But it has to begin some where. Is it not that a thousand miles journey begins with a single step? The vector of learning of our students should have to be made in right direction. Otherwise their efforts, time and money goes astray.

Innovation - Generates Jobs

Cambridge Research Park, Limerick University research Park, Harburg University Park in Germany, technology based spin-offs from Sophia Antipolis, university park in France, Oulu Business University Park in Finland etc are world famous examples which have benefited most of the students, industry and academia. The author has personally verified by visiting them. China, Taiwan have installed such parks in their institutes and thereby currently have successfully been converting brain drain into brain gain. An OECD study recently reported that :

Those nations which lead in introducing innovation tend to win jobs from those who lag.

Joblessness in India is increasing due mainly to lack of innovation. Insufficient innovative activity in India is due to shortage of people possessing innovation skills because innovation is not taught in colleges. This is cited as a key factor behind under performance of Indian economy and fast growing unemployment

India must recognize the full scope of the innovation phenomenon without which proportion of sick industries will increase and new born companies will be handicapped at birth itself.

Can Indian academics teach innovation skills by international standards? Can they teach skills of discovery and skills to generate technologies equal to their counterparts abroad? Certainly Yes! They have the potential. Can India hope to become a developed nation with out learning innovation? Should we keep on teaching sun set technologies? Can we hope to reform education without adopting innovative strategies? We can not generate employment without NTBF. Can students acquire innovation skills without infrastructure for innovation? We essentially need a swimming pool to learn swimming.

Conclusion

A new enterprising society in the world is coming into being. Institutions should therefore focus their attention on reorienting students for closer integration with the world. Mobility of academicians at international levels is advocated. This has remained our serious deficiency in the past.

Education and training in universities, colleges and polytechnics have a major influence on nation's capacity for innovation. The role played by them, however is not satisfactory. Much needs to be done. Scientific methods like in developed countries need to be introduced. Innovation policy needs to be evolved. Can they produce NTBF, and how many, is a pertinent question which they should be asked.

How much knowledge is acquired and stored in brains is important, but how well innovative skills are learned deserves priority. India in globalization should deviate from traditional methods of learning and take a lead in sharpening the innovation potential of students. They have missed opportunities in the past because necessary infrastructure and direction for self employment were not available. Now at least they should not miss.

If India does not become a center for technological innovation then there is no other way to become a developed nation. If we develop systems in colleges to produce new knowledge and new technology, then there is a fair chance to convert brain drain into brain gain.

The knowledge infrastructure proposed in this paper is a profit center. It generates wealth much in excess of consumption. It is found to subsidize education and research, besides improving the quality and relevance. It should therefore be installed forthwith in each university, college without any delay. Government should play its central role.

If India desires to become a technological super power, then higher education institutions must have to throw away the old shackles, and install new innovation and entrepreneurship culture to create NTBF. This is no more an option but compulsion.

Resources are not in short supply, but the visions. Universities must generate leaders and brand new ideas to enable industry to win.

"The innovator makes enemies of all those who prospered under the old order and receives only lukewarm support from those who would prosper under the new."

Innovation is about creating value, about increasing productivity and growing economy. Insufficient innovation is at the roots of low productivity.

Education Institutes in India must recognize the full scope of the innovation phenomenon.

How to Set up a Patent & IPR Center

Patent and IPR center should lie at the heart of the institution.

Need and Importance

Research conducted by students and faculty in BE, ME, PhD courses, and research projects funded by AICTE / DST often result in publication of papers in national and international journals. This is good, but better is if research findings are exploited commercially. Research should flow to market as fast as possible. This increases utility of research done, productivity and competitiveness of industry. The financial returns from investment in institution increase. Intellectual capability and skills of students for discovery of new knowledge, new technology and new theories go up. This encourages the researchers. The patent and IPR center if established will facilitate flow of brand new technology to industry and make them more competitive. It will make them more qualitative, purposeful and relevant. The confidence of students will go up, and they become competent by international standard. This increases the innovation capacity of India and in turn generates more jobs; realization of national dream of 2020 is facilitated. The aim of TEQIP will be better fulfilled. Today in the absence of such a center, innovation skills are not developed, which is a serious deficiency.

Rating of an institution at international level is measured in terms of patents obtained, and hi-tech start ups. World class institutions are essentially doing these things. Industries are flocking round them in search of new ideas. Now good :

Students dream to obtain patents.

Government of India has set up the office of Technology Innovation Forecasting and Assessment Council [TIFAC] in New Delhi. The mission is to propagate patent culture in industry and in institutions. The center if established will give a Philip to institutes of technical education.

FUNCTIONS

1. Collect literature, patent laws, books, journals from India and abroad.

2. Keep up to date information from world over.
3. Conduct awareness programs, for industry personnel and students
4. Build an inventory of patents issued in India and abroad.
5. Make industry aware of patents available. Develop a habit to use patents
6. Display patents for use of students, staff and industry
7. Explore innovative potentials of students and faculty. Inspire them
8. Make an inventory of innovators and users
9. Survey the needs of industry
10. Explore commercial value of research done in institute.
11. Provide a common platform for innovators from industry and institute.
12. Prepare a list of patent attorneys
13. Study patent laws in India and abroad. Suggest improving them.
14. Do benchmarking with similar centers else where in the world.
15. Remain in network with institutions where patenting is done, like NCL Pune, IISC Bangalore, European patent office, TIFAC New Delhi.

Staff Required

To begin with the center may appoint two full time officers, one with technical and other with law background. Trained officers are not normally available. They may have to be deputed for training to TIFAC, NCL Pune. They may have to attend conferences in India and abroad.

An advisory committee from faculty and industry may have to be appointed to monitor the progress.

Budget

To cover the salaries of officers and staff, office stationary etc may come to about Rs. 20 lakhs/ year.

Out Put Expected

The center may create a culture of discovery and patents, Seminars, debates and discussions, meetings with industry personnel etc. About 5 patents and 3 start ups may be targeted from second year.

Conclusion

The center will increase innovation capacity of students and India. India will become more competitive. More employment will be generated.

11

Operating Manual For Systems Improvement in An Educational Institute

Mediocre teachers are easy to be found and easy to be appointed. They teach nothing other than how to be more mediocre.

Synopsis

The paper outlines in brief the need and importance of preparing an operating manual for systems improvement in higher and technical education institutes. Institutions else where in the world are using it from several years. But in India it is not yet a practice. In competitive environment, now institutes cannot afford to ignore. Autonomous institutes, deemed universities, private universities, are coming up in increasing numbers. All these are spending huge sums of money, consuming scarce human, physical and financial resources, but fail to come up to student's expectations. Thousands of students are going abroad. They are paying huge amount as tuition fees to foreign universities. Our institutes although spending huge resources are not able to achieve international standard. It is mainly because they lack scientific approach in governance, and do not use operations manual, to achieve the desired quality at competitive cost.

The contents of the manual include vision statement, quality policy and objectives. It prescribes delineation of the duties and responsibilities of all employees. Authorities, powers and privileges, with accountability of each one need to be pinpointed. Good systems are at the roots of success. An attempt is made in this article to identify in brief, internal and external systems. Methodology for the preparation of the manual is given.

If the institutions do not prepare manuals, they stand a high risk of slipping down in rank in favor of foreign universities, waiting at the doorstep. Without the operation manual, institutes with all the resources at their command, will not be able to contribute effectively.

Introduction

World over, people are experiencing brain race. To be able to win, government is promoting the scheme of autonomy, deemed university, private universities, and permitting foreign universities to come in. Top Management is having ambitious plans and programs to make the institutes' world class. Government of India has started a modernization program known as "Technical Education Quality Improvement Program" [TEQIP], with the assistance of World Bank in selected institutions.

Public and private institutions are keen on becoming preferred in world market. They are showing modern vision, values, commitment and vitality for transformation to world-class level. This is good but not enough. This thinking must percolate down to all the levels. Operations manual that is a written document provides the necessary common guidelines, rules and regulations, powers and privileges and working procedures. It transfers the dream down the line. The purpose is to involve all stakeholders, facilitate participative decision-making and management, reduce administrative and bureaucratic delays, and make most of the physical, financial and intellectual capabilities.

From experience in the world operations manual is found to be an effective means of communication to motivate and mobilize support and cooperation from all. Universities like Oxford, Cambridge, MIT, and Stanford have become world class only because they have been using scientific approaches like operations manual in governance. Any Indian Institute can also become world class for which necessarily it will have to prepare and use the manual. It is good to have enthusiasm, it is good to have physical and financial resources, but it is essential to have scientific approach in governance. TEQIP project has also prescribed preparation of operation manual for those institutions, which are covered under the project.

Often the systems and procedures in the institutions are found to be incompatible with the visions and missions. There is a mismatch and vagueness in accountability, duties responsibilities and authorities. Valuable time of employees, especially professors is spent for less productive purposes. Operations in the institute are over centralized. Principals are over burdened. Professors are not empowered adequately. Governance leads to piecemeal random approach without operations manual. Resources remain underutilized. Target is missed. In competitive environment it falls too short of the purpose.

Usage of manual is found to provide an aid to synchronize functioning of all the people and make optimal utilization of physical, financial and especially intellectual resources. It makes the institution more capable and deserving. It thereby attracts funds, endowments, and scholars. It sets a tone of scientific culture, so essential to become competitive. It creates a work place designed to think great. It creates the most effective workflow. It allows people to concentrate both on their individual tasks and work together in a team. It is filled with innovation and creativity. It allows the institute to recruit and retain top-notch talent. This is what operation manual can do. Can an institute

Which is aspiring to show better performance afford to ignore?

Operations Manual is prepared more for the following purposes.

(a) Giving a formal shape to the short and long-term dream, quality policy, quality procedures, and communicating the same to all stakeholders namely trustees, students, parents, industry, faculty and staff. It is to increase organizational capability.

(b) Identifying precisely duties and responsibilities of each and every one working for the institution. It identifies all the jobs that need to be done and presents them, in a sequential integrated manner. It gives a holistic view.

(c) Presenting rules and regulations, powers and privileges, and accountability. The purpose is to synergies efforts and to make people work with joy.

(d) This makes people more productive and gives them courage and confidence for accepting change and making most of it.

(e) The manual helps in describing and implementing quality policy.

(f) Providing improved governance of policies, practices.

(g) Providing documented base of quality planning for quality audit.

(h) Providing continuity of the quality system and its requirements during changing circumstances.

(i) Manual is a useful training material for employees.

(j) Presenting the quality system to external agencies such as National Accreditation Board, AICTE, ISO, State and central government, NPIU.

(k) Increasing confidence level in public, students and staff.

(l) Obtaining higher economic rate of return from investments, attract funds and endowments.

(m) Attracting scholars, teachers, and make it a preferred place of study and work.

(n) To attract industry for consultancy, technology licensing, and placement of engineers.

(o) To make systems and procedures compatible with visions and missions.

QUALITY POLICY AND OBJECTIVES

Customer Focus. The institute's policy is to satisfy all customers, internal and external. The declared vision is to satisfy each and every student, parent, industry, alumni, faculty, and staff. They are the valuable customers. It believes in understanding their minds, expectations, developing happy relations.

Feedback from students, industry, faculty and staff in this regard is obtained at regular intervals analyzed and used for reformation. Feedback given by students and other customers enables the institute to understand, their expectations, and opportunities [blind spots] for improvement.

Improve Quality of Inputs [Enablers] - Output will automatically be superior to maintain good health one has to eat good food. Providing quality inputs is essential to obtain quality output. Ensuring the quality of inputs that is to say "quality assurance" is the approach, followed by the institute. It is the human capital, which makes all the difference. Improvement in human resource inputs is therefore given top attention.

Design Systems Scientifically, The institute strongly believes in systems improvement. 85 % success is found to come through scientifically designed systems; People perform better if systems are good. Good systems are a prerequisite to create joyful environment for learning and working. It intends to transplant good systems from world-class institutions elsewhere in the world. The institute believes that increased funding alone does not improve quality. It has to be accompanied by systems improvement.

Create Quality Cell to Conduct Quality Audit

Quality does not come by accident or by chance. It requires a conscious and deliberate persistent effort. The institute intends to establish a quality assurance cell, with qualified staff. The cell conducts surveys on customer satisfaction by using statistical tools. The surveys indicate the opportunities for improvement. Benchmarking possibly with the world best is then done, to emulate best practices. Findings are reported to governing board.

Team Approach

The institution believes in team working. It is the teams and not the charismatic leaders that build great organizations. Good leaders and good teams help to achieve peak performance. Boss and sub-ordinate relationship in the institute is not useful. There are team leaders and team members. All play their respective roles voluntarily like the players in a football team. Smart work rather than hard work is preferred. Every one is expected to work with excellence. Participative decision-making and management is encouraged. Administrative and bureaucratic delays are reduced. Governing Board shall empower various functionaries. It will delegate necessary financial and administrative powers to all concerned.

Adoption and implementation of systems approach: Quality policy and procedures are described in detail in the manual. They are designed fo institution as a whole and for each constituent department. It is prepared after thorough discussions with all concerned. Preparing by just a few persons in isolation is discouraged. Benchmarking of all the existing activities and processes against other counterpart institutions in ongoing search for best practice is done. Benchmarking is the beginning of quality improvement.

When approved by the governing board the manual is printed and circulated to all for use. Care is taken to see that all concerned understand the document. Training programs are conducted for top, middle, and lower levels from time to time for smooth implementation. Quality audit based on planning of quality policy and procedures are conducted at regular intervals. Department of quality assurance is created which works round the year. It undertakes first reformation of those systems, which are easy. Manuals are revised from time to time.

Incentives and Recognition of Merit

Care will be taken to see that incentives are provided for meritorious.

Quality Planning and Quality Audit is a on going Journey

The culture of continuous self-assessment is to be consciously developed. It is not a one-time job. It uses data about existing systems and makes refinement through questionnaire and personal interview from time to time. Policies, procedures, report formats, instructions are subject to change. Benchmarking with the best in the world is made and best possible practice selected for adoption and implementation.

Internal Quality Audit

The quality cell shall establish and maintain documented procedures for planning and implementing internal quality audits to verify whether quality activities and related results comply with planned arrangements and to determine the effectiveness of the quality system.

Internal quality audits shall be scheduled on the basis of the status and importance of the activity to be audited and shall be carried out by personnel independent of those having direct responsibility for the quality being audited. The scope of audits is determined with regard to the importance of the activities in question and the knowledge of any existing or likely problems. The audit frequency for quality system, product or process is, normally twice a year.

The results of the audits shall be recorded and brought to the attention of the personnel having responsibility in the area audited. The management personnel responsible for the area shall take timely corrective action on deficiencies found during the audit.

This is to be done by quality department, by means of continuous monitoring, planned reporting back on actions or direct follows up in conjunction with the audit being performed the next time, as required. The result of the follow up is documented in the audit report form. One copy of the audit report including the notes during follow up is filled and kept by the quality department.

The results of internal quality audits form an integral part of the input to management review activities.

Organization Structure

The manual should give the organization structure. Duties and responsibilities, along with authorities, and accountability of each employee should be given. All the persons from top to bottom like chairman, trustees, principal, professors, librarian, registrar, finance officer, clerks, laboratory staff etc. should appear in these statements.

Feed Back

Opinion surveys from customers are of vital importance for reformation. Feed back formats should be well designed and given in the manual. Feed back from students, faculty, staff, governing body members, industry, university, government administrators, alumni, etc need to be taken at regular intervals. The feedbacks so obtained are analyzed and conclusions drawn. The governing body so as to initiate the process of reformation utilizes the conclusions.

METHODOLOGY

The manual is prepared with the involvement of all concerned. It has not to be prepared in isolation, by handful persons. The document is usually prepared in the institute by persons in quality cell, preferably under the guidance of a consultant. The document is released for use after approval from the governing board.

The document covers all the activities of the institute, including UG, PG, doctoral programs, research, innovation, industry institute interaction, patenting, IPR, entrepreneurship, fund raising, and all other activities, which are related to the institution.

Department Manual

Keeping in mind the above principles every department will prepare its own systems manual. It will be done jointly with its all employees. In preparation it will ask following questions and provide answers. Each department shall prepare its own quality manual suited to its needs.

(a) What is being done in the department
(b) When it is being done
(c) Who is doing it
(d) Where it is being done
(e) Why it is being done
(f) What is the sequence
(g) What are the forms and records
(h) Can the processes be improved
(i) Conduct surveys of expectations and understand opportunities for improvement
(j) Analyze them and draw conclusions
(k) Benchmark them with better elsewhere in counterpart institutions for establishing best possible practice
(l) How the activity, task can be performed in a better way
(m) What preventive actions needed
(n) What are the instructions of the department
(o) How records can be maintained in a better way
(p) Circulate the draft document to all concerned
(q) How to conduct internal audit.
(r) How and why to conduct training program for people at all levels

(s) Prepare job description for each post, authorities and responsibilities

(t) Are the professors and staff as competent as those in world class institutes

(u) Do benchmarking and find out what ought to be done?

(v) Prepare a plan, implement and monitor

(w) Some of the processes for examination are given below

Some of the activities performed by the department, which need to be examined, are Lectures, practical, industrial training, examination, tests, attendance, project work, innovation, patenting, publication, book writing, consultancy, testing, special lectures.

Record keeping, stock keeping, dead stock and consumables, equipment purchase, maintenance, house keeping, working hours.

Preparing long range plans and yearly plans, auditing with the involvement of all is desirable. They develop a feeling of belongingness. Helter skater working is avoided.

Upgrading skills and knowledge of all the faculty and staff on continuing basis is the top priority activity. The people become multi skilled, versatile to produce more and better output.

Facilitating co-operation with in the institution and out side, for development is important for success. This makes the institution more deserving and earns reputation. Quality manual is a tool to keep the institution up to date by both national and international standard.

Characteristics of a good Head of the Institution

He is technically competent. He is a leader and not a boss. He is impartial. He is above cast creed and religion. He is a good organizer of seminars, conferences. He builds a team of followers. He creates a spirit of unity. He is loyal to his job. He loves students, faculty and staff. He is not corrupt. He devotes 40% of his time to routine activities and 60% to professional activities at state and national levels. He delegates powers to professors and others. He values education.

Conclusion

In WTO regime, when foreign education providers are destined to come in India, some of them by virtue of their superior merit may get preference over the best of Indian institutions. Our institutes then may be labeled as mediocre. Indian intelligentsia may then be rated low. This may hurt the pride of nation. To avoid an unhappy situation, Government has started the TEQIP project. In competition some of the Indian institutes may overtake the best of foreign. This program for effective working has prescribed preparation of "operations manual". However even those institutes which are not covered in project but desirous of upgrading would have to prepare manuals. Dream of India to become a developed nation by 2020 depends on how quickly and ably institutes adopt the system. Indian institutes are under a great threat from coming of foreign universities. They may capture the education market. Preparation of manual now is essential for survival and growth.

References

1. Guidelines for developing quality manuals, IS/ISO 10013: 1995 of Bureau of Indian standards.
2. ISO 9001: 1994, Quality systems- Model for quality assurance in design development, production, installation and servicing.
3. Guidelines on implementation of Reforms, of National Project Implementation Unit, Government of India, February 2006.
4. B M Naik, Quality assurance in Higher and Technical Education: Can we afford to ignore it? Published in University News, Vol 44 No 30 July 24-30, 2006.
5. Prem Vrat, Quality System for Excellence in Engineering Education, University News Vol. 43 No. 39, September 26-October 02, 2005.

American institutes have gone ahead of European because they practiced globalization and liberalization early.

12

Private Universities - End of Monopoly Regime

We teach to invent, to innovate, to research. We teach to find which is not known. We certainly teach what is known but more essentially we teach students to find unknown.

Private universities, although new to India, exist in the US from hundreds of years. Almost half of the 3500 US universities are private. They are managed and maintained either by the church, industry, or philanthropic organizations. The standard of education in them and the quality of research output vis-à-vis that of the state controlled universities is superior. The best university like MIT Boston is private. The US has progressed well and due share of credit goes to private universities. Many important inventions and innovations have taken place in them. Human civilization would not have advanced so much, if there were no private universities. Today, private universities in the world earn a large proportion of patents and IPR. Following article explain the need and importance of establishing private universities in India.

ENTRY OF FOREIGN UNIVERSITIES

Universities form foreign countries like U.K. USA, Australia are entering India in a big way. People do have a craze for foreign degrees. Special counseling sessions by foreign universities are being held in metro cities. The proposal of private universities being discussed and debated in India needs to be examined under the influence of arrival of foreign universities. India would have to strengthen its higher education system, both private and government, so as to face aggression. Foreign universities are making an entry so as to capture education market, which is so abundantly available in India. In such a case education will be much more expensive. Students would have to pay much more, than both government universities and private universities. Already thousands of students are going abroad each year by spending big amount. It is now for Indians to consider whether to have foreign universities which are much more costly or private although costlier than government universities. India has signed an agreement in WTO, according to which from 1st January 2005 foreign universities are permitted to come in, so also Indian universities can go out. When India has made university sector open to private foreign universities, how it can stop it for those of Indian origin?

WHY PRIVATE UNIVERSITIES?

India needs private universities to strengthen its own education. This will be achieved through competition to government universities. Private universities can bring new life and blood through competition, which government university can not.

Government universities have rendered very valuable service, so far. All universities in India are state funded and hence state controlled. They enjoy monopoly. Students have no option. Their performance, by global standard is however far below. Neither the students nor the employers are happy. They are over centralized, bureaucratic, and monopolistic, thwarting and impending ideas of students and professors. They kill the innovative talent of students and faculty. They care only for their bosses, ignoring the needs of students and industry. They are far too behind their counterparts in the developed world. It is because of their poor performance that many students go abroad for higher education. They are using outdated structure of affiliating colleges. They are giving admissions, and degrees but not latest knowledge. Therefore they appear cheaper but truly are not. The limitations of government universities lay in their government structure. They are managed and maintained by people who are not qualified for the purpose. If India wants to become a champion in higher education, it must create competition in institutions. There can not be a champion without competition. Monopoly of present universities must come to an end. That will be the beginning of improvement. Mere presence of a competitor can force an incumbent to lower prices and improve services

Private universities can bring competition and initiate new innovative projects - to make most of world wide opportunities. Private universities are more enterprising by nature.

The organizations / innovations like research parks, innovation centers, incubators, campus companies, venture capital companies etc which exist from almost 50 years in universities in advanced countries have not yet reached the Indian universities, which offer only irrelevant courses. Consequently, the educated unemployed are growing. There are six lakhs in Maharashtra alone. The competition in Indian economy is far too low mainly because of mediocrity. The students are still required to go to UK and US for higher studies. How long they will have to keep going? They are going from Gandhi Nehru period. How long we should fill the coffers of foreign universities? The answer lies in setting up private universities, and bringing competition to the state controlled universities, Private universities are cut for entrepreneurship. India will miss opportunities in patents and starting of New Technology Based firms, if private universities are not started or delayed. We do not have innovative mechanisms so far mainly because we do not have private universities.

Private Universities Are More Responsive to Market. They cater efficiently to the rising demands in terms of quality and quantity. State universities need to be supplemented by private universities.

Because State universities have limited resources they need to be supported by private. In the newly emerging knowledge society, the need and importance of efficiency in higher education needs no emphasis. The proportion of students taking to higher education in India is only 6% but it is rising fast at the rate of 12% per year. In the US this proportion is more than 50%, Korea has 37% and Thailand 12%. In the fast paced globalization, if India has to compete the only option is to augment its private universities. This is the only way to get a competitive advantage. State Universities are subordinate to Government. They often play the tune of political masters, who keep changing.

Private Universities can take Long-range View of Education.

Because their management does not depend on government they take long range view. The Government, which is elected for a short period, does not pay the required attention to higher education, which essentially demands long range planning. The vice chancellors most of the times are appointed on political considerations. They bring politics in universities and the scholarship is driven out. Research is given a back seat. Private universities, if installed, will break the monopoly of the present universities, which is so essential for progress.

Who will provide remedies to remove the weaknesses in state universities? Only private universities can come to its rescue. They can bring improved methods of work and capital investment from the world over especially from NRIs. Any delay in such timely intervention would take away our huge education market to foreign universities. Autonomy to colleges is prescribed by National Education Commission way back in 1986. But it is not yet implemented. The Government is not willing to part with the powers and pass them to colleges.

Private Universities Can avoid political intervention

They keep pushing forward their academic missions and visions regardless of the political party that comes to power. The vice chancellor is not appointed by the Government but by the university board. With a humanistic aim they admit meritorious students from anywhere in the world. They bring about a cultural exchange between the nations and enrich the human civilization. Most of the private universities abroad are reported to be making more productive utilization of resources. They get donations, so much so that every year they start new research projects and new courses. Almost only 50% of the university budget is met out of student fees. The rest is met out of donations and patent IPR royalties.

The fees prescribed by US universities are much higher. It is because they maintain a high standard of laboratories, library and education. They do not get financial aid from the Government. The students get loans from the banks and scholarships from philanthropic organizations. In India too loans are new available.

Private Universities Can make private college scheme more successful

In India there are private self-finance colleges affiliated to state controlled universities. This is a case of partial privatization; the final responsibility of quality rests with the university. Colleges many times tend to play mischief and follow unethical means to encourage students to copy in examinations and even buying degrees like the episode of the Nagpur, as it may affect reputation so much that the university stands the risk of closure.

However, a fear prevails that the private universities may indulge in malpractice and sale of degrees. This has not happened in the U S or anywhere else. The system of controlling academic standards of the university, world over, has now changed to the scientific method of accreditation adopted nationally and internationally besides ISO.

Private Initiative Can make research and education more productive

As per the Bush Commissions report 1945, "Science - The Endless Frontier" U S universities have been strengthened for research. They are primarily knowledge generation centers, where students learn by researching. In this system quality of education is found to be the best, so also the research aspect. Cost wise, research subsidizes education and education subsidies research. Institutes are granted status of university only if they have a proven ability of knowledge generation and not merely teaching. India will have to install such systems for innovation. There are associated risks, like in any good project, but the gains are tremendous.

Private universities inherently are more enthusiastic and co-operative to industries. Private universities are friendlier with industry

Private universities if started bond between industry and institutes will become thick. Flow of technology will take place to industry and national productivity will increase. The expected synergistic relationship between the two will happen. Brainpower of Indian students will be used in India to solve Indian problems. Patent culture is more likely to pick up.

Private universities are good to promote export and reduce import

We have been buying technology and goods from foreign countries and they are selling from many years. Now the situation is proposed to be reversed. This cannot happen without starting of private universities. There are greater risks in not starting private universities. Indian universities can reach out to foreign, only if they are private.

Private universities take away poverty from poor

They can bring vibrancy to rural areas. Some people are making hue and cry that the private universities will educate only rich. And gap between rich and poor will widen. Poor and deserving students need not hesitate to take loans for paying fees. They will get proper education like in foreign; worth the fees Government has liberally started education loan schemes. This is the way for poor to become rich. When students go in private universities many seats will become free for poor people in government universities. Is this not a benefit for the poor?

Private universities have many other sources of income, for ex. earnings from patents, donations, consultancy, and research projects. Many campus jobs become available to students. The turnover in campus goes several times more, bringing income, scholarships to students. The students from poor family background are in fact better attended in private universities.

To win in global competition and to fulfill rising aspirations of the people, India cannot afford to ignore the proven model of private universities.

Private Universities are more successful in producing leaders

India is rich in resources yet we get goods from foreign countries. We have abundance of manpower. Yet the wanted cutting edge technologists are not available. There is a huge population but enterprising leaders are not available. Our conventional universities are producing followers. They bring technologies from abroad and teach here as traders. They do not have well springs of new knowledge, new technology and patents. They are like departmental stores or Relay centers. India needs private universities to create leaders, who create new theories, new technologies patents and IPR.

If India does not start private universities, Will it cause any damage?

Certainly yes it will. Many students will miss opportunity to take higher education. The overall intellectual capability of India in world comparison will remain low. The existing universities due to lack of competition will not improve. More and more students will go abroad for higher education. It will be a big drain on financial resources, besides brains. Universities abroad will flourish, and Indian universities will sink. Money form people in India instead of coming to our universities will flow out. Poverty in India will tend to increase. There will be plentiful manpower in India but unemployable. India's position in world instead of improving is likely to deteriorate. India is destined to miss vast opportunities if starting of private universities is delayed. The employment and income generation in India will get a setback. The present rising wave in software will also be adversely affected. If the above damage is to be avoided it is urgently necessary to start private universities. It is no more an option but compulsion. There are almost no risks in starting private universities. There are much greater risks in not starting private universities.

India Needs to Promote Private Universities To Excel in World

It is believed, the world over, that universities are international organizations. Although they get grants from Government yet what to teach and how to teach is not the business of Government but that of the university. Universities should render academic advice to Government and not the other way round. Private universities in industrially advanced countries were the first to give Phillip to scholarship. Nations like USA and Japan came forward to start private universities. It is these private universities, and not the state universities which have become a moving force, of their economies.

Starting private colleges is good but not enough. It is essential to start private universities

Government universities are not able even to declare the results of examination for three months. Now in WTO regime monopoly enjoyed by the universities in India and elsewhere in the world is being, abandoned. They are being exposed to competition not only domestic but also international. This is the beginning of worldwide improvement. Internationalization of higher education is taking place. This is too good for the younger generation. Private universities from, abroad and from India in this will play important role, which should be viewed as a positive sign. Private universities alone can take india on top of the world. This is the only way. Private universities in USA have taken their universities ahead of European universities, so are the findings of a evaluation report. In India too, private universities will take us ahead of our counterparts elsewhere in the world.

PRESENT STATUS

Maharashtra Government has issued the ordinance No XXII of 2004 on 16th August to provide for establishment of self Financed Universities in the State, to regulate their working and functions and for matters connected therewith or incidental thereto. The bill is yet to be presented in state assembly. The select committee is examining it.

The private university bill was presented in Parliament in August 1995. It was passed by Loksabha but unfortunately rejected by Rajya Sabha. The Supreme Court has already given green signal.

Supreme Court in the case of Chattisgarh has given stay in the matter. The Government of India is re-examining the proposal. This is with a view of better implementation.

Private University is a worldwide trend with high merits. However, it has to be implemented carefully. Otherwise a good scheme is likely to go in disrepute.

Universities, in India unfortunately are tending to become pawns in the hands of bureaucracy. Universities tend to become salves of the Government. It is only on account of this that there are many ills in higher education. More is expected from universities, which they are not able to give. Because most of the times bottlenecks are at the top like appointment of vice chancellor is not on fair considerations. The common man is unhappy. Blame for ills in higher education is passed on to teachers wrongly. Appointment of a non-academician like Divisional commissioner or Police commissioner as V C is against the fundamental principles of management. Such persons are experts in their fields but do not and cannot understand the pulse of academics. What will happen in match if selection of cricket team is done by government officers and ministers instead of cricket control board?

Private universities which do not have interference from government, provide a cure to the problems in higher education. They attach more value to academics. This explains the urgency of starting private universities. The implementation however is not that simple. Discovery and Innovation skills are the distinguishing features of university organizations from other government department. But government treats higher education like any other government department. Consequently the nation is being left behind in brain race. These are the things stopped forthwith.

CONCLUSION

Prime Minister Manmohan Singh in his speech on 15th August 2004 said, I quote.

"Higher education should not be the prisoner of either bureaucracy or ideology; it must develop on the foundations of professional excellence and intellectual integrity."

These are the words of wisdom, which need to be remembered and acted upon by the educationists and education administrators.

Bureaucracy is hi-jacking the interests of higher education. This is not desirable, in public interest. Dr. Radha Krishnan as chairman of UGC in 1948-49 wrote.

"We must resist, in the interest of our democracy, the trend towards the governmental domination of the educational process."

University system, in public interest, need to be pulled out of monopoly, and bureaucracy. It is necessary to expose it to competition locally and internationally. Setting up of private universities will restrict entry of foreign universities, which is essential in public interest. It will mark the beginning of a new era.

Creating knowledge based society in India demands a transnational effort. India has adopted the route to create the most dynamic and competitive knowledge based economy.

References

1. M A Tutkane, University Education: Reflection or Pathfinder of Society, University News 42 [46] November 15-21 2004.
2. B. M. Naik, Positive Aspects of Privatization, the Hindu, 7th Nov. 2001.
3. P. R. Dubhashi Privatization of Higher Education, University News 30th June 1997 Vol. 135 No. 26.
4. B. M. Naik Private Universities, Sakal 3rd Feb 2004- in Marathi.
5. Liksatta 25th November 2004.

6. Loksatta 26 April 2001.
7. Loksatta 21 July 2004.
8. Higher Education in Crisis, Economic Times Editiorial, 23rd December 2004.

13

Quality Assurance System in Higher and Technical Education

Total Quality Management [TQM] approach emphasizes quality assurance, by providing quality inputs. It has made a change in performance of organizations around the world. TQM enables to develop self-assessment culture, so essential to be progressive on sustained basis. Quality improvement involves the statistical tools, consumer research, goal setting, teamwork, problem solving, Human Resource Management, and strategic planning. This paper reviews different aspects of quality assurance, steps involved in implementation of TQM and Organizational frame work for implementation.

NEED AND IMPORTANCE

As many as 130,000 students in the year 2009 went to USA, UK, Australia, New Zealand, Germany, for higher education. The trend is increasing. It is because education in

India, of the quality in foreign, is simply not available. Each student has to spend around Rs. 15 lakhs per year. Yet they are going. We need to make introspection to build our institutions qualitative and competitive by world standards. This is essential to avoid brain drain and to achieve the dream of becoming a developed nation by 2020. India can fulfill the aspirations of younger generation, if and only if, it leads in quality, in research, innovation, IPR, patenting, and hi-tech start ups etc.

Both the students and industry have become quality conscious. They are willing to pay necessary cost. People expect more, but universities are not able to give. They put blame on shortage of finances. Truly they are not and expending resources, unproductively. Many institutions have five star infrastructures but the academic culture is obsolete. For example, the capacity utilization of installed facility in most of the institutions is too low. Most of them open in the morning at 10 and close at 5 in the evening. The counterpart institutions in developed countries open at 8 in the morning and close at 11 in the night. The libraries remain open twenty-four hours, round the year. Indian institutions are spending money, effort and time but fruitlessly. It is because there is almost a complete lack of scientific approach in Governance, which is the theme of this article.

Total quality Management approach emphasizes quality assurance, by providing quality inputs. It has made a change in performance of organizations around the world. Japanese economy became a powerhouse by using Total Quality Management. Dr. Deming one of the pioneers is practically worshiped in Japan. World best institutions are using TQM and by virtue of which they have reached high standing. It is necessary for the governing boards to prescribe TQM. They should provide visible unwavering support for implementation, Alignment of all the people in the organization to world-class vision is necessary. The curricula need to be made matching with the requirement of tomorrow and day after.

There are professors and staffs who like to contribute in a full way to improve. But there are circumstances, which prevent them from reaching their full potential. What kind of circumstance? TQM identifies them. It is for policy makers sitting in AICTE/UGC, with out any delay, to initiate steps for installation of quality assurance cell. Accreditation will become meaningful only if the cell for quality is set up.

Imperatives of TQM

Quality can be improved by external agencies like AICTE/ UGC through inspections. It has however, to be supplemented by internal efforts, with in the institution. It is here that quality assurance plays a key role. Having resources, enthusiasm, and common sense is good but adopting scientific quality assurance method is essential.

The students in both private and public institutes deserve the best possible quality, so as to fulfill the national dream of becoming a super power. It is the duty and professional responsibility of governing boards, trustees to provide best possible education.

Professors and administrators have to be competent by international standards. They ought to have professional commitment and an obligation to employ world best practices.

The competitive imperative stems from competition prevailing in education. Best students and best faculty can be attracted only if the institute is professionally managed. The institutes only there by can remain on top.

Institutes have to be accountable to government and society. TQM enables them to become more accountable.

The cost of ignoring the quality assurance is too high. It is in terms of letting the nation lag behind in world brain race, resulting in low standard of living. The institutions tend to lose best teachers, best students, and reputation.

TQM can't be purchased. It has to be practiced step-by-step and developed by conscious efforts. This cannot happen overnight. It does not provide instant success. It will throw up new difficulties and challenges. It is a slow process, but the benefits are long term. TQM enables to develop self-assessment culture, so essential to be progressive on sustained basis.

PRINCIPLES OF QUALITY MANAGEMENT

Quality assurance believes in "prevention is better than cure." Eating good food is essential for good health. With this logic the method prescribes control on inputs. Traditional Quality Control concept is obsolete. It is the lack of application of scientific systems that hold up quality and not the shortage of resources.

Efficiency of the systems is at the roots. Institutions where systems are good, people tend to work efficiently. Bad systems are found to cripple the innovative people.

Quality is systems improvement. It is the systems, which matter.

Systems improvement is not a one shot affair. It is an unending journey.

It requires a deliberate and persistent attempt in a systematic way.

Quality does not come by chance or by accident.

People are not the problems but the systems.

Quality is every one's job, from top to bottom.

Quality is continuous improvement, [Kaisen] i.e. working slowly and steadily, like tortoise that won the race.

Quality comes when the leaders are passionate.

Quality comes through strategy of better Human Resource Development.

Quality is empowering professors.

Quality is fear reduction in the minds of employees.

Quality is recognition and reward.

Quality comes through better teamwork.

Quality is measurement of input, output by using statistical methods.

Quality is systematic problem solving.

Quality comes through opinion surveys for understanding customer needs by statistical methods.

Quality comes through Benchmarking, i.e. by comparison preferably with world best. What the counterpart institutions else where in the world are doing, and how are they doing? What do the teachers in best institutions do? Are they passionate about teaching and research?

Quality comes when every one does work in correct way, right in the first instance. It requires hard work, but essentially smart work.

Quality is meeting or exceeding the customer needs. If you do not satisfy the customers some one else will. If institutions do not offer better education students will go somewhere else.

Inspection does not improve quality. It hurts.

Quality improvement involves the statistical tools, consumer research, goal setting teamwork, problem solving, HRM, and strategic planning.

Quality goes beyond Accreditation. Accrediting agencies, program reviews, standing committees, local inspection committees, and control minded governing boards and well intension task force all alone by themselves will never be able to improve quality. Most of these quality causing mechanisms view quality from inspection perspective, which is defeated scientifically.

Inspections do not result in decrease of the number of defects. In fact they increase.

Accreditation measures quality, like the thermometer.

Impressing pre requisites of quality on the minds of people, government and people's representatives is necessary. If quality is important it must be well articulated, so that legislators make it obligatory.

Organizational Frame Work For Implementation

It requires creation of a cell in the institution.

It requires a team of leaders to develop vision.

It requires office of quality assurance.

It requires implementation team.

It requires internal and external networking.

It requires advisory team.

It requires support form top.

It requires planning.

It requires design of questionnaire and feedback from customers.

The word total in TQM stands for, total number of systems, total number of persons, activities, customers, stakeholders, and inputs and out puts.

Satisfy all the customers and quality follows

Some of the customers are listed below :

Students.

Faculty

Alumni

Industry.

Staff.

Government

Society etc.

Aim of the institute should be to satisfy each and every customer with out an exception. The institute has to respond to multi customer environment. Developing happy customers is a sign of quality. TQM leads to making the institute preferred.

The leadership of an organization must, by word and deeds convey the message that customer satisfaction, through a process of continually improving quality is the responsibility of every member of the organization. Inappropriate systems create problems, regardless of person or persons. Therefore systems should be attended with utmost care. Incentives should be given to remove deficiencies.

Remove the barriers that rob the people of pride of their work. Do not ignore any one, for ignoring is demoralizing. Make sure that expectations are clear and well understood. This creates a positive environment. The expectations must become tangible and ubiquitous. It is impossible to feel ignored if some one is paying attention.

Quality circle is a mechanism to involve all from bottom to top. Small groups of people analyzed and evolve solutions to current problems.

Solving problems in such a way that they do not continue to occur is the essence of TQM. Reacting to crisis, known as "fire-fighting approach" is not good.

A little praise goes a long way for most of the people, to keep them prideful. Individuals are like flowers, which need watering regularly, without which they wither. People become mediocre without encouragement and by abandonment. If maintained prideful they deliver quality.

There were two stonecutters. One was emotionally involved in building a temple. He was found doing a fine job. The other stonecutter was rather sour, disgruntled. He was also involved in building the temple. But he was not doing his job as fine as the other. He was seen unhappy because he did not know the noble cause for which he was working.

Systematic approach to quality management is necessary. This is given by TQM. Institutions need a new approach to managing human and fiscal resources. Quality management is not one-shot affair but an ongoing journey.

Increased funding will not improve quality, if we do not allocate resources wisely. This demands TQM. If we do not use funds to promote distinctiveness, and if we are not able to create customer satisfaction, the investment is unproductive.

DIMENSIONS OF SERVICE QUALITY

ACCESS: Maintaining customer driven office hours is desirable. Providing efficient telephone, e-mail service provides easy access. Effective communication with customers is important.

Keeping Customer informed: Explaining in writing what services will be provided by the institution, what are the costs and visions of the institution in long range and short range. Assuring the customer of the intentions of the organization is essential.

Competence: The institution should spell out and justify how it is competent, having the necessary skills and knowledge. It should demonstrate its excellence in its teaching job through statistics of results. Appropriate indicators should explain the research capabilities.

Courtesy: Politeness treating students with dignity and honor. Extending equal treatment to all is desirable.

Credibility: Honesty, trust worthiness, having fair policies in recruitment of deserving candidates.

Reliability: Consistency of performance and dependability. Getting rid of incompetent employees, reducing billing errors.

Responsiveness: returning phone calls, replying letters, resolving complaints on time are the usual weaknesses.

Security: Freedom from risk, danger, doubt, assuring physical safety, protecting individual's privacy.

Tangibles: Physical evidence of service, maintaining campus grounds, acquiring appropriate technology deserves greater attention.

Knowing the customer: Providing individual attention, and developing means to listen obtaining feedback at regular intervals.

Customer Focus: Institutions must change their attitudes in favor of customers.

There can be no culture of quality without consistent and persistent distributed leadership though out the organization.

AUTONOMY IS ESSENTIAL

As institutes needs considerable degree of autonomy, and flexibility so that it has the freedom to teach and freedom to research, without political or any other kind of interference, so that creativity and imagination are encouraged, and so that resources including the time and energy of faculty staff and students are used effectively. The institute also needs the involvement of state as a force for meeting the public needs, as a force for change, and as a force for accountability. The problem therefore is not to eliminate the state's role but to perfect it.

As a leader do you hear the customers?

Do you issue only circulars or obtain feedback? Feed back loop is essential.

Do you meet employees formally and also informally?

Do you conduct customer surveys, to assess how satisfied they are?

Do you simply talk on quality or engage in deeds?

Are the curricula fit for tomorrow and day after?

Do you change the minds of employees with new ideas every time you meet?

VISION STATEMENT

Vision statement ought to be stimulating, unifying, guiding, and distinctive. It is the foundation on which the "house of quality" is built.

What is the unifying distinctive vision? It is a vision, which touches the hearts of people inviting their emotional involvement. It provides organizational rallying force. It evokes a meaning with reference to the institution proper. It allows an institution to enjoy a unique position in the higher education environment.

Vision statement communicates key values for today as well as for the future. Vision statement provides a sense of purpose, for which the institution exists.

Vision Statement of a typical world-class institute, says

It needs to be recognized internationally.

The institute wants to be the world best place to study and work.

It intends each student to learn at least one additional language, to have three months experience in foreign country, show tolerance towards culture, beliefs and faiths of others.

The institute wants faculty to have international experience and to increase international research projects by 50% in coming five years, and to involve students in each of them.

The institute wants to know, what clients ten years from now expect, and to excel their expectations.

The institutes want to solve problems and meet challenges by a team, regardless of their level of jobs.

Institute aims at producing leaders, pioneers in technology.

It intends to produce start-ups in high technology. Raise the target from 20 to 40 in coming two years.

The institute today obtains 150 patents every year. It intends to raise the target to 200 in coming year.

It wants to discover newer technologies for the welfare of human kind.

It intends to expand its net to countries in Asia, and China.

Existing vision statements in most of the institutes in India are meaningless, because connecting links between vision and operating systems are missing.

The top people must articulate quality in speeches, and weave if with public relations. The top management should make their institute unique by becoming outstanding.

Every one needs to connect his duties and responsibilities with others.

SOLVING PROBLEMS

Each president's office is a magnet, which attracts problems. The buck stops there.

Solving problems is not the answer to improving the quality. The solution lies in understanding and continuously improving the processes that give rise to problems.

Take processes in hand for improvement first which are easy. One should attempt difficult processes in the course of time. Do not attempt all at a time.

7.1 85: 15 Rules

85% what goes wrong in an institution is due to poor systems. Only 15% fault is attributable to individuals.

The process is incomplete without closing the loop, known as feed back loop.

The responsibility for quality in higher education does not lie at the top alone but with every one in the organization.

Empowering people with in the organization to improve quality is essential. If you do not empower people to improve quality, you can loose both the customer and employee.

If you do not empower people, you encourage and reward sloth ness.

If you do not empower people you will become inundated with bureaucrats and manuals.

The organization becomes a collection of under achievable.

Quality Management needs to be viewed from others point who receive higher education services, and not from the viewpoint of those who provide.

Make a five-year quality improvement plan.

Motivation alone is not enough to generate change.

It essentially requires academic freedom to maintain a distance from a whole host of evils, both real and imaginary.

The implementation team will prepare a Quality Manual.

Quality Policy, Quality Procedure, Quality audit be conducted every year.

STEPS INVOLVED IN IMPLEMENTATION OF TQM

Conduct awareness programs.

Make a survey of expectations of the customers, and assess how satisfied they are, through well-designed questionnaire.

Discuss the results of survey openly.

Prepare vision statement with the involvement of all.

Identify the processes, and systems in the institutions and outside.

The systems are for example.

Internal systems for:

Admission,
Teaching theory and practical
Examination,
Practical training, Recruitment of faculty and staff
Promotions
Pension benefits
Dealing with unions
Finance and Account system
Purchase system
Campus maintenance
Hostels etc.

External systems:

Interaction with industry,
Interaction with international institutes,
Industry,
Research,
Commercial exploitation of findings of research.
Links with university,
Links with government,
Fund raising etc.
Each of the process needs thorough examination.
Questions need to be raised,
How well is existing process doing?
Why does the process exist?
How does it compare with the processes else where,
Preferably with world best institution?
Who benefits from the process?
Does the customer benefit?
What are the inputs and outputs?
What is their quality?
What are unfulfilled expectations?
What incentives are needed?
Do you celebrate success at each step?

What are opportunities and strengths?

What are the threats and weaknesses?

Have you prepared vision statement in joint meetings?

Have you conducted interviews with the people who are benchmarks?

Each system has

(a) Inputs

(b) Processes and

(c) Outputs

For improving the system one has to make analysis, benchmarking, and use of "Planning-Development-Control-Action [PDCA]" cycle, on continuing basis for each of inputs, process, and outputs. Histograms, flow charts, pie chart, and other statistical methods are strongly suggested. Decisions should not be based on intuition but necessarily on statistics.

To summarize

The future of our children and grand children is bright only if the institutions are professionally managed by using TQM.

TQM is essential for survival and growth. If they do not do so forth with, the governance of education in India will be labeled outdated and inefficient. Indian education may go in the hands of foreign universities. Implementation of quality management systems should be done preferably with the help of a consultant. This ensures success.

Professors and staff should be trained and empowered.

TQM is made compulsory in England for all organizations, which draw financial aid from Government. Should this be a hint for India?

TQM enhances capacity utilization. Cost per unit of out put is reduced. Economic rate of return from investments is increased.

Indian academic community should take an initiative.

There is none from India in the 100 world best universities. MIT, Wisconsin, and Oxford, Cambridge is all using TQM, and so they are world class.

Many institutions in India are spending money far in excess but due to lack of TQM approach they do not excel.

Implementation of TQM does not require money; it results in saving.

The members of legislatures, governing boards should immediately take a drive to I Use TQM.

Should the National Knowledge Commission prescribe TQM? Yes.

The responsibility for using TQM lies with the policy makers sitting in the governing boards, AICTE and UGC.

References

1. R. P. Mohanty, R. R. Lakhe, Handbook of Total Quality Management, Jaico Publishing House, 2004.
2. Edward Sails, Does TQM Have A Role in Education. The Journal of Engineering Education, October 2005 Vol. XIX No 2.
3. P. Prema, Quality Assurance in Professional Training of Teacher Educators: Challenges and Strategies, University News, Vol. 42 No. 32, August 09-15 2004.
4. M. Aruchami, Quality Imperatives in Higher Education, University News Vol. 42 No. 05 February 02-08, 2004.
5. Romesh Verma, Quality and Relevance in Education, University News Vol. 42 No. 10 March 08-14, 2004.
6. Prem Vrat, Quality System for Excellence in Engineering Education, University News, Vol. 43 No. 39, September 26 October 02, 2005.

14

Science Park Valuable Tool To Tap Knowledge

Science Park Generates Welath and Employment

Science Park is a new invention. It has come to be known as a major source for creation of new wealth. It has proved to be very effective in tapping the valuable knowledge of academicians working in higher education institutes for commercial purpose. Science/Technology Parks are found to be especially useful in employment generation, industrial development, and in making education more relevant and purposeful. Having realized the importance, the department of science and technology Government of India launched the scheme way back in seventh plan to begin with, in only a few universities and engineering colleges. Based on the experience in India and abroad, it can be said that a vigorous attempt now need to be made in the current plan to establish parks on a large-scale basis, especially in less developed regions.

A science park is defined as an industrial complex, close to a place of learning, like university, engineering college, polytechnic or a research laboratory. It is designed to encourage formation of knowledge or technology-based industries in a high quality and pleasant environment. It has a function of transfer of technology and business skills to enterprises. It provides accommodation to tenant companies on rental basis. It aims at reducing the time-gap between invention and its commercial application.

Research Park differs from Science Park in the sense that it prohibits all manufacture except for prototypes. Various companies are welcomed to establish their research centers in the park adjacent to universities. The research personnel benefit most from interaction with each other and with the academicians in the university. Often they undertake collaborative research so as to compete in the international market, although they compete with each other in the domestic market. Innovation centre consists of a group of buildings close to a centre of academic excellence, providing accommodation and other facilities on a short-term basis which enable newly-started firms and small business firms to develop ideas. It does not provide accommodation to an enterprise once it has grown. It is like a nursery of plants or an incubator.

Business Park provides high quality accommodation in which a wide variety of activities such as manufacture, showroom, distribution, etc. can be performed. Business Park does not have links necessarily with higher education institutes or does not have tenants which deal in high technology.

Techno polis in Japan provides a high quality infrastructure with all kinds of services needed by a firm. Techno polis is established for starting hi-tech industries in rural areas near the universities and research laboratories and where rail, air, road transport air communications are available. Recreation facilities schools, sports, etc. are especially built up if not available.

In the US, three very different patterns of parks emerged at MIT in Boston, at Stanford University and at the Research Triangle Park in North Carolina. The growth of Boston Park is clearly associated with MIT, through the formation of hi-tech business in the surrounding area. Graduates and former staff of MIT have been the single most important source of spin-off entrepreneurs in the region in electronics and related industries. The growth was spontaneous at a time when employment in textiles in the region was declining. The other two have grown out of a clear policy and initiative taken by Prof Terman at Stanford and Prof Luther Hodge at the Research Triangle Park. The commonality in them is that both of them have been sponsored by universities. Initiatives were also taken by federal, state and the city governments. Almost each university in the USA has a park attached to it on a land of more than 200 acres.

Japan is implementing, "The Techno polis Strategy", to develop its backward regions under which 26 Silicon Valley's are installed. They emphasis more on development of high value-added products and services, techno polis is designed to become the engine for Japan's economic growth in the 21st Century.

They consist of (i) new university (ii) research park, (iii) joint research consortia, (iv) venture capital foundations, (v) office complex with latest tele-communications and (vi) recreation facilities.

In the UK, there are more than 50 parks fully operational and some more are under establishment. All the parks taken together house more than 5000 enterprises, employing more than 40,000 qualified scientists and engineers. Most of the enterprises on the park are knowledge-based and deal in high technology like micro-electronics, computer hardware, system software, CAD/CAM, consultancy, etc. The entrepreneurs are in the age group of 28 to 35 years with 20 percent of them from universities and polytechnics.

On-park enterprises are found to perform far better than similar off-park enterprises. The failure rate is hardly 2 per cent. Most of them have links, both formal and informal, with higher education institutes. The firms which are backed by universities are more successful than others. Academics have proved to be more resourceful in giving ideas of innovation. Almost every enterprise has produced a new product/patent in the last two years. Export has totaled 20 percent. New technology based firms find it much more easily to start on the park. Value addition made by them is much higher than firms elsewhere.

Cambridge University, which was once orthodox in the academic value system and was initially hesitant towards installation of park, has also found it an extremely valuable addition. It has further enhanced the scholarship and prestige of the university, besides transforming the total economy of the region. The attitude of the university authorities and the Government has undergone a complete change.

A major contribution to Science Park has come from academicians. Parks have given a stimulus to academics to start a business. Without a science park most of the academician owned enterprises would not have been started at all. The attitude of young scientists towards entrepreneurship has also improved and the brain drain from UK has been arrested. More and more firms are being established on the seed bed of science parks.

Science Park has emerged as the best agency for employment generation. Employment on a sustained basis of high quality environment, productivity income and prospective in nature is generated on the parks. The old jobs, lost owing to the decline of textile and steel industry, have been made up far in excess by the parks. The performance of conventional industry on account of the emergence of parks has also improved. Parks have been pumping continuously new technologies in industry.

The role of the Government has been central to the establishment of science parks in all countries in the world. The higher education institutes have undoubtedly been the leaders of this change. The universities, IIT's and engineering colleges in India would also have to perceive the role being played by their counterparts elsewhere in the world and adopt an attitude favorable for promoting entrepreneurial culture. They would have also to aim at playing a leading role in initiating the installation of science parks in India.

The service conditions of academic staff would have possibly to be reviewed so as to enable them to commercialize their knowledge. This would certainly pose problems which, however, are possible to be resolved. Researchers and academicians would have to be permitted to associate themselves with business, perhaps on a part-time without jeopardizing teaching and their academic pursuits.

The state industrial development corporations which are setting up industrial estates in big cities and smaller towns have recorded a slow growth and high rate of failure. The level of technology employed by enterprises in these estates is often outdated, resulting in sickness. It is recommended that a task force be appointed for expeditious installation of science parks in the industrial estates.

Technology Park Gives Quick Returns At Enhanced Rate on Investment. It Brings Strength to the Process of Industrial Development.

Science and Technology Park and Its Relevance To India

More Innovation More Progress **No Innovation No Progress.**

Science and Technology Park is a worldwide movement to promote establishment of new technology based firms. The purpose of the article is to bring out the important aspects about this new invention and the impact it has caused on economy of those countries and relevance to India. The article also presents the concept, utility, feasibility and future scope of such parks in India and explain how it can help to solve some of our chronic problems like unemployment, irrelevance of education, industrial sickness, brain drain, etc. what has been the new approach towards such parks elsewhere in the world, what has been done in India, so far, and what is contemplated in Current Plan, will also be presented.

It needs no emphasis that science and technology has come to be known as a prime mover of economy. Obviously, therefore, the Government is attempting to develop India as a technology oriented nation. It has devised numerous schemes to promote industrialization and granted huge financial resources for the implementation. India has third largest technical manpower in the world along with vast natural resources like minerals, iron ore, coal, land, water etc. However, the output from industrial sector, although increasing is not commensurate. The productivity is far too low by world standards. It is not that the people work less or are less intelligent. What is lacking is that what Dr. Termen at Stanford University, US in 1950 observed

"Industry needs access to high-quality research in order to be competitive in international market. Academicians ought to commercialize the results of their research for the overall good of humankind."

With this philosophical approach the concept of Science Park was born around 1950 in Stanford U.S. Now North Carolina Research Triangle Park, adjacent to three universities, is occupying 6500 acres of land. There are more than 900 PhDs employed in this park. It is evaluated that each one is adding value more than $1, 26,000 to the local economy.

There are more than 3000 affiliating companies to M.I.T. Boston, for exchange of scientific ideas. They owe their origin to MIT. Each company is paying royalty of about $1, 00,000 to the M.I.T. in return. Emergence of new technology – based firms with the partnership of leading edge experts in higher education institutes is becoming the trend. This is obvious from the fact that now *new industrial complexes, world over, are coming up only around Universities.*

Technology transfer from academic and research institutes within the country to industry for improvement of productivity have been a major concern of the Government. The available technology in universities, I.I.T.'s engineering colleges, NRDC, and CSIR laboratories is not put to fuller use, and brain drain takes place. This is largely because there exists no organizational mechanism like Science Park to affect the transfer of technology. The transfer is left only to a chance.

Consequently, in spite of availability of talent and technology in the country, technology continues to be imported. There are structural arrangements, well-defined systems and procedures for such imports and hence it takes place more frequently resulting into thousands of foreign collaborations. The priorities have been all along in favor of collaborators, providing only disincentives to the indigenous academic and research institutes.

In industrially advanced countries there are "technology parks" attached to science and technology universities which are found to be very effective for the purpose of technology transfer. Such an organization is a missing link in India. The Department of science and Technology has started a scheme of Science and Technology Entrepreneurs Park, "STEP".

It may not be out of place here to discuss the organizational structure of Technology Park, functioning. In the U.K. several such parks are flourishing in that country including Research Park at Herriot Watt University, Aston Science Park University of Birmingham, and Science Park at Bradford University and Technology Park at Cambridge University.

These parks are run not by engineering departments of universities alone but by the autonomous organizations established specially for the purpose. The management rests with directors from associations of industry, municipalities, banks, financial institutions, and the university etc. The parks are attached to universities, but independently managed and maintained. University and park are interdependent. Universities function as energizing force for their progress. New business and technology ideas come from research in universities. Scholars are working in both of them.

The role of engineering departments of the nearest university is like a "promoter and catalyst". The parks are physically situated in the immediate vicinity of a university campus, which facilitates easy communication between professors and entrepreneurs. The laboratories, library, computing centers of the institutes are shared also by entrepreneurs on payment basis. These parks provide the entire infrastructure like space, electricity, water, telex, telephone, security, etc. Some common services like typing, marketing, etc. are also provided. It provides all the infrastructure, venture capital, raw material and guidance for every enterprise. Because these facilities are taken care of by the organization managing the technology park, the entrepreneur can concentrate on functions of his enterprise without any loss of time. The heads of the technology parks are experienced and highly motivated people.

The prospective entrepreneur often a graduate student makes an application to the management for space in Technology Park. A large number of such applications are received which are then scrutinized, and selection is made by a committee of experts. The criteria for selection are that the project should be using advanced technology not otherwise easily available.

The university faculty is also encouraged to take active part in the establishment and running of these enterprises. Some of their students also take part and earn while they learn at the university. Some professors go on deputation to technology parks keeping a lien on their services at the university.

The technology parks have been taking part in international exhibitions and, therefore, even small enterprises automatically become known in the international markets. Some parks also have marketing companies, which undertake marketing of products. Likewise other specialized services including personnel, training, recruitment are also provided to small entrepreneurs. The small-scale companies enjoy a good deal of freedom and autonomy to try out innovative ideas. When these entrepreneurs grow, into a big company they transfer themselves to bigger industrial estates. Thus the technology parks function like nurseries.

The size of technology parks is growing every year. Many professors have themselves become entrepreneurs. They may even permanently migrate to industry. Almost every university in the U.K. today has a technology park attached to it, and has succeeded.

In U.K parks have come together and formed a Science Park Association. It has evaluated the performance of all the parks and their contribution to national economy.

The higher education institutes have undoubtedly been the Leaders of this change. The universities, IITs and engineering colleges in India would also have a valuable reservoir of knowledge, experience and talent much of it is at leading edge of new technologies, but for want of Science Park it remains underutilized.

Because of low failure rate of enterprises on park, and high employment and economic growth, Science Park fulfills the most important objective for nation building. In the face of large scale sickness in small scale industry and grim unemployment situation, in India, establishment of Science Park, merits high consideration for vigorous implementation. In the Current Five Year Plan period Technology and economic progress are fundamentally linked with each other and to translate technology into business, especially for rural development, Science Park offers a much better proposition.

Science and Technology Park is a new invention. It provides a high class infrastructure and environment in the vicinity of higher education institutes where qualified scientists and engineers can professionally grow. It has come to be known as a major source of creation of new technology based firms. It has proved to be very effective in tapping the valuable resource of knowledge of academicians for the growth of professions and productivity. The scheme is found to be especially useful to promote employment industrial development and making education more relevant and purposeful.

In India, many engineering colleges offering graduate and postgraduate education have reached a stage where establishment of a technology park can prove immensely useful to them as well as students passing out of these institutions. It is not enough now to just produce engineers and technologists from institutes located in industrially backward areas. It is essential to offer them an environment like that of a technology park so that they can take firm roots in their regions, start enterprises and not migrate to other places.

Science and technology parks are more pertinent for qualified scientists and engineers. especially in the age group of 22 to 35 years, academicians in engineering colleges, IITs, universities and polytechnics. Parks are also important for Government administrators, banks, who are vested with powers of decision making.

India needs such a scheme most. The steps taken by the Department of Science and Technology, in setting up parks are in a right direction, and it is hoped that in current plan period the scheme will be invigorated and many more parks will be established to help to raise the masses above the poverty live.

Technology Park is a Means To Poverty Eradication. It Leads To Teaching Valid Knowledge And Quickly Transfering It To The Real World of Work.

RESOURCE GENERATION THROUGH TECHNOLOGY PARK

Unless and until there is a major academic reform in the engineering curricula, it will not be possible for the students to stand to pressure of international competition in Technology and win in 21st Century. Today, the academic courses are not oriented to entrepreneurship. Even after studying for four years the students are required to undergo rigorous training in industry. They have to start learning the practice of engineering from beginning. Why do only professors decide the curriculum? Why there is no involvement from industries in academic reforms? Why is there no interconnection between industry and technical institutions? Why is entrepreneurship, in spite of vigorous efforts, not growing at expected rate? Why is capacity utilization of knowledgeable people so low? Why is innovation so low although talent is available? How to arrest the brain drain of engineers and technologists? Why is our industry dependent on technologies coming from abroad? All these questions can be answered by studying the "Technology Park" scheme, which is first established in U.S.A. and U.K. and is now doing a good job world over. Technology Park organizations not only provide a link between industry and educational institute but do much more for human welfare.

ORGANISATION STRUCTURE

It is important to understand the organizational structure of "Technology Parks" functioning in U.K. and elsewhere.

Following are the typical technology parks which are popular for their high achievement.

1. Research Park at Herriot Watt University, Edinburgh.
2. Aston Science Park, University of Birmingham.
3. Science Part at Bradford University.

These parks are run by the autonomous organizations established specially for the purpose and managed by directors from Association of Industry, Municipality, Bank, Financial Institutions etc. University is often the promoter.

The parks are physically situated in the immediate vicinity of university campus, which facilities easy communication between professors and entrepreneurs. These parks provide the entire infrastructure like space, electricity, water, telex, telephone, security, etc. Some common services like typing, marketing etc. are also provided. It provides all the infrastructure, venture, capital, raw-material, and guidance to every enterprise. Because of these facilities being taken care of by the organization of Science Park, the entrepreneur can concentrate on major functions of his enterprise without any loss of time, the heads of the technology parks are experienced and highly motivated persons.

FUNCTIONS

The objectives of Science Park / Technology Park are

1. To facilitate the transfer of technology from laboratory to industry as quickly as possible and to reduce the lead time between invention and commercial application, which improve competitiveness of industry?
2. To provide a platform to the entrepreneurs for starting enterprises, such that they have not to waste their time and energy on establishment of infrastructure and they could focus on technological advancement.
3. To establish a close relation on continuing basis between institute and industry and permit theory to influence practice for its continued up gradation, and to remain competitive.
4. To create an environment in which high-tech knowledgeable people feel happy to work and live and contribute at high pitch of their efficiency.
5. To facilitate technical education to remain more relevant, purposeful, up to date and cost effective.
6. To provide a pipe line for the flow of technology from college to industry. Transfer of technology is not left to chance but a formal well defined and efficient proper method is provided.
7. To provide safety to clients from exploitation and cheating by some unscrupulous consultants.

8. To facilitate development of in house technology and to reduce our dependence on foreign technology.
9. To ensure that the resources, financial physical are allocated to genuine entrepreneurs, and to transfer their energies in technological areas, by virtue of location in one place. The sickness of industries, which presently is a wide scale problem, would be reduced.
10. To step up capacity utilization of scarce facilities installed in laboratories, and of human capital in colleges.
11. In the absence of technology park, industrialists have a tendency to use imported, although old technology. The trend could be reversed for better new indigenous technologies and make it available much cheaper and quicker.
12. To provide experience and parental care to young knowledgeable enthusiastic entrepreneurs, to nurse them to use latest technologies till they grow.

METHODOLOGY

The students who have an inclination for business and industry make applications which are then scrutinized. Selection is made by a committee of experts. The criteria for selection normally are that the project should be using high-tech, should require inputs from university professors, library and laboratories.

The professors of the universities are also encouraged to take active part in the establishment and running of enterprises, many of their students also take part and earn while they learn in university. Some professors go on deputation to Technology Park keeping a lien on services in university, especially those who have innovative and bright ideas, which are not acceptable to any entrepreneur for implementation.

The technology parks have been taking part in international exhibitions and therefore the names of small enterprises put up their patents and IPR in the international market. Sometimes in this park there are marketing companies, which undertake marketing of products, like wise there are many specialized services like personnel, training, recruitment etc., which are provided by small entrepreneurs.

These small-scale companies are enjoying lot of freedom and autonomy to try out innovative ideas. When these entrepreneurs grow, into a big company, they often transfer themselves to bigger industrial estates. Thus the technology park functions like a Nursery of Industries of young Entrepreneurs under the supervision of university professors.

The size of Technology Park every year is growing, and they are acquiring additional lands for the purpose. Many professors spin-off and become entrepreneurs in high-tech. They may get permanently migrated to industry. Almost every university in U.K. today has a technology park attached to it, and they are proud of their success in arresting the brain drain from country through this scheme.

Now they have such parks in Boston, Ann Arbor, Palo Alto in America, there are more than forty companies which spin-off every year from MIT Electronics laboratory alone, and thirty companies from its instrumentation laboratory. In 1972, MIT even incorporated a development foundation to launch new companies that would use MIT technologies. Technology parks have facilitated them to modernize their industry. The textile and steel industries have gone away and the same are replaced completely by electronics, and computer industries, in which the margin of profit is much larger. Some observers have reported that the main driving force behind entrepreneurship in Technology Park is the academic staff in engineering departments of universities. Universities have functioned as "Incubators" and have attracted entrepreneurs, young men and women from far off places to their regions. Nearness of enterprise to knowledge center is a very important factor for successful working of an enterprise and hence big industrial complexes have grown around technical universities.

There is now an international association of technology parks. Every year, they meet and exchange experiences.

Relevance of Technology Park to Backward Areas

In industrially backward regions, for example, there are now many engineering colleges offering degree level education. Students passing out from usually take jobs in Government or Public/Private sector undertakings. They migrate to industrial belts like Mumbai and Pune.

Many desire to start enterprises in their regions but they lack capital, experience and environment, and so they migrate to places elsewhere. In backward areas, it is not enough now to produce graduates and post-graduates. *It is essential to offer them an environment like Technology Park so that they take roots in this region, start enterprises and do not migrate to other places.*

It is this first class material "Human Capital" coming out of colleges the "Bain Power Factories" which is a critical input to industrialization. Experience in the world elsewhere like Silicon Valley Corporation, Manchester, Birmingham etc. has made it clear that modern successful industrial complexes could grow as "Spin-Off" of research and knowledge based institutes. Universities in backward regions have to show vision for future; have to make a note of this. For planning of future development they have to think of providing avenues to technologically competent youths. It is a right time to conceive a scheme like "Technology Park" to redirect the future work force to High Tech., in which the pay-off is much higher and working environment much superior.

Such a park, if developed, will undoubtedly promote employment generation for all kinds of people in the region and raise the income and their standard of living. There is more of freedom, money, scope for growth and prosperity in High-Tech entrepreneurship. Graduates and post-graduates in engineering are increasingly taking to entrepreneurship. If this is to grow and their efforts to bear fruit, establishment of **Technology Park** is the only way.

Steps Involved in Establishing A Technology Park

1. To develop awareness of Technology park amongst teaching faculty.
2. To develop awareness amongst the key persons in organization like District Industries Center, MSFC, SICOM, Municipality, MIDC, Industries association, Banks, etc.
3. To appoint a steering committee to float a collaborative company of college, Banks, MSFC, MIDC, DIC, ST etc. and establish project directors office to form a co-operative society or a separate public limited company for this purposes.
4. To raise share capital and obtain loan from funding agencies.
5. Purchase of twenty five acres of land & constructed two sheds of about Rs.10 Lakhs.
6. To provide the entire infrastructure like water supply, electricity, telephone, telex, central office, etc.
7. To select entrepreneurs and their projects.

New Technology Based Firms (NTBF) Ought To Flow From Colleges To Industrial Estates
India Became A British Colony Not Because of Warriors Like Lord Clive and Waren Hasting, But Because of Scientists Like Neuton

RESEARCH BASE FOR GROWTH CENTRE AND INDUSTRIAL CLUSTER

LEARNING from the experience of other countries, it can be said that the growth centers and industrial clusters currently being established in India would have to be competitive not only by Indian standards but by the standards of recent industrial complexes being established elsewhere. For this, they essentially need to have a research base and should have structural bonds with academics elsewhere.

THE academic research institutes have a vital role to play in both establishment and running of clusters and growth centers. From the experience elsewhere in the world and in India, it can be said that enterprises in growth centers need to have easy access to the latest research, so as to remain competitive. Without a strong research base in science and technology in each growth centre, they will not be able to achieve the desired objectives.

The aim of setting up the growth centers / clusters is to promote industrialization of backward areas with concomitant infrastructure development, thereby bringing about balanced growth in such areas. Each cluster / growth center is proposed to be located in large area and will be provided the necessary industrial and social infrastructure, at par with the best available in the country, with big investment.

Guidelines for the preparation of project proposals have been sent to various states by the Centre and the same have also been published. *It is observed that there is a missing link in this scheme, namely, that of an academics connection with the cluster and growth centre.* A critical examination of this scheme in the light of experience all over the world so as to avoid mistakes is essential.

NEW TECHNOLOGY

With the rapid rate of change of technology, it is observed that for revival of the economy and employment generation there is a need to establish new technology based firms (NTBF) and to restructure the existing industry. This would have to be driven by the latest science and technology available in universities, technical institutes and research laboratories.

A recent OECD publication observed that a nation which lags behind in "technological innovation" will tend to lose jobs to those countries which lead in introduction of new technologies.

In view of this the scheme of growth centre ought to have an innovative character.

Technology change today is so fast that product cycles have become much shorter and obsolescence quicker. The opportunities in the national and international markets are immense, but they are short-lived. To cope with this situation demands flexibility in technological and organizational capacity, which, in fact, is now the limiting factor for growth. It is not so much the availability of raw materials, finance and markets which determine the feasibility, but the ability of people to generate and assimilate newer technologies. This is an overriding factor which needs to be attended to in implementing the scheme of industrializations.

RESEARCH BASE

This demands "research base", strategic alliances for research, collaborative arrangements and joint attempts by industry, Government and academic institutes. This has given rise to the establishment of "research parks" on university campuses. Consequently, science and technology institutes, which were earlier on the periphery of development, have now, by virtue of their increased influence on competitiveness, moved to the centre.

Due to increased communications the world is now a global village and national economies are tending to become international. The growth centers and industrial clusters would have, therefore, to be designed so that they are globally competitive.

Quite often, when there is a foreign collaboration, there is only import of equipment, and the effort to assimilate technology and adapt it to the Indian situation is rare. This is largely because individual enterprise technologically is often too week. The common research base, if installed for each cluster/ growth centre, will fill up this gap.

These themes are related time and again in national and international level conferences, yet it is feared that the critical linkage of frontiers of science and technology with establishment of industrial centers in India is being lost sight of.

A look at industrialization in the US indicates that the startups are coming up around universities. Special foundations have been set up by MIT to aid entrepreneurs.

Japan and many other countries are currently setting up "Silicon Valley's" in their backward areas. They essentially consist of new university, Research Park, venture fund foundation, housing complex, rail, road, air communications, and an office complex providing technological and management guidance.

The focus of techno polis is on productivity-enhancing investments in new resources and development of hi-tech laboratories. They are investing heavily in research and technical education. High tech industries like electronics, computers, genetic engineering, biotechnology and new materials are given preference. There is an emphasis on creating a high class work environment.

SCIENCE PARKS

The UK Science Park association has done an impact evaluation and reported that these parks are the ones which have drawn heavily from the expert knowledge of academicians and added greatly to the process of industrialization, besides making higher education more relevant and purposeful. They have also been instrumental in arresting brain drain. Most of the parks are joint projects between city councils, banks and universities the joint effort is found to provide a single window approach much desired for speedier implementation.

Germany has also placed considerable emphasis on restructuring its industry in order to boost international competitiveness, in particular in the field of technological innovation. Innovation centers and research institutes are specially set up attached to universities by providing facilities of basic research and development. The Daimler Research Centre forms the hub of such a scheme, employing more than 2000 S & T personnel. In 1987 the research institute of applied knowledge processing at the university of Ulm was established and similar ones at other places. Medium sized companies are in the process of housing their R & D departments in Government-sponsored science parks adjacent to a university.

WINNING STRATEGY OF CANADA

The Science Council of Canada has outlined a strategy for "winning in a world economy, according to which the most valuable resources for economic renewal are people with knowledge of frontier science, technology and technology management who operate on broad horizons and who can cross the usual discipline boundaries. *The success of a nation in international competition depends now on turning intellectual strength into marketable commodities. It has set up a Research Park, MaRS [Medical and Related Sciences] in Toronto University. It houses around 3000 PhDs.*

Learning from the experiences of other countries, it can be said that the clusters and growth centers currently being established in India would have to be competitive not only by Indian standards but by the standards of recent industrial complexes being established elsewhere. For this, they essentially need to have a research academic institute and should have structural bonds with academics elsewhere. A cluster/growth centre with good infrastructure but without a research base is like a healthy man without vision.

This means that either the growth centre should be located in the vicinity of proven academic institutes or such institutes should be specially set up in them. In either case, an investment in creating a research base is essential. Of course, a new institute to be fully functional would need more time, besides money. Therefore, locating growth centers/clusters in the vicinity of an existing academic institute sounds logical.

Any Company Unwilling to Commit the Funds and Efforts Required by Strategic Alliances with Academicians will not Likely Reap The Benefits of New Technology.

As a Result Those Companies Most Likely will not be a Major Force in Industry Ten Years From Now.

15

Expanding Horizons in Higher and Technical Education To Adopt New Visions of New World A Challenge

Today success in the global market place means creating and applying new knowledge- which is to say new technology faster than one's competitors. World winners will be those who develop talent, technologies, techniques and tools so advanced that there is no competition.

Synopsis

Which government does not want to generate hi - tech employment, high pay international jobs, spur industrial growth, and make education globally competitive? Then it must install research parks, incubators, Patent and IPR to facilitate commercial exploitation of sunrise technologies. Class room teaching is good but not enough. Industries, world over, are seen flocking round the advanced knowledge centers to obtain brand new ideas for global competitiveness. Institutes must have original knowledge springs like well water springs. They must have a mechanism to convert intellectual strength in to usable goods and services. Role of higher education has emerged central to industrial and economic development, in creating India's future. Association with industry, venture capital firms, international agencies who succeeded in this cause is essential.

The paper prescribes "dream big" for universities and colleges. They should aim at technology generation, technology diffusion, which is achieving high significance in enabling a nation to win. The paper emphasizes adoption of new organizational inventions like Research Park, which when implemented will contribute to India's international competitiveness. The institutions should have now to look beyond the traditional lines of teaching and learning and adapt to corporate development, and help industry to win. They should have to restructure themselves to become fountain heads of new knowledge and new technology. They should deserve the status of "Light House" for industry. People demand world class education. How can this be done? Synergy between industry and academics in this cause is vital. Parks have enhanced the scholarship of universities. They jointly can give economic and political stability to India. Will industry- institute interaction become a national priority? The paper recommends reforms in the light of experience elsewhere in the world.

1.0 Introduction

World experience tells us that now the economic development is technology driven. The limiting factor for growth and prosperity of a nation is not oil, nor land, nor minerals but the scientific and technological capability of people. Industrialized nations by virtue of technological superiority are found capturing the world market and emerging as epicentre of interdependent world. Industrialized nations through knowledge especially of emerging technologies are amassing wealth. 80 % of world's wealth is possessed by G-8 countries. World Bank observed that wealth is flowing today from developing to developed countries because of level difference in technology. Besides, advanced nations yield economic and political powers. Solow the Nobel Laureate observed that the GNP of USA doubled between 1909 and 1949, and that 85 % of the growth was attributable to technology change[1].

Those nations, organizations and individuals exploiting the latest technology are likely to win- others may work hard, may have essential resources to draw on, but will lag behind without technological capability and adaptability.

2.0 Scientific Infrastructure "Research Park" and its Relevance to India

True that India is late starter in engineering and technology and so it lagged behind. However, after independence it has made a laudable progress. But, it has yet to go a long way. It is today distinctly a technology follower. The technology development plans of most of the companies in India are propelled by foreign collaborators. Universities and academic institutions are too weak in research, and innovation. They have remained reflection centers teaching that knowledge which comes to them from abroad. They do not have "well springs" of new knowledge. Besides, they have remained away from industry. There are systems and procedures for import of technology, but there are no systems developed for technology generation and transmission from institutions within the country to industry.

Industry Institute Partnership world over, is observed to be critical to success. The World proven model of Silicon Valley was initiated by Prof Terman of Stanford University. Research Triangle Park in North Carolina was initiated by Prof Luther Hodge of Duke University. MaRS innovation district in Toronto, is evolved in partnership with Toronto University. This model for technological and industrial development has been adopted now in many east- west countries. The role of government in so doing has been central. The universities and other higher education institutes in the respective regions have undoubtedly been the leaders of this change. The underlying principle given by Prof Terman being that-

"Industry so as to remain competitive globally needs access to first class research in universities. So also the first class researchers in universities need access to industry so as to commercialize their research findings."[2]

Thousands of Research Parks are now installed in Japan, Taiwan, China, U K and elsewhere in the world. They are found to provide a high class infrastructure in the vicinity of higher education institutes where qualified scientists, engineers and entrepreneurs can professionally grow. Research Parks have come to be known as the maternity homes for safe birth of hi-tech industries. It provides a fertile ground for creation of New Technology Based Firms [NTBF]. It has proved to be effective in tapping the valuable resource of new knowledge for the growth of professions and productivity. It is an engine of development reducing lead time between invention and commercialization, giving new direction to human civilization. India so far has been trying to catch up technology race from behind rather than riding the crest. If it adopts research park scheme it will be able to ride. It will move new knowledge and new technology continually to economy like blood supply to our body. The economy will thereby have more knowledge/technology intensive business. India must recognize the role of new technologies and universities responsible for generating them. Research scientists and engineers if attracted to good infrastructure of research parks they will not migrate to other countries. New knowledge industries keep coming around universities.[3]

Where do Indian institutions stand in technology generation and diffusion? How many engineering colleges and universities offering education at graduate and research levels have corporate development as a vision and mission to carry out technology transfer to industry? Department of S & T Government of India has installed more than twelve parks in universities. They are doing very well. But they are too few for a big country like India. Doing research is good. But what use it is if not exploited commercially? Many institutions have now reached a stage where establishment of innovative endeavors like Research Park, technology incubator, patent & IPR center, entrepreneurship development center can prove immensely useful to them, to industry as well as to students passing out of these institutions. It is now not enough to produce just engineers and technologists but it is essential to produce leaders in technology, and leaders in industry that too by international standard. To win in world economy it is now necessary to produce technology pioneers, for which innovative infrastructure like research parks are absolutely necessary. Education charged with the spirit of discovery and innovation alone can move a nation forward. Future belongs to those who understand this. The purpose of this article is therefore to prescribe innovation, creativity and commercial exploitation of research which are the present day deficiencies of Indian economy. This will necessitate installing units as stated above as integral components of institutions. Industries, venture capital companies and institutes must come together to set up such parks. The "Stand Alone" policies of industry and education must be done away with. This is today's Guru Mantra.

3.0 Reforms Needed to Create Future

Knowledge is power. It changes lives of people. It converts a liability in to an asset. The world, due to rapid advances in science and technology, is changing fast. Change is accelerated by globalization, privatization, and liberalization. Survival of fittest in competitive world is tending to become the law. People have to cope with high velocity environment on local and global planes. Institutes of technical education, under these stormy changes, have not to perform the way they performed in the past. They have to depart from old style to enable the people to assimilate emerging, technological advances and use them so as to win jobs and earn income in competition at world level. They have to facilitate increase in scientific and technological capability of people. It is they who produce scientific and research personnel to do discoveries. Institutes must have to be adaptive, constantly changing, and using world class strategies. Courses, curriculum and methods of teaching must have to change with times. Their visions and missions, policies and practices, systems and procedures must have now to be constantly changing to fulfill local as well as global needs. World experience says Institutes ought to provide economic stimulus for regional development. Even political development of nations depends on capacity of institutions in what and how they teach[4].

Where do the Indian institutes stand in world list? They are far too low, like India in Olympics. They are progressing. Yet thousands of students are going for higher education abroad, to be humiliated? Why? The education in India is yet not aligned to the needs of globalization. No longer well being of a nation and its future destiny are constrained by its geography, population, natural resources. Knowledge especially of science and technology has become the prime mover[5]. Science and technology represent the new driving force. Economic prosperity, energy supplies, manufacturing capacity, health, public safety, military security, political stability and environmental quality all these and more will depend on knowledge owned and possessed by the people, women and men in the community. Scientific knowledge with usage does not deplete but multiplies. This is the unique beauty of knowledge resource. India will be strengthened by learning to compete in S & T in this flat world.

3.1 Education must be compatible to globalization[6]

Technical education ought to be qualitative and cost competitive not only by local standards but by international.

Many opportunities and challenges are arising in the areas of research, innovation, manufacturing, sales etc on global plane. The borders of education are expanding ocean like. How to prepare people to make most of them? Do the policy makers have to be outward looking? Do they have to take in to account the global dynamics in respect of technology, industry, economics etc? Yes, certainly they have to. It is essential, without which design of system will be imperfect. People can harvest opportunities ably only if they are well aware of what is on horizon and how to prepare in advance? They can make most of the situation if they are educated and technically trained and not without it. On the whole to win in world economy technical education must have to be compatible to globalization.

Education must be world class to enable people to win in interdependent world[7]. People are ready to pay for in terms of time, effort, and money. But Universities and colleges in India are not able to give. Why? This needs examination in depth. Their frame of work is old, out dated, primitive, and dysfunctional. They lack in creation of new knowledge, discoveries, and creative endeavors which are now the integral components of modern institutes elsewhere in the world. They lack in organizational capability. They lack in global visions and missions. That is why Indian institutes do not stand high in world list, and thousands of students every year go abroad. From experience elsewhere in the world, it can be said that higher education has to be necessarily coupled with research and innovation. Multifaceted research facilities like, technology incubation, patent & IPR, start ups entrepreneurship, Research Park have become now the integral components. They are observed to have a deeper impact on quality of education. Quality in Institutes is now critical and related to improving economic and political security of India. Do we realize this?

3.2 Institutions must now change their orbit[8].

They must jump up to creating hi- tech enterprises, hi-tech world class entrepreneurs, producing not just engineers but more of M Tech and PhDs. Institutes must take active hand in corporate development, by virtue of research become a "light house" for industry. The center of gravity of operations must have to shift from UG to advanced education like PG, PhD and post doctoral. This is what National Knowledge Commission 2006-2007 has recommended. Without them India cannot hope to become a super power, and achieve its declared dream. Without research, innovation, technology transfer Indian institutes may keep on producing engineers but they will be just followers and not leaders. They will not be able to create new India which people dream. Will India create a brand name in innovation? Without it India will lag behind in brain race

Attempts for reforms are being made in India through Technical Education quality improvement program [TEQIP]. Techniques of industrial management like Total quality Management [TQM] are being implemented. Leaders in industry are being appointed as chairman and members of board of governors. These efforts are good but not enough. Hi-breeding by way of transnational collaboration is necessary. Role of academicians in reformation is crucial. The authors say leadership skills on the part of academicians to establish and run institutes in world class manner need urgently to be developed. It is ultimately the academicians alone who can change the scene in institutes. First class professors need to be recruited and deputed to world best institutes and enabled to grow to the international standard. Professors and researchers need to be respected more. Science and Technology need to be accorded more budgets, comparable to those in developed countries. The establishment of new institutions like new universities, new IITs, IIMs, as declared by government has to be designed and implemented not in a routine manner but in a world class manner. These institutes must be designed with the involvement of world best professors, regardless from which country they come. We did this in IITs and so they shine.

3.3 Education must be Enterprising,[9] oriented to producing Entrepreneurs like Narayan Murthy, Bill Gates

An institute exists basically for two purposes. First, it exists to educate people, to make them more competent to do jobs using the state of the art technology. Secondly it exists to conduct research, innovation and use their findings in various vocations and professions. The purpose of education is to instill knowledge in those who undergo education. The purpose of research is to discover to create new knowledge, new theories, new technologies etc. so as to raise human civilization to greater heights. Institutes are also expected to train professionals to do professional practices more efficiently, to do consultation, technology transfer, assist students in career planning and contribute to broader social agenda among other things. They must promote entrepreneurship.

The role models of students should have to shift to becoming world best entrepreneurs. But these are not the things; they were expected to do in the past. These are now the new additions in their roles. Modern institutions unlike in the past have now to target to build a learning society consisting of learning organizations and continuously learning individuals. They have to play different roles in a variety of ways. All institutes however may not do all that. They may choose to do what fits in their visions and missions, and fits in their respective resource availability.

Education should reach to Excellence which comes through research and innovation Institutes which engage themselves simultaneously both in research and teaching are found to show excellence and hence are preferred by scholars. It is this kind of institution which tends to excel in competition and attains the world class status. People want world class education. But where do we find world class education? It is available in only a few institutions like IITs. Many universities and colleges are not able to give. Students are going abroad by spending huge sums of money. According to one estimate the total drain on foreign exchange, every year is equivalent to the cost of establishment of 20 IITs. The purpose of education in changing global context must therefore be understood by people who matter most to bring about changes. Only those who realize this win.

Teaching and research ought to go together[10]. An investment of rupee one in research in an educational institute does double duty. Firstly, it produces research output in the form of new knowledge, new technology, contributing to human civilization. It enhances economic competitiveness. The students at younger age are more agile and productive in research. Catch them young, becomes possible. Secondly, it results in elevating the educational standard of students and thereby quick dissipation of the findings of research to society, making it competitive. It is thus giving double profit. Research funding in an education institute is adding greatly to human capital making them innovative lifelong. Developed nations follow this strategy and hence they are found to be more progressive. India should therefore learn to invest with priority in research in institutes of technical education. There is lot of potential lying idle in youths in these institutes. Will India succeed to utilize it, remains to be seen?

3.4 Research Subsidizes Education, and Education Subsidizes Research

A modern institute is a place where teachers simultaneously do research, and where researchers do teaching. It is observed that in these institutions teachers teach the latest and researchers discover unknown faster and better. The new sunrise knowledge, which they discover, flows automatically to class rooms. They tend to teach tomorrow's knowledge today. They remain ahead of time. Professors conduct research with the help of students at a cheaper cost and in lesser time. Students acquire research and an innovation skill which they use life long, is the prime gain. It is the best economic proposal for any nation. Teaching and research are thus found to be complementary to each other. Hence they must go together. Students learn to cultivate habit to dream high and possess tenacity to fulfill the dream. In the absence of research in an educational institution professors tend to teach sunset technologies i.e. yesterdays knowledge today, throwing the new generation behind time.

This however does not mean that teaching institutions and teaching professors are not necessary. They also have a place in society. There are jobs which do not require research skills. Working knowledge is required to handle in marketing, purchase and manufacturing. They are quite large in number. Teaching institutions do important job of providing people for them. Such institutions and professors in them however need continuous updating. They must have to undergo retraining at the hands of researching professors.

Nations with higher knowledge level are found economically more secure. Emphasis on technical education in developing countries to elevate technology level therefore achieves high importance.

Are researching professors passionate to teach? Students ought to learn not only the known knowledge and known professional practices but learn to discover unknown. They ought to elevate professional practices constantly to newer heights. The professors and students rightly form a wider community of close knit researchers; build a team to become think tanks for the society. Thus an institution fulfils both teaching and research functions in a most efficient manner. It is this intimate connection-the idea that professors bring cutting edge knowledge and expertise to the class room that makes the institution relevant and purposeful. Institutions which are involved in only teaching remain teaching shops teaching "parrot like" that which is obsolete, irrelevant and comes to them from other researchers mostly in foreign. They have therefore no first hand experience and hence lack force in teaching. Researching professors are found highly passionate to test and teach new knowledge to students. Institutions are thus the testing grounds, of forthcoming technologies and generations.

Teaching and Research have no Force without being Tied Together.

There is a school of thought that those who pay more attention to research tend to neglect teaching. They believe students are put to disadvantage. However, this is a myth. How much time a professor should devote to research and how much to teaching is an art. This has to be left to the judgment of individual professor. It is observed on the whole that students prefer to have instruction at the hands of researching professors. All world class institutions excel simply because professors in them are research oriented. They have excellent bond with students. They function in an autonomous manner. In such institutions there is always a tension between teaching and research. The tension is like the tension in rope of a bow only on account of which arrow moves forward with force. Education gets force on account of this tension.

3.5 Modern Institutes should be multifaceted[12]

Technical education institutes have no longer to be simple. They have to be reformed much beyond class room teaching and learning. They have to e necessarily multifaceted complex organizations in part driven by technology and, in part mirroring other organizations in the world. Increasingly, they have to cater to peoples demands such as research skills i.e. generation of new knowledge, technology innovation, patenting & IPR, lifelong education, technology incubation, technology transfer, entrepreneurship, start up companies, venture capital etc It is these aspects whose presence in campus is adding to institute's reputation. They create and add tremendous value in learning environment. Students at UG, PG, and doctoral levels get thereby inspired to dream high, learn even that which is beyond curriculum and learn to be innovative and creative to take paths not trodden by their predecessors. Research, patent & IPR, entrepreneurship etc enable to get more value out of investments in an institution. They increase the financial rate of return. Institutes become more viable. They succeed in attracting more and more funds.

The paper emphasizes the urgent need to establish on priority basis the units like Research Park- Technology Incubator- Patent & IPR centre- Entrepreneurship Development Centre, Technology Transfer Centre, Venture Capital Fund, Innovation centre etc on the campus. This is to set a tone of discovery, innovation, creativity, spin-offs, new technology based firms, create technology pioneers etc in economy. Without this the paper argues that India, in spite of its potential will lag behind.

Attracting best talent in P G, PhD matters. A nation cannot win economic war with only soldiers like B Tech degree holders. Captains and Generals with M Tech PhD degree are needed. In India not many scholars however are found to be attracted to post graduation and doctorate courses. Why? An analysis will indicate that due to poor infrastructure and poor knowledge availability at institutes, value addition being made through these courses is less than the value addition made by working in industry. Besides, the students have also to forego the salary income. The institutions are deficient in respect of multifaceted activities. Many students in competition prefer to go to universities abroad. Indian institutes to that extent are losing talent, and hence lagging behind. They need to be made attractive enough in comparison with their counterparts abroad. Also they must have to offer what industry can not in terms of research, innovation etc. Without innovation infrastructure, institutes will not be able to produce captains needed to win in world economy. Achievement oriented missions in Indian institutes need urgently to be practically built on big scale. Capability building is a big challenge to reach to world class standards. Institutes ought to be empowered with autonomy to do all that and to award degrees of B Tech, M Tech, and PhD.

Number of PhDs awarded by an institution has become a differentiating factor of one nation from the other. It is now the critical measure for economic development. By virtue of this they alone tend to become a "light house" for industry and to bring prosperity to the nation. The purpose of an institution thus goes far beyond and extends to nation building and building humanity. Many institutions in the world attract scholars from anywhere and everywhere in the world. This is the strategy worth emulation.

Do we give research grant to professors at the time of appointment?[13] If yes, it will attract better talent in professorship to increase university value. Education is not necessarily synonymous with teaching. One can acquire knowledge by reading, researching, experimenting, discussions, etc. Being taught in a class room is only one way of learning. Similarly new knowledge can be developed through the simple act of thinking like Gautama Buddha. An institute is one place in society where inquisitive minds assemble to brainstorm, leading to breakthroughs yielding enormous benefits to society. It is a place where a student motivated by questions like why and how can find answers. An institute to be excellent has necessarily thus to be multifaceted. It must grant funds for research right at the time of appointment. Many institutions in the world are doing and this is the best way to become world class.

3.6 Should Institutions be autonomous and transnational in character?

Yes, without which they will not be able to bring about changes. The mandate to an institution is to preserve, discover and carry knowledge from one generation to the next. This mandate cannot be fulfilled without financial resources and grant of autonomy. It is for the Government to allocate adequate funds out of public exchequer, yet grant autonomy i.e. liberty to think and liberty to act and not intervene in its internal matters. It is obviously because Government is least qualified in academics, it cannot steer the direction and hence it should not interfere. Public private partnerships are being evolved to make most of knowledge and financial resources available in any society for the cause of technical education. Transnational partnerships for both research and education are also growing. They must grow so as to tap and bring together good work being done everywhere and anywhere in the world. Experience tells us that transnational research linkages are vital to effective teaching. It creates favourable environment for achieving excellence. Nations are prosperous where institutions are autonomous and transnational in character, multifaceted and free to conduct teaching and research in a multiple way. Institutes should keep control of their destiny in their own hands; hence they should necessarily be autonomous. If control goes elsewhere it will then not be able to do justice to its vision and mission.[14]

4.0 Make Governance and Leadership fit for new visions

Improving governance and leadership of institutions so as to install Research Park is essential. The old style of working and thinking does not suit. Bringing corporate principles of management in academic institutions is a trend. It is good but not enough

How does an Institute differ from an industry? Can industrial management practices work well in academics?

Management of a small institute worth the name is much more difficult than management of a big factory, so said Pandit Jawaharlal Nehru in 1959 on the occasion of laying the foundation stone of IIT Mumbai.

Institutes are meant to produce leaders, leaders for the nation and leaders for the world. This is what American universities are doing. Many leaders in many countries have received education in USA. Today's leaders were students yesterday. Some of the students of today are going to be the leaders of tomorrow. An institute deals with human beings who create future engineers to run factories. An industry on the other hand deals with machines and materials for profit. They produce goods and services, which is much different from producing leaders. An institute attempts to unfold the capabilities lying dormant within the students. Professors are research scientists working for a much broader aim like developing human civilization. Factory managers on the other hand are in service of factory management. Industries do processing on non living materials. There is thus a vast difference between the two. Skills needed in factory management and institution management is much different.[15]

4.1 Management strategies need modifications to fit new visions[16]

Factory methods and strategies for improvement like TQM do not apply as they are to academic institutions. They need to be modified so as to suit and achieve the humanistic and scientific excellence of an institute. The spirit of academics should not be lost while implementing TQM. The quality of education leading to excellence does not have external referent like in industry. In globalization links between the institutions with the government of nation state are weakening although they provide funds. Links are strengthened with bodies which work for humanity. Institutes are more in the service of humanity in general. Personnel from industry who are associated with academic institutions in their management should have to bear theory of education in mind.

The strategies employed for successful working of a factory therefore do not necessarily apply to all activities in an institution. Institutes are not for profit like factories. That is why they are registered not under companies act but under charitable trusts and society's act. However, of late institutes for profit are on horizon. They are under debate and discussion.

There is a school of thought that institutes must remain institutes and industries must remain industries. Each has a separate reason to exist. There are some common purposes for which they may have to come closer. Industries need to have a continuous flow of competent manpower, new knowledge and new technology so as to remain competitive globally. It is the institutions which are legitimately meant to supply. Industries have R & D cells. All the research which the industry needs cannot however be done all alone by itself. Some research of fundamental nature for public good has to be necessarily done in institutes. Professors need freedom to think and freedom to act much more than in industry. They do research not alone in private interest but also in public interest. They need more mobility and sharing of research experience across the world. To be a successful leader in industry is one thing. To be a successful leader in an academic institution is quite another. The skills needed, knowledge and mind set needed for each is much different. However, there are commonalities.

Industries cannot do all the long range research they need to be competitive by themselves. They essentially need support of universities. To illustrate.

The invention of Geographical positioning system [GPS] was initiated in Cambridge University by a UG student named kleppner under the guidance of his professor. This invention today is found to have a high impact in automobile sector. The impact came after a period of 50 years. Universities do not take a short range view like an industry. Return on investment in academics is not immediately apparent. Economic analysis indicates that the returns from research to the institute are about 20%, to the nation 50%, and much greater to global society. The impact of research done in institute is on a much larger plane from which many industries world over draw benefits. This is not the case in isolation but there are innumerable cases of them. Larger public interest has to be kept in view in coming of industry and institute together. Industries are benefitted most by conducting research in universities. They must cash on research in universities and support them financially.

5.0 What can we conclude?

Waves of technology are sweeping the world. Now is time for India to dream big and take a jump start in creation of new technology. This requires creation of hi- tech enterprises, technology and business incubators, entrepreneurship, research parks, Patent & IPR, Venture Capital Fund, Continuing education Centres, etc. Enterprising institutes have a deeper impact on improving the quality of education making it more relevant and purposeful. Scope of PG, doctoral and post doctoral courses must be widened. Institutes ought to expand and look beyond conventional horizons to what their counterparts elsewhere in the world are doing.

Indian universities and colleges must have to study the strategies, visions and missions adopted by world best. Internationalization should become the trend. Can we create world class centers of excellence? This will decide India's future.

The Indian economy can flourish only if there is a culture within the country which is favorable to innovation and technology transfer. Is finance for innovation available? The priority given to S & T in national budget, although increasing, is still far from adequate. Research, education, and industry are isolated from each other, which constrain their growth. Venture capital is not available for innovation in universities and there is a fear for failure. How many patents are obtained every year by each university/college? How many NTBFs are born in university? How many pioneer technologies are developed? These are the pertinent questions now to be asked.

India dreams to become a technology power in the world which could be made possible by adopting world best policies and practices and not without them. The sermons of National Knowledge commission must forthwith be heard and implemented.

Institutions must be governed, managed and maintained by following world proven academic principles. Permitting mobility of professors and establishing transnational collaborations between the institutions is essential. Professors should be enabled to rise to international standard for which suitable schemes must be designed.

"The success in international competition depends now on turning intellectual strength in to marketable commodities"

References

1. Abheek Barman "Fund a lab and grow" Economic Times , 2nd May 1997.
2. The role of science parks in the promotion of innovation and transfer of technology, Proceedings of the science parks association, Annual Conference 6-7 April 1989.
3. "Great minds meet at MaRS Center - Taking Canadian innovation to world" - University of Toronto Research Park "MaRS" in Toronto – Canada Research Park.
4. The Role of American University. The Creation of the Future, book by Frank H T Rhodes, published by Cornell University Press.
5. Rising Above the Gathering Storm Report published by National academy of Sciences US, 2007.
6. National Knowledge Commission report 2006-2007.
7. Globalization, The Impact on our Lives book by Rob Bowden, Rain Tree Chicago Publication.
8. Creating knowledge, strengthening nations- The Changing role of Higher education, Edited by Glen A Jones, Patricia L McCarney, and Michael L Skolnik- University of Toronto Press.
9. Naik B M 2004, Technological Innovation in Educational Institutes, The Indian Journal of Technical Education Vol 27, No. 2, pp. 59-61.
10. Innovation and Technology Transfer, News Letter of the Institution of Engineers [India] 1998.

11. The Human Nature of a University, book by Robert E Goheen, Princeeton University Press. 1969.
12. Global Visions & Missions in Technical Education, Book By B M Naik, 23 Meher Nagar Garkheda, Aurangabad - 431005- India published in 2008.
13. Higher Education in Canada, Edited By Charles M Beach, Robbin w Boadway, R Marvin Mclnnis published by John Deutsch Institute for the Study of Economic Policy, Queens University.
14. University of Ontario- Research and development Park at Sarina Lambton campus and London campus- Canada- web site.
15. Universities for Sale, By Neil Tudiver published by Canadian association of University teachers.
16. Op cit-Ref 4.

16

Strategic Planning – A New Tool For Creative Management of Institutes

SYNOPSIS

With the adoption of privatization policy in education, in India and abroad, a new class of people, "Educational Entrepreneurs" has emerged. They have initiated, vigorously, critical examination of the old values, institution missions, work methods, needs of education etc. demanding a change in the perceptions of people. They are ambitious and wish to outwit in local and global competition and to make the most of the opportunities.

They generated a much needed competitive environment for themselves as well as for Government and aided institutes. Institutions now have developed a strong will to win. But, mere will, enthusiasm are not enough. They ought to have the skills of planning, monitoring, and evaluation without which they will not be able to stand in global competition.

The article therefore prescribes the adoption of strategic planning, without any loss of time, for all institutions including those which are managed and maintained by Government. This is not now an option but compulsion, without which they will become dysfunctional.

The chapter presents, in brief, what is meant by strategic planning, what is a mission statement, how to arrive at it, who are stakeholders, how to assess their expectations, how to prepare strategic plan and how to implement it. Forces which Hi – JACK the planning process are identified. Strategies which have worked well in India and abroad are also presented.

WHY STRATEGIC PLANNING

Our institutions are lagging far too behind the world standards. Most of them have become teaching shops, like coaching classes. They have very little research base. Consequently, they continue to teach old, outdated, and irrelevant. They have almost no ability to teach the state of the art. Very few faculty members have M.E. and Ph.D. qualifications while elsewhere in the world most of them are PhDs. The interaction between institutes and industry is weak. What is wanted by industry is not taught and what is taught is not wanted. There is a mismatch between the two, leading to low productivity in both the industry and institutes. The syllabi, laboratories, library and other infrastructure of Indian institutes are far too weak by world standards. The output from our institutes in terms of quality and quantity is far too low.

If the institutes are not performing as they should, if they are not coping with the change, if they cannot satisfy the educational needs of youths it is largely because they are lacking in usage of strategic planning. It is observed, at most of the places, that the limiting factor for better performance is not the availability of resources but the vision of people who work for institutes and the same could be created by this new tool of strategic planning. Many institutions want to bring about organizational change and take them to greater heights but they simply cannot do so, because they lack in capability to use the technique of strategic planning Refer figure 1.

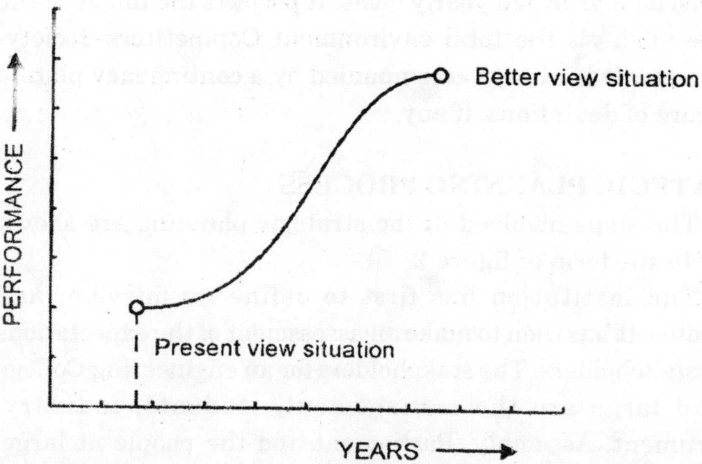

Fig 1 : Shows the Need of Strategic Planning to move from present view situation to better view situation

In the absence of strategic plans, different people think and act differently in inconsistent directions not knowing that they are operating at cross, nullifying each others' efforts. Often, people remain unprepared for changes, unprepared for competition and hence they fail. New strategies and new directions are badly needed without which Indian Institutes, the industry and economy as a whole cannot have good future. Adoption of strategic planning is found from experience to develop a competitive spirit amongst the employees, make them oriented to goals, targets and global opportunities. Today in, the absence of strategic plans, most of the institutes do not have well defined missions and even if they have missions they are not connected with activities they perform, hence their performance is low in spite of high potential. It is management tool used extensively in industry. Now is the time for institutions to use.

WHAT IS A STRATEGIC PLAN

Strategic plan is a written document of declared intentions. It is a pattern of consistent actions of today and tomorrow, detailed on 5 year and yearly basis. It projects the image of the college vis-à-vis the total environment Competitors-Society-Region etc. It is always accompanied by a contingency plan to take care of deviations, if any.

STRATEGIC PLANNING PROCESS

The steps involved in the strategic planning are shown below in the form of figure 2.

The institution has first to define its mission; and mandates. It has then to make an assessment of the expectations of the stakeholders. The stakeholders for an engineering College by and large are the management, students, industry, Government, Assembly, Parliament and the people at large. Appropriate proforma will have to be designed, got filled up, from the concerned and then analyzed.

Next and the most important thing is to assess the Global environment, to know, who are the competitors, what strategies they are adopting, and then identify the strategic issues, then make (SWOT), strengths, weaknesses, opportunities and threats analysis.

SWOT analysis is required to be done throughout the organization; starting from a small laboratory to a big department and ultimately aggregating for the college as a whole. It has to be participative, top down and bottom up. Every individual and department has strengths. We have to be aware for our strengths and apply them to harvest the opportunities.

While doing so we have to guard on our internal weaknesses and the external threats. Are our internal systems and procedures matching with objectives? Are they up to date? Are internal people co-operative? Is the external competition manageable? What are the forces which may Hi-Jack the people and organizational strengths? These are some of the questions which need to be answered.

Various options will come out from the exercise above so as to meet the stakeholders' expectations. These options will

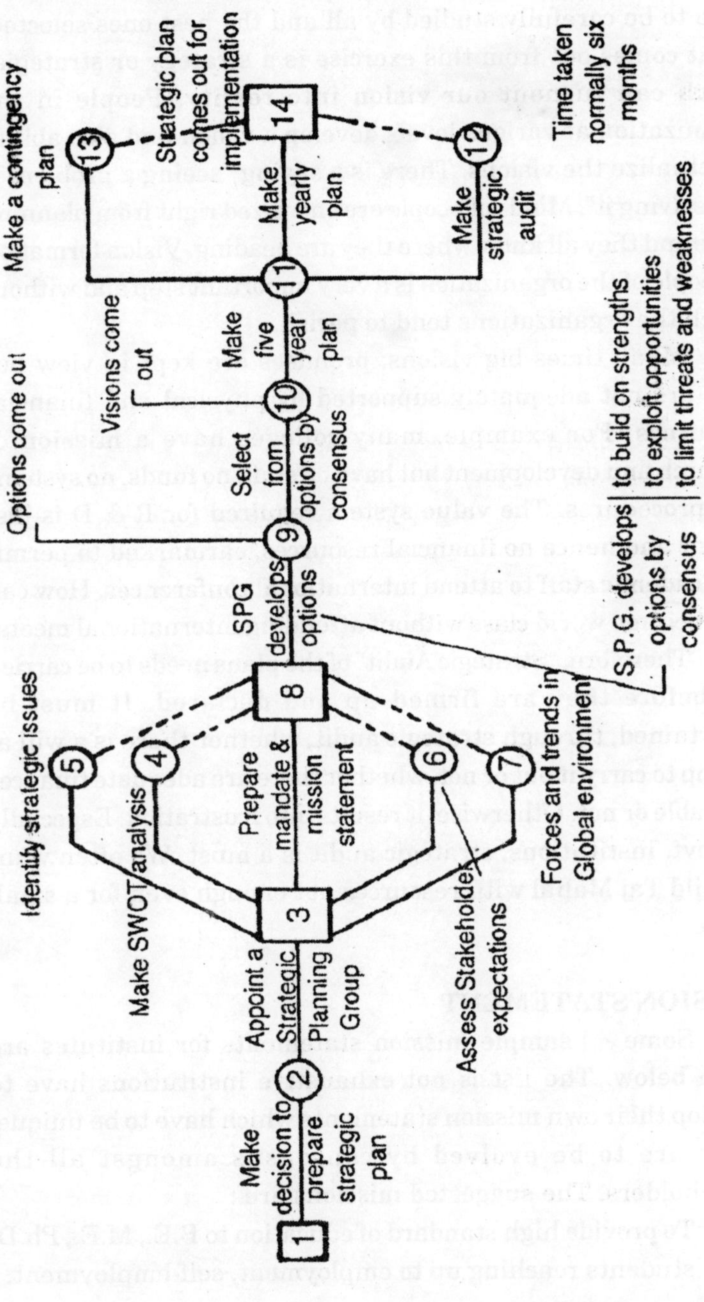

Fig. 2: Shows the Steps in Strategic Planning Process in the form of PERT

have to be carefully studied by all and the best ones selected. What comes out from this exercise is a strategy or strategies which can turnout our vision into reality. People in the organization at various levels develop a vision and also ability to actualize the visions. There is a saying "seeing a problem is half solving it". Minds of people are energized right from planning stage and they all know where they are heading. Vision formation in people of the organization is a very important step and without which the organizations tend to perish.

Many times big visions, promises are kept in view but they are not adequately supported by physical and financial resources. For example, many colleges have a mission of research and development but have no staff, no funds, no systems and procedures. The value system required for R & D is just absent and hence no financial resources, earmarked to permit the academic staff to attend international conferences. How can they become world class without attending international meets?

Therefore, "Strategic Audit" of the plans needs to be carried out before they are firmed up and declared. It must be ascertained, through strategic audit, whether there is a will at the top to carry it out or not, whether there are adequate finances available or not. Otherwise, it results into frustration. Especially in Govt. institutions, strategic audit is a must. We often want to build Taj Mahal with resources not enough even for a small house.

MISSION STATEMENT

Some sample mission statements for institutes are given below. The list is not exhaustive institutions have to develop their own mission statements which have to be unique. They are to be evolved by consensus amongst all the stakeholders. The suggested missions are :

1. To provide high standard of education to B.E., M.E., Ph.D. students reaching up to employment, self-employment.

2. To provide employee's security of working with job satisfaction, acknowledging the right to be informed and consulted in all matters which affect them.
3. To conduct education with due care for the environment.
4. To remain on forefront in technology and transfer the same to industry to maintain them competitive by global standards.
5. To provide testing consultancy to industry.
6. To provide continuing engineering education to in service engineers and maintains them competitive.
7. To bring about regional development, community development.
8. To provide equal opportunity in education to all.
9. To provide new technology to industry to improve its productivity.
10. To generate employment and income of the people.

Mission statement has a effect in involving people, gaining employee-commitment to achieve goals and targets. It however, necessitates a process of education, to continuously upgrade the quality of people.

The mission statement is an outcome of a long drawn process of debate and discussion amongst the stakeholders, over a period of about six months.

Some Current Strategic Issues of Engineering Education Institutes

The first and foremost issue is how to increase the competency of people working for colleges and bring them at par with their counterparts in developed countries. There are teaching staff members, administrative and laboratory staff, whose capacity needs to be upgraded by undertaking suitable schemes. If schemes are drawn out and colleges make investment in their employees this is likely to increase their commitment and loyalty. Today, big institutions are in the hands of small men.

Secondly our institutes and people are too inward looking so also the students. They lack in international perspectives. The issue is therefore how to orient them to Global standards.

It is not enough, if only a few employees and management people think strategically. All employees have to acquire the mental skills to think strategically. Ways and means will have to be devised to promote strategic thinking in whole organization.

Developing a style of management suitable to local culture and bent of mind of the people is an important issue. The style of management would have to be different at different places flexible and participative to achieve the goals. It will have to provide relevant information to all at appropriate times. Systems would have to be designed fir for the purpose.

One of the important issues is how to increase relevance of education to regional needs. How to make curricula oriented to people's needs? In this case, the participation of industry is needed which is quite difficult and is a challenging issue to be resolved.

Today, the institutes are highly deficient in technology transfer, research, continuing engineering education, etc. How to develop an innovative character for the institute is the big issue to be addressed by key persons. One of the prime issues is yet how to meet growing needs of technical education of the vast masses of people, in terms of quality and quantity. The priority given by Government in budget to education is too low, only 3% of GNP is allocated as against 10% by many countries. It is said that lack of budget to education has failed the nation.

STRATEGIES SUGGESTED

One of the successful strategies in institution development is to tap the innovative and creative talent of employees especially the teachers. It is predicted that knowledge based organizations will lead in future and hence our strategy should be towards usage of new knowledge, intellectual capital is a valuable asset which a knowledge organization should try to possess. Networking of knowledge workers leads to synergetic conditions, and now the organizations should take special efforts to create networking.

Next, the institute should adopt a strategy of listening to students, industry personnel and people. Listening means obtaining a feedback, positive or negative, which is very useful to maintain equilibrium? Proforma may be designed and got filled at regular intervals, analyzed and corrective action taken wherever necessary.

Thirdly, the learning ability of the individuals and the organization as a whole is very crucial to make the organization flexible enough to adopt to change. If there is no learning, the people become stiff and often resist change. If they are continuously learning they are more susceptible to change and remain in tune with time. Lifelong learning is a very important aspect to be attended to reduce inertia of people. This strategy may be adopted especially for non-teaching employees, who tend to be neglected, and they create bureaucratic hurdles.

Fourthly, grant of autonomy to people keeping a central control is a good strategy to motivate knowledge workers less of hierarchy, less of departmentalism, more interdisciplinary working helps to succeed and hence these strategies are suggested.

Making the work measurable of each and every employee in the organization has to be tried. What is not measurable remains uncontrolled leading to waste and less efficiency. It is not easy to achieve this, but still it has to be aimed at, and given a fair trial.

WHY STRATEGIC PLANNING FAILS

All strategic plans are not implemented as they are, partly implemented and partly not. This is due to a variety of reasons, such as political disturbance, natural calamities, and non-availability of funds, organizational bureaucracy and departmentalism. The plans prepared are often HI-JACKED. The managers, however, should not feel frustrated.

Hidden Agenda, invisible strategies, in the minds of people is yet another potential danger. Key persons make strategic plans out of formal process, with the help of the sixth sense.

It also fails when top management and strategic planning group get engrossed in current problems and spend insufficient time on long range planning and the process become discredited amongst other staff. It is also on account of the failure of the management to create a favourable climate.

SUMMARY

This chapter has presented how urgently Indian Institutes need to prepare the strategic plans. It has outlined a few missions, issues and suggested possible new approaches which the institutes may follow. The institutes have to take a stock of their capabilities, short-comings, policies and vision. They have to share the same with the people, who work for them. This is the way prescribed in strategic planning to improve performance and productivity of institutes. It is hoped that this will provide some guidelines for the preparation of the strategic plans. Thanks to the new class of educational entrepreneurs who have put institutes in top gear of competition and thereby made it compulsory to use the technique of strategic planning.

Strategic planning has helped industry to perform better. Now it is the turn of academic institutes.

17

Find a Worthy Purpose and Means Will Follow

HIGHER AND TECHNICAL EDUCATION IN CRISIS

In a liberalized economy a phenomenon is observed that Universities from countries like Australia, USA and UK have taken out an aggressive drive to market education world over, including in India. They have opened technology transfer and marketing departments, as companies have, to make sale of education. They are advertising frequently in newspapers and holding meetings with students, parents and management of colleges in India. They are opening learning centers and giving affiliation to private colleges. These outside universities which have proven experience, reputation and credibility with employers, especially multinational corporations, are more likely to attract the best of our students. To a great extent, in globalization and liberalization, if we do not upgrade our institutions they are likely to capture our better students, and our colleges may be left with mediocre. Our Universities may then become like Zilla Parishad or municipality schools. Thus, there is an external pressure on our higher education system to improve and compete globally.

To compare the situation with industry, it is observed that multinational companies in liberalized economy have been, since long coming to India and posing threat to Indian companies. It is also resulting in technology transfer, collaboration and improvement in our companies in respect of products and processes. This is viewed as a welcome development for it is beneficial to consumers although putting pressure on producers to manufacture goods of international standards at competitive prices.

A somewhat similar situation has arisen now in higher education. Our Universities and especially engineering education institutes which are crucial to national economy have to face counterparts? They need to understand the methodology of functioning of Universities in foreign countries and emulate. The students and employers who are customers are presently very dissatisfied with the present approaches of the universities and colleges which are not teaching what is wanted and also not assuming the legitimate role of providing technology to Industry.

If we look at Universities in countries like Germany, U.S.A. Japan there is a striking difference in respect of research. These Universities offer flexible courses permitting students to learn what they like, giving access to students in national-level research projects. Besides, the professors for example in Germany have two hats, one in University and another in National Research Laboratory. Similarly, the senior research scientists in research laboratories have on reciprocal basis Chairs in Universities. This kind of integration of University with research laboratory is said to be a great strength, in taking the country technologically forward. It is a missing link in our country.

Their Universities have also marketing and technology transfer departments which play a key role in regional development. They have their own technology parks and University companies to give technology push to economy and escort students for jobs in industry. The proportion of students studying engineering is much large : 15 to 20% of the total student population as against only 7% in our country. Universities generate 33% of their income through research contracts and patent sale. These missions and visions are conspicuously absent in our Universities.

The present Universities in our country on the other hand have very little interaction with industry and regional development authorities. Industry has no confidence in research capability of Universities. The vital element of innovation is missing from higher education. The relationship between the university and Industry truly has to be complementary to each other. Industry and institutes be interdependent and revitalizing each other. But the actual situation is far from desirable. The leaders in education and leaders in Industry along with government ought to react strategically taking into account the policies and practices elsewhere in the world and restore the desirable relationship.

When food problem in India was acute in 50s and 60s it was predicted by the World Bank that people would die in 70s and 80s out of hunger. Thanks to the strategic and unique measures taken by the Government like establishment of separate agricultural Universities to do research, education and extension in an integrated manner. The agricultural Universities are not only educating students but they are also developing new varieties of seeds and scientific practices and carrying them to farmers. Without this, the agriculture in India would have remained primitive and the food problem would have become more acute and people starved.

Similar situation has arisen now in the industrial production and productivity which is far too low by world standards. We are importing technologies more and more from abroad and yet the industry is becoming sick is obvious for how long can we remain competitive on borrowed knowledge? We have to learn to do research in Universities and provide access to young students to do research. Without this the higher education is less likely to improve and the workforce for industry and economy may remain less competent despite the potential. It is high time that we go for technical Universities integrating the three, namely, education, research and extension like in Germany and Japan, This is also recommended by UNESCO in one of its reports especially for developing countries. It is further emphasized in the report that the 5 year plans of national development and universities should have closer co-operation with the Universities. AICTE has approved the scheme.

Today, the Universities in India are doing only policing trying to prevent copying in examinations. They have become only controller of examinations rather than the seats of research and learning. Autonomous states to University departments and colleges is prescribed by the new national policy on education 1986 but till today not much progress in this field has taken place. It is mainly because our leaders in education both in colleges and Universities are lacking knowledge and confidence in this new system. Unfortunately, they are not with the world in this respect. The coming of foreign Universities in India will give them an opportunity to see from closer distance their strategies and management styles and it is hoped that this should induce good effects in our system.

To conclude, coming of foreign Universities in India is a boon for students in higher education and a golden chance for institutes to learn better policies and practices. We hope that our Universities will welcome them and associate closely. A major overhaul is needed in higher education, especially technical, to make it globally competitive. It is hoped the Government and industry will take bold steps to set up Technical Universities like agricultural Universities to integrate research, education and extension. It may certainly cost but the costs of not doing are prohibitively high.

Prof. Michael Porter in his book "The Competitive Advantage of Nations" based on studies in ten developed countries wrote that countries are industrially advanced which have emphasized engineering education. Secondly, those nations which have more of Technical Universities are more advanced. Thirdly, the model of Technical University is more productive and effective for technical education than a comprehensive or multi faculty university. Fourthly, the nations where universities and CSIR like laboratories remain in network, share research facilities and findings provide access to research to young students are more advanced.

Effective Professors often are those who take
Initiative to participate in networks with industry
And research organizations world over.

18

Performance Planning and Appraisal: Why and How?

Rewards For Extra-ordinary and Punishment To Defaulters Needs To Be The Culture

The paper prescribes the exercise of 'GOALSETTING' for every institution and every individual as it is central to Performance Appraisal. A model is prepared and presented, which needs to be adopted for implementation after debate and discussions with all the concerned. It is strongly recommended that rewards and punishments should be related to the outcome of performance appraisal, without which the purpose of appraisal cannot be fulfilled

The national policy on Education – 1986 (NPE) had given considerable stress on improving quality of technical education. It considers the teachers as the pivot of the system.

The teachers have to perform multiple roles of teaching, research, consultancy, development of instructional resources, administration, student services, acquisition and development of expertise in their chosen field of specialization. In order to promote the excellence in technical education the national policy on education recognizes the need to perform such multiple roles by the teachers. Therefore, the performance planning of teacher is a very important aspect from view point of technical education. The NPE also stipulates the introduction of performance appraisal system for teachers, which will make the teachers accountable for their work.

SET-GOALS-THEN MEASURE AND MEET THEM

One important role of a technical institute is to impart education to the students to enable them to acquire up-to-date knowledge of their fields, so that they become an asset for the socioeconomic development of the nation. In the present situation many new technologies are emerging. The rate of change of technology is so fast that an individual faculty member or institute can easily suffer from obsolescence if the faculty or institutes is not sensitive enough to all these changes and don't adopt ways for coping with change at both individual and institutional levels. All this requires an effective method of performance planning for individual faculty. The first step in performance appraisal is to define the job, various duties and various expected goals for individuals as well as for institution and the criterion on which performance will be judged. The various primary functions of a faculty member are –

(i) Institutional activities: These include scheduled teaching in class room and laboratory, development of teaching materials and methods, student advising and counseling, conducting examination assessing answer books etc.

(ii) Academic research: This includes the supervision at Bachelor, Master and Doctorial levels, carrying out research work and publishing the work in journals.

(iii) Consultancy: To take the live problems from industries and work on it, and transfer technology to industry.

(iv) Student's activities: To take part in various extracurricular activities, to guide the students for their future plan, various opportunities, etc.

(v) Continuing Engineering Education.

The University grants commission strongly urges for good performance by teachers because teacher performance is linked with the task of maintaining and co-coordinating standards. The various factors which influence the quality of education and its contribution to the national development are the quality, competence and character of teachers. The various problems which will affect the performance of teachers are –

- Self competence.
- Attitude towards the work.
- Sensitivity to change in environment.
- Delegation of authority.
- Lack of clear definition of his role in total educational system.
- Performance appraisal system.
- While doing the planning for teachers the following points should be taken into consideration.
- It should be specific, clearly mentioning the various activities of the teacher.
- As far as possible the objectives should be measurable in some way.
- Every objective should have a time limit on it.
- The objective should not be beyond the capability.
- Plan should be challenging so that they get a job satisfaction.
- To ensure good performance the existence of an effective performance appraisal system is a must.

PERFORMANCE APPRAISAL OF A TEACHER

Performance appraisal makes the teacher accountable for his work. To carry out the performance appraisal of a teacher, it is necessary that teacher should know what is expected of him, how much is expected of him and what happens if he does better or bad. An effective performance appraisal system for faculty is vital for optimizing the contribution of individual faculty member to the institutional performance. The NPE has recognized the need of formulating the performance appraisal system for teachers which should be open, participative and data based. The AICTE will evolve feasible staff appraisal system and corresponding norms, through extensive consultation with state government, Director of Technical Education, Institutions, professional bodies and teacher's representatives.

"If we don't step up the challenge of finding and supporting the best Professors, we will undermine everything else, we are trying to Improve technical education".

(a) Existing system and its deficiencies

The present scenario of faculty appraisal in technical institutions, although widely varying, have deficiencies which are in brief as under :

The present system of performance appraisal is most unscientific. It consists of preparing confidential reports annually by the Head of the Departments.

The report appraises the person rather than the work done by him. In the recent days a self assessment form is to be filled up by the teacher, which is again reviewed by the Head of the Department. The confidential report gives vague and ambiguous terms. One cannot interpret the meaning from these statements; the reports are the opinion about the individual. This can be taken as a personal criticism. There is no communication of the appraisal to the teacher at most of the places. If adverse communication is made the teachers are found to revolt, and reply back. Another demerit of this type of appraisal is that the lack of scholastic authenticity on the part of the appraiser. As teachers in technical institutions belong to a wide spectrum of disciplines, no single supervisor has the academic competence to evaluate all of them.

(b) Proposed performance appraisal system for engineering college teacher.

As the performance appraisal is a system of controlling the work, not the people, due care should be taken while

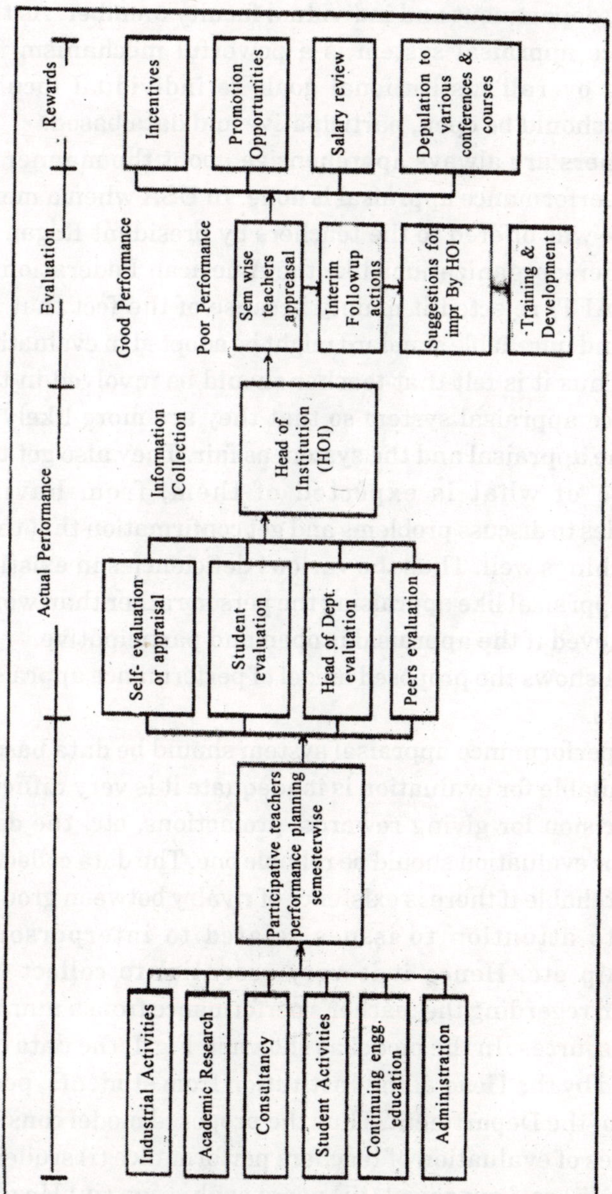

Fig.1 Block diagram representation of proposal model for Performance appraisal of a teacher.

formulating it. The performance appraisal involves the institution, department and individual faculty member. As the performance appraisal system is a powerful mechanism for translating overall institutional goals to individual faculty member, it should be open, participative and data based.

Teachers are always apprehensive about the manner in which the performance appraisal is done. In USA when a merit pay scheme was offered to the teachers by president Regan in 1983, teachers; organizations like the American Federation of Teachers (AFT) rejected it mainly because of the fect that an uncertain and unreliable standard might be adopted in evaluating teachers. Thus it is felt that teacher should be involved in the performance appraisal system so that they are more likely to consider the appraisal and the system as fair. They also get the knowledge of what is expected of them, from having opportunities to discuss problems and get confirmation that they are doing things well. Thus the various deficiencies in existing system of appraisal like appraising the person rather than work, can be removed if the appraisal is open and participative.

Fig. 1 shows the proposed model of performance appraisal for teachers.

The performance appraisal system should be data based. If data available for evaluation is inadequate it is very difficult to take decision for giving rewards, promotions, etc. the data available for evaluation should be reliable one. The data collected may be unreliable if there is existence of rivalry between groups, inadequate attention to issues related to interpersonal relationship etc. Hence it is very essential to collect the information regarding the teacher's performance from a number of reliable sources. In the model as shown in Fig.1, the data can be collected by the Head of the Institution from students, peers and Head of the Department. Thus the proposed model consists of four types of evaluation of teachers performance (i) students evaluation (ii) self-appraisal (iii) peers evaluation (iv) Head of Department Supervisor evaluation.

Before evaluating the teacher's performance, preparation of a suitable work plan for each teacher is very important activity in the whole process of performance planning and appraisal. The Principal and all Heads of the Departments should conduct a meeting of teachers in each semester to prepare the work plan of each teacher. Before planning meeting, each teacher should prepare his plan for the semester taking into consideration the overall goals of the institution. The activity plan should be as far as possible easy to measure (quantified) for monitoring and evaluation. Otherwise evaluation becomes complex. The activities should be based on position, need, experience, and ability and relevant to the needs of the institution. This plan of the teacher should be approved by the Head of the Institution in the planning meeting. If the performance planning of the teacher is specific, realistic, time limited, measurable and challenging then further activities can be implemented very smoothly. So implementation of performance planning and appraisal in a careful manner is the need of the hour.

For the measurement of the performance of a teacher, the performance appraisal meeting should be conducted for each semester by the Head of the Institution which should be participative by senior group of teachers, the four types of evaluation already mentioned should be taken into consideration for studying the poor performance and good performance. For each type of evaluation a detailed questionnaire can be prepared and filled in by student, self, supervisor and peers. In student evaluation the students should be selected from each group like academically very good, average, good in extra curricular activity etc. the questionnaire for student evaluation should have questions on teachers as follows :-

- Preparation of the subject
- Presentation of the subject
- Personality, character, punctuality
- Readiness to help the students

- Classroom management, use of various modern teaching aids
- Behavior with students, participation of student activities, both extra-curricular and co-curricular activities.

For each question, some credit should be given. For each type of evaluation percentage given should be fixed. Similar questionnaire can be prepared for other types of evaluation also. Then total percentage obtained by the teacher should be used to decide the performance of the teacher.

If the teacher gets above 75% then he should be given grade "Excellent," for 60 to 75% "Best", for 50 to 60% "Good" and for below 50% "Poor". If the teacher gets excellent and best grades for consecutively three years he should be given increments, promotion, etc. If the teacher gets poor grade for successively three years then he should be given punishment accordingly. For improving the performance of poor teacher. Head of the Institution should conduct interim follow-up meetings. In the meeting, the teacher should give the reasons for his poor performance. After hearing the causes of poor performance he will suggest the way for improving the

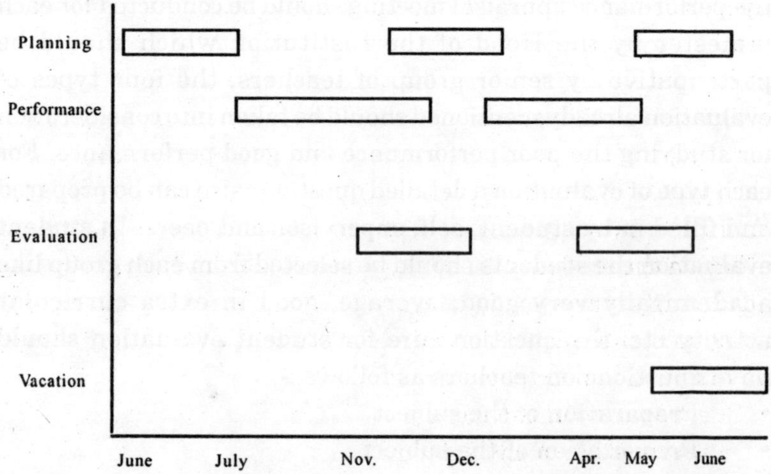

Fig. 2 Performance Planning and Appraisal Cycle.

performance and if needed he may be deputed to training and development courses.

Fig. 2 shows the Bar Chart of performance planning and appraisal cycle for one academic year. Normally for any institution first term period is July-November and second term period is December-April. For each semester, planning and evaluation should be made. In the month of June-July planning of teacher/institution should be done and then between July to November teachers have to work according to their planning. Then in the participative appraisal meeting for the first semester (i.e., in November-December) the evaluation of the teacher and preplanning for the next semester can be made. The Bar Chart also shows these activities for the second semester.

CONCLUSION

The paper has presented the urgent need of 'GOAL SETTING' for individual and for the institute at the start of every semester. Performance planning must precede the appraisal. The system ought to be OPEN, PARTICIPATIVE and DATA BASED. Rewards to meritorious and punishment to defaulters must be integrated with the system. It is illogical to expect outstanding performance without outstanding rewards and vice versa.

The aim of performance planning and appraisal is to facilitate the teacher and the institute to contribute most to the best of their abilities.

Introduction of PADS in College cannot be a casual affair. It has to be a conscious attempt for which setting up a task force is strongly recommended. The task force would have to be well trained in Goal Setting and Performance Appraisal.

19

Students Need to Acquire Innovation and Entrepreneurship Skills for Global Competitiveness

Professor is the hero in an education institute. He needs to be enabled to rise up to international standard. This is the responsibility of college

Every Student Should Aim To Become Not Just An Engineer But The World Best

It was presumed in good old days that new technology could be discovered only abroad. Our students, colleges, universities, and industries were expected to become only copy cats. We have been as a result, constantly buying technologies and they are selling. But now, Indian talent has become conscious of its capabilities. It has become ambitious to discover new technologies ahead of others. Indians in Silicon Valley have made a mark. It is observed that students, who sow the seeds of innovation in their minds in college days, are better suited to become successful leaders, in service career. Students who aspire to become leaders in technology and leaders in industry should have necessarily to acquire skills to generate new technologies, new products and new processes and obtain patents. Students should resort to innovative non conventional thinking. Good merit in examination is necessary, but not enough. Creativity is essential. Education without skills of innovation and skills of entrepreneurship is incomplete in modern sense.

DO YOU HAVE A COLUMBUS SPIRIT?

Do you have an urge to discover unknown? Do you have the spirit of inquiry and spirit of adventure? Knowledge memorized and stored in brain is important, but more important is the ability to discover unknown. Ideas are the real capital. You need ideas to succeed. Idea generated is opportunity generated. Ideas come from innovation. A skill set for technological innovation, organizational, resource or market innovation, is essential for every engineer so as to become a leader in his chosen field of specialization.

There is an acute shortage of creative engineers. Engineers as humble servants are plentiful. Can you dream to become" First Mover"? Opportunities to be so are abundant. Opportunities are found to galore. Winning leaders can see opportunities where others can not. But where are the winning engineers in India? You can be one of them. Most of the students learn in a passive way, what is handed over to them by teachers. They do not question why and how. They should show greater initiative to take active hand in discovery of new technologies, new products and processes, organization and unexplored markets. They essentially have to acquire the existing knowledge and yet think differently, consistently so as to become the leader. Winning leaders are essentially good learners. If you want to be a world class engineer, you have to be world class learner. Try to become an engine and not a Bogie.

HOW TO BECOME WORLD BEST?

The capabilities of Indian people are pretty high, but most of the times they remain unexplored, because of lack of innovative spirit. Hon. President Dr. Abdul Kalam wrote "the young generation should dream high to become world best. Unless there is a dream no big achievement takes place." Visions are in short supply and not the capabilities. Intellectual resource of Indian youths, in the past remained under utilized due to lack of high aims, and not due to lack of resources. Our accomplishments were limited by our thinking in smaller terms. Now is a time to think big. Innovative thinking provides a drive to move forward. Beware! You young engineers matter most. Your future and the nations future is very bright if you cultivate the habit of innovation and bring about reforms in whatever you do, wherever you live. Innovative engineers are never a drag. They are always wanted. In fact India is suffering from the deficiency of creative engineering. Will you consider with priority to be innovative? An innovative person never remains unemployed. On the contrary he is more in demand. He has a mission in his life, which gives him extra energy and purpose to live. An innovative person constantly strives to improve. He is always dissatisfied with the existing state of affairs. He wants to create new, and again new. The innovative spirit in him does not permit him to sit idle. He contributes to uplift the human kind. Human civilization is progressing on the strength of such innovative persons. Are you one of them? If so, you are bound to win.

TRY TO ACQUIRE NEW VISION OF NEW WORLD

Most of the students soon after graduation are looking for jobs, possibly in Multi National Companies. Very few dream to be entrepreneurs. On the one hand there are so many educated unemployed and on the other hand there is an acute shortage of innovative entrepreneurs. The resources are in abundance, so also the demand for goods and services. Availability of finance is plentiful. Opportunities are practically unlimited. But it is the foreign companies which are making most of them. Can the Indian engineers not widen their visions to make most of their capabilities? They ought to become enterprising, like their counterparts in developed world. What is the role model before our eyes? Is it Bill Gates? Dr. Abdul Kalam, Dhirubhai Ambani? Bill Gates started his enterprise while he was a student. Apple Computers, HP like many companies were started while the promoters were students. While you are young and energetic, you can become an entrepreneur easily. Need you any help, institutes are always there to support you.

WHY NOT HIGH TECH START-UP?

Now that the Government has taken massive drive to promote industrial development, Industrial estates are being set up even in small and medium towns. Government has adopted de-licensing policy. Financial capital is being made available along with subsidy. Help to prepare Project reports is provided and all kinds of guidance extended. Can the university educated persons not think of establishing high tech start-ups? They should use their expertise and start New Technology Based Firms [NTBF]. The opportunities in industrial field in India and abroad are in abundance. They should show bold attitude. Without NTBF you will remain number two in the world. Command on hi-tech and command in entrepreneurship makes enables you to become number one.

Students should learn to capitalize on innovation. This will enable you to become number one. This is good for you and for the good of nation. Students should incubate their ideas for industry, under the guidance of professors, while they are students. This is the latest established trend in the world that universities are becoming the maternity homes and giving birth to healthy industries. It is reported that such entrepreneurs are more successful. In such cases the congenital defects in industries are avoided. World class institutions, in India like IITs, NITs and some state colleges have started Technology Incubators, Business Incubators, Research Parks, and Innovation Centers, Venture Capital Foundations, Patent and

IPR centers, in their campuses, based on experience of developed countries. You can benefit from them.

INNOVATION IS INDISPENSABLE TO WIN

Technology parks, Special Economic Zones are being set up in every state by Government and private agencies. Many foreign enterprises are coming in them. There is a greater need of indigenous companies. Research based companies make better fortune. They are needed most in India, at this juncture of time. Students should therefore think of starting knowledge companies also termed as research based companies utilizing the expertise available in universities and transferring the same to industry to improve their productivity. The strengths of research institutes and engineering colleges need to be integrated with the industrial development. There is a gap between the two which the young students should try to bridge. It is realized that, Industry so as to remain globally competitive needs access to first class research in universities. So also the first class researches in universities need access to industry for application of findings of their research. There are only two alternatives in this competitive world, namely to innovate or die.

AIM TO BECOME CAPTAIN OF INDUSTRY

Thousands of students every year are going abroad for higher education. What do they learn there? Can you not learn that in India? They learn skills of innovation, skills of generation of new technologies, skills of patent and IPR. Can you now learn these things in India? You can certainly learn. Now government has started a massive program for reformation of engineering education, in IITs, NITs, and various other engineering colleges. They are being upgraded to world best level. Various centers of excellence are being installed in them. India aspires to become a destination of technical education in the world. Institutes have now new visions of new world. Institutes are being equipped in respect of infrastructure for innovation, so as to build India a developed nation by the year 2020. Now it is expected that the students change their mind set in favor of innovation and entrepreneurship rather than to work for MNCs. Here they mostly work in supporting role and remain contented with high salary only. It is never too early to start an enterprise.

BEHAVIOURAL SKILLS MATTER

Students ought to possess the knowledge of culture, living styles, languages spoken, etc of different countries. They must have to show tolerance to the religions, faiths in human values, beliefs, castes etc. of others, so as to operate on global plane. They must help to keep human civilization together and not divide. A new kind of knowledge based society is emerging in the world. Students have to contribute to shape it well. The competency of engineers in international environment is measured in terms of, technical skills and behavioral skills. Students ought to be good in respect of both. Often behavioral skills weigh more. Written communication, oral communication, etiquettes matter equally. They must enrich the work environment for themselves and others. Do you add value to the work culture? Do you dress well? Winning engineers transform negative energy into positive energy.

HUMAN CAPITAL COUNTS

Students have to be innovative to see the incoming opportunities ahead of others. They have to think strategically. India possesses the largest pool of youthful workforce and high quality human capital. Availability of working age population elsewhere in the world is less. This is our competitive advantage. Students ought to harvest this global opportunity. Whole world is available as a market for your skills. You have to develop your self for global needs. Education without skills of innovation and entrepreneurship is incomplete in modern sense.

According to a news item published in Economic Times, on 19th May, 2003. "India slipped to 21st rank from 13th in number of scientific output." The PhDs produced in engineering are only 293 [1998 as against China 2900, and 5930 in US. Engineers with BE degree are like soldiers, M Tech., Ph.D. are like captains and generals. What should be your choice?

Economic Returns Come From Knowledge Diffusion

Research out put in universities often results in wonderful publications, but rarely does it result in commercial exploitation. Thesis remains on library shelf. Universities think innovation is the business of industry. They do not go nearer and remain away from market. Universities are found to ignore innovation. As a result the students do not learn the skills on innovation. Indian economy due to lack of innovation in technological fields is lagging. Invention when commercially exploited is known as innovation. It leads to creation of new products, new processes. It improves the productivity and industrial competitiveness. It is an activity which gives birth to new ideas to reduce the risks of business failures. It is an essential pre-requisite to create and run an industry in an efficient manner. It is the innovators which lead.

INNOVATION IS PLEASURE GIVING

Professors and students when they see the application of their research in industry, they get thrilled. They get a kind of satisfaction and an inspiration to do research more and more. They get that satisfaction which by earning any amount does not come. Innovation thus provides a kind of fuel for research and makes advanced education fruitful. Innovation enhances the utility of research done, and the rate of return on investment. Financial and research links between industry and universities if properly established, they drive the economic growth and innovation faster. A formal policy on interaction between the industry and institutes is being built. Younger generation should have to make a conscious effort in this direction.

BENCHMARKING WITH THE WORLD BEST

What are your counterparts elsewhere in the world doing? What are there achievements?

MIT Boston has a technology licensing office [TLO] in which about 200 people work. The author has personally visited this office. The students and professors of MIT every year earn about 100 patents and lot of royalty. Our students on internet should get in touch with their counterparts not only in USA but in other countries also. Quality and relevance of education is reported to have improved mainly because of the presence of patent culture in the campus. Enterprising culture is imbibed in students, which leads to spin-off of companies. Around ten companies are born every year in MIT. Institutes have become the maternity homes, where good baby care is taken and companies are born without any congenital defects. Benchmarking works as a driving force on the path of progress. It is a spring board for taking a jump. Out students should try to know what the level of achievement of their counterparts is. This can broaden their visions.

A NEW ENTREPRENEURIAL SOCIETY IS COMING INTO BEING

Individuals should focus their attention on preparing themselves fit for the same they should deliberately create a favorable mind set. If the students care for making India center of technological innovation, then there is a hope for India to become a developed nation by the year 2020. The infrastructure like patenting is a profit business. It should therefore be installed forthwith, in each university, college without any delay. Government should play its central role. Young engineers should be aggressive to grab opportunity in patents. The whole world is tending to become a knowledge society. Winning engineers should look at patenting as an opportunity. Young generation should accelerate the arrival of new technology, and prepare others to absorb faster.

VENTURE CAPITAL IS AVAILABLE IN PLENTRY

If you have a brand new idea for business, if it is untested and untried in India, you may write a letter to any of the venture capitalists. You have a project idea and they have capital. You can join hands with them and take equity. They help you to refine your ideas. If your project makes profits you share them. By any chance if it fails, the loss is borne entirely by the venture capitalists. They win in nine out of ten projects. The loss of one is paid out of profits from nine. You do not loose any thing what so every. This is the beauty of venture capital. It is the venture capitalists in Japan and USA who have taken the industry forward. Now it has come to India to help you. You need not have Tata and Birla parents. What you need is to have a business idea whose time has come. Resources are not in short supply, so also the capabilities.

THOSE WHO DARE WIN

Let me now present on story. A kind had a beautiful daughter. When she became of 17 years age, the king wanted her to marry. She agreed on the condition of SWAYAMWAR. The boy should be able to swim across the river. The king announced and invited young boys. They assembled on one bank of river. The beautiful princess was standing with a garland on the other bank. There were many shakes, crocodiles, frogs in the river. So the young boys, who came to win the hands of princess, were not ready to jump. The king was disappointed. After waiting for one hour suddenly one frail and weak boy jumped. He swam across the river. The marriage was celebrated with great pomp and show. The other boys who were standing on the bank were stronger, deserving and more competent. Yet they lost the golden chance. They were repenting. When the boys were standing around the Hero, one boy asked *him* how he dared to jump. He said, really I did not myself jump. Some body from behind pushed me. Then I had no alternative than to swim. Any of them could have swum across, but no one showed daring the princess was none other than the "opportunity. Do not wait for some one to push you from behind.

20

Engineering Education: Where and How it Should Reach

"Good Institutes so as to Create Educated Citizenry are a Pre-condition For National and Regional Development"

The paper presents the objectives of engineering education in this time of dynamic economy and fast changing technology. It analyses the existing system of engineering education in India and points out its inadequacies. Reforms are suggested to be able to achieve the desired objectives.

INTRODUCTION

Science and technology is advancing today at a much faster rate than at any previous time. There has been a mushrooming of scientific findings in the last two decades, and new dimensions to professional and technician skills have become open. As a consequence demands made on engineering education have greatly changed. Rapid advances in science and technology have rendered the existing system insufficient for engineers and technicians both in respect of quality and quantity. As is economic, social, and technological development necessary we need to review the existing system and tailor it to suit the requirements of today and possibly those of tomorrow. In this article it is attempted to explain the objectives of modern engineering education, and the ways to achieve them.

OBJECTIVES OF ENGINEERING EDUCATION

Engineering profession has certain obligations to society. To continue to offer services in improving living and working conditions, devising ways and means to effect saving in efforts and materials, safety to society and so on. The forefronts of basic sciences are continually advancing and opening new areas for engineering endavour. An engineer has to be alert and be able to assimilate and translate the advances of science in engineering practice. Thus engineering is far from static and essentially a creative profession. Engineering education has therefore a goal to prepare men fully competent to do the professional practice independently and further raise the same to new heights through practice and research. It follows that education in college should produce engineers who can do the function of engineering analysis, design of construction, production, or operation. He should also be able to bring the designed project in reality. Further engineering education should inspire the student with necessary spirit, and enable him to deal with new situations with fundamental approach on his own initiative and confidence. He should develop a desire and sense for involvement and taking an active hand in changing things in the profession. Thus the aims of engineering education lie much beyond training and employment. The new situations they have to handle in profession often involve social, economical, political and technical elements. Problems are seldom in well defined form. An engineer has to be able to sort out the problems, and simplify the same without loosing its essential nature. Further he should be able to think of a right approach to attack, evaluate and test the results at each stage.

EXISTING SYSTEM AND ITS DEFICIENCIES

The existing system of engineering education in most of the colleges in our country seems to be an extension of the high school system, wherein it is contended that learning is proportional to attendance in class room. In engineering colleges 75% attendance is compulsory. Many students attend classes out of this compulsion and consider class room to be a place of entertainment instead of learning. Of the same class there are many divisions, instruction being repeated for all the divisions in all the subjects as in high school. Curricula remain static for years. Teachers teach the subjects with a narrow outlook without any reference to the practice of the day. Teachers are isolated from professional practice and research and have no opportunity to be directly involved in them and remain in contact with the forefronts of the scientific developments in the subjects. A teacher who somehow keeps himself abreast though passively of the developments by reading journals and so on has no opportunity to deliver the advance material to students, because it is not included in the curriculum and obviously not asked for by external examiner. Students are more examination minded and have therefore no interest in listening to such things of advance knowledge.

Inspite of the fact that several Indian Standard codes have been evolved and adopted, universities have not yet insisted on instruction in the use of these codes, which is a thing to be done every day by a practicing engineer. The teacher is not many a times the examiner for his students. University believes more in external examiner. The teacher has therefore no opportunity to know the performance of his students in examination and adjust his teaching for the next batches.

Learning process aims at examination, wherein students have to memorise the subject matter and reproduce the same mechanically in the paper. Learning is wrongly considered to be a passive process as if students absorb knowledge from what their teacher says. It has also become a narrow speciality of the subject. For example learning to design plate and shell roofs. Students learn mathematical derivations and such other treatment to a very great extent, without adequate consideration to the methods of its construction, economic, and other feasibility aspects to bring type design in reality. It therefore does not take place as a liberal art for the profession. Students do not come to know the problems involved in the practical application, and are therefore labled as theoretical engineers. They do not come up to the problems in profession while taking education and are obviously not prepared to meet them. One often hears too many complaints about the irrelevance of the offerings of the engineering courses. Obselete and outdated knowhow is taught at many places, and for current and advance knowledge there is no time for learning. It is therefore no wonder if products of our institutions cannot step in and stand independently in profession. Those who are supposed to create and provide jobs for others become themselves a burden to society. Best judged students of colleges desire to be hirelings, and the second grade men with forced circumstances form the cadre of employers and decision makers. Engineers produced by our colleges are poor in practical respects and that they should take lessons from practicing engineers. It is a common grievance of the people emerging out of colleges that all their education is a passive experience and they are not prepared to take active hand in changing things and bringing about a different social order.

REFORMS NEEDED

The contention that learning is proportional to attendance does not hold good in case of higher education. Students seeking admission to engineering courses have brilliant career. Learning to them is largely a matter of stimulation and guidance, rather than tuition. Today there is great deal of over instruction in the college and students are reluctant to attend all that. Regardless of how a teacher teaches every student learns at his own rate that too at his own initiative and efforts.

It would therefore be right to abandon the attendance system in class room. Engineering students recognize the responsibility of preparing drawings and such other works themselves. Therefore insistence on doing the drawing within the four walls of the college should be given up. For better learning to take place they need more of freedom and less of supervision. They should have liberty to do it at home or in college. The number of theory lectures for each subject may be reduced allowing more of free time for self learning. Through lectures they should receive a good introduction to each chapter of the subject and its full scope along with the knowledge required for professional practice and latest developments. What is given in text books may be passingly referred, as students have no interest in listening to them. They understand it better by reading the well written books themselves. A good academic freedom to students and staff is a practice in Germany, USA and many other developed countries. It is indeed the backbone of their so successful education system. They experience that academic freedom is very essential to develop creative thinking in the young and energetic minds. When students drive their studies themselves and by self initiative they are prepared best for getting actively involved in profession and attempting to raise the same to new heights, as is the primary objective of engineering education.

To enable teacher to deliver right type of material to students through lectures, he needs to have association with the professional practice and also research in the field. It is an observation that when a teacher divides his time equally in teaching research, and professional practice he is prepared best to lecture in class room. Being in contact with profession he experiences problems and after sorting them out-puts them to research in his faculty. He could also evaluate and test the outcome of research at each stage and extend the same in practice. This knowledge gained from research, and supplemented with that from experiences flows automatically in classes and the young prospective engineers are greatly benefited by that. While passing out from college they come up to the forefronts of scientific developments in each subject. A synchronized relation and feedback system in teaching research, and practice is best possible in this way. A professor is then rightly able to serve as a source of academic impulses in the society. Engineering college should then justly become a seat of learning, and a leading unit in the process of economic and technological development. In developed countries this system prevails. Every institution engages itself in teaching and research. It is therefore the need of time that our engineering colleges do not limit themselves to merely teaching but apply themselves also in research, as is being done in foreign countries.

Most of the industries in our country are functioning in collaboration with companies in foreign countries. Development plans of these industries, howsoever minor they may be, are, implemented with the help of their counterparts. Today there is a potential of knowhow available, with laboratory equipment at engineering colleges, which can be gainfully utilized for such work. But where are the systems and incentives? But because Government allows industry to run to their collaborators indiscriminately the knowhow at colleges remains idle, does not grow and in turn education suffers. It would therefore be right to curtail foreign collaboration at least to the extent of development plans and divert the work to colleges. Participation of college staff should also be invited in the preparation of Government project designs. Today engineers of the departments such as B&C, I&P D, CPWD, etc. prepare the engineering designs of the projects, and also check the same. Because checking is done by the same department which prepares it, it has become just a formality, and mistakes are carried in execution. In fact purpose of checking designs is best served if it is done by-a different agency. If checking of designs of Government projects is directed to college staff, they will be able to bring fresh view points in the design, and do it best in the light of latest developments in the subjects. This is turn assists the cause of education. Today students seeking admission to engineering colleges have little background of industry. Particularly those coming from rural areas whose number is large. They have absolutely no idea of the field in which they want to make career. In the absence of any practical training before admission they cannot decide their interests in the branch of engineering, they choose. They find it difficult to correlate theory they learn with the practice. Introduction of practical training before admission and during vacations will enable the students to better appreciate the lectures. Teachers need not spend time and energy in describing elementary things. Workshop practice in colleges may be altogether stopped. Six months practical training should be prescribed as precondition for admission. Training could be according to the branch of engineering, which would be naturally different for different branches. The idea of practical training is usually acceptable, but a difficulty is often put forward that the industry is not ready to accept the responsibility to train young prospective engineers. Industrialists do not want to suffer even slightest inconvenience in the cause of education and yet expect to have well educated and trained men from colleges. Government should therefore in national interest make it obligatory for industry to impart practical training to students, as it is obligatory to observe labour welfare.

The curriculum of courses should look more forward than behind. New subjects such as advanced computer programming, advanced mathematics and so on should be introduced, management Science is achieving importance in the technological age. Knowing only engineering design is not enough. In executing the design he has to deal with labour, salesmen, fellow men etc. who bring to him new problems daily. An engineer should therefore learn modern scientific methods of projects planning and scheduling such as CPM/PERT, and more important to get well along with others. He must also learn public speaking, public relations, and psychology to give him confidence in his management duties. Syllabi of the subjects need not be spelled out in details as is the case today. They should be broad in nature giving just an outline of the subject. Details of curriculum may be left to teachers, who on having freedom may add or delete things as they deem fit from time to time and with reference to the practice of the day. Thus curriculum will not remain static but change with time.

To bring students more in active participation in learning, group discussions, attending seminars and symposiums should be encouraged. Curriculum should include project report writing and a dissertation. Dissertation should be a sole creation of the student and done preferably after all his theory papers are over, he should find a problem for himself, work on that and draw out conclusions. Students derive great pleasure from their original creation, and they should be permitted to do so. Memory oriented examinations will have to be stopped. Questions set should be aimed t testing the candidates intelligence and critical faculty and not merely his capacity to memorize facts and figures, special seminars and orientation courses if necessary should be organized to train examiners for the purpose.

CONCLUSION

In this time of dynamic economy and fast changing technology, engineering education should reach to intellectual self-reliance, that will enable young engineers to face bravely and resourcefully situations not scheduled in the curriculum. To be able to achieve this goal conventional method is not an answer. Practical training before admission and during vacations will have to be introduced. Government should make the necessary legislation that industry accepts this as corporate social responsibility to train young engineers. A change in the basic approach to the establishment of engineering colleges is necessary. Professional research will have to be introduced in colleges. Foreign collaborations should be restricted and industry should be made to refer to colleges for their development problems. Integrity of teacher should be considered beyond reproach, and he should be given full hand to experiment and do the curricular reform.

Where once nations measured their strength by the
Size of the armies and arsenals, in the world of
Future knowledge will matter most.

21

India Needs Industry Oriented Technical Universities to Win in World Economy

The chapter presents need and importance of integrating engineering education, with research and industry in the context of rapid technological change and external pressure of globalization. It brings out inadequacies in the present system and suggests reforms for institution building so as to make Indian education competitive. The industry institute interaction is very crucial nowadays to improving competitiveness. The chapter suggests that technical universities on the lines of agricultural Universities be set up forthwith, so as to carry out education, research and technology transfer in an integrated manner.

There are more than 2300 engineering colleges in the country turning out about 2 lakh engineers per year. The number of post graduates produced are however, very few, around five thousand and the doctorates are far too few. Today, success in industrialization depends not only on the number of engineers but on their depth of knowledge. The post graduates and doctorates in advanced countries have proved to be a major force in generation of new technologies. Almost half of graduates with them go further for post graduation and half of them again for doctoral and post doctoral research. Are we producing only soldiers in technology without a matching number of captains and generals? It is mostly on account of the lack of research base in engineering colleges that the Indian Industry is dependent on imported technologies. The development plans of most companies are propelled by collaborators.

The high-tech industry today demands engineers with skills for innovation and skills for generation of new knowledge and skills for generation of newer technologies. India needs now technology leaders, "first movers" in high tech start-ups. Can engineering colleges under present multi faculty university system produce them? Are the policies of engineering education and policies of industrial development compatible?

Most of the engineering colleges are teaching oriented and not research oriented. They are affiliated to multi faculty universities which are not at all industry oriented. They lack vision in relation to the speed and direction of industrial growth. They are not sensitive enough to market demands. The engineering faculty is one of the many faculties and often does not get the priority as well as resources it deserves. The syllabi are revised too late, the conduct of examination takes long time, and the results are declared late. Semesters do not begin on time. The engineering colleges in this system are not able to perform to the level they should and they are capable for. They remain busy in routine things. For innovative works, they are left with no time, energy and money. The innovative ability of students and professors is thwarted, impeded and stifled. Some of them, out of frustration go abroad. How long they should keep going? Can all students go? It is essential now to build industry oriented technical universities, so as to make most of our intellectual resources and win in the world economy. Technical universities will enhance the utility of growing number of engineering colleges. They will accelerate the pace of development.

A trend towards establishment of technical universities since first industrial revolution is observed in developed countries. Germany with a population of about ten crores has 84 technical universities. Japan with 12 crore population has 200 technical universities, U.K. In the recent past has elevated all its polytechnics to the status of technical universities. U.S.A. with 30 crore population has more than 1000 technical universities. U.S. universities have focused their attention on industrial needs. This has paid them dividends. Why can't country like India have at least one hundred technical universities? Do we realize that multi faculty universities are consuming more funds and giving less output? Do we realize that they are less purposeful, less productive than technical universities? India needs industry oriented technical universities most, so as to capitalize faster on emerging technologies. Do we realize that the opportunities missed are more valuable than the cost of establishing technical universities? We urgently need to make policies for education and industrial development compatible to each other.

Michael Porter in his book "The competitive advantages of nations" from comparative study of ten developed countries wrote that nations are industrially more developed which have more technical universities. The model of technical university is more powerful enterprising and yet cost effective than a multi faculty university. They are more focused on industrial development. Industry in collaboration with such universities have ventured for establishment of research parks, incubators, patent transaction and Intellectual Property Rights help centers, technology licensing centers, venture capital foundations etc... They have successfully spun off many new technologies and new technology based start-ups like APPLE, HP etc. These innovative activities in technical universities have, in the last twenty years, made a very valuable contribution to the economies of those nations. The universities have moved from periphery to the center of development. We have missed such opportunities because we do not have industry oriented research universities. Are we trying to do jobs with yesterday's organization structures, systems and procedures? Is the governance and leadership in education behind the time?

A phenomenon is observed that universities from countries like Australia, USA, and UK have taken out aggressive drive to market education world over including India. They have opened marketing departments to make a sale of education. They are opening learning centers and giving affiliation to existing colleges in India. These outside universities have proven experience, reputation and credibility with employers, especially Multinational Corporations. They are likely to attract best of our students. In the era of globalization and liberalization, we can not stop them from coming. If we do not upgrade our institutions, they are likely to be reduced to municipality schools. There is an external pressure on higher education to improve. Status quo is too dangerous.

Indian industry when compared with its counterpart in developed countries is yet to go a long way. Although the population of India is 16% of worlds population, its industrial output is around only 1%, per capita income is 450 US$, which is one of the lowest in the world, with 25% people living below the poverty line. The industrial productivity, although increasing, is too low and India ranks 43rd in the world list. A study conducted by CII (1999) observed that Indian companies do not tap new knowledge from engineering colleges and universities because they do not know what industry needs. If industry oriented technical universities are set up, they will go nearer to each other and the relationship between the two will be mutually supportive.

A CASE FOR TECHNICAL UNIVERSITY

Compatability Between The Policy For Technical Education And Policy For Industrial Development Is Essential

In order to become a significant economic power in the 21st century, it is essential for India to restructure its engineering education without further loss of time and integrate the same with indigenous research along with horizontal expansion of industry. The rapid changes in technological scenario, faster development of newer technologies along with their judicious applications in industry demand a fresh look at traditional organizational structure of colleges and universities. The age-old methods, structures, linkages and values which served well at one point of time, are nowadays totally outdated and no more relevant in today's context. Strategic restructure, as well as reorganization of technical education by establishing more and more technical universities, is the pressing need of time. In this paper, it is reiterated that without revitalizing the technical education by establishing technical universities, Indian economy and industry, howsoever desired, cannot grow and become globally competitive. Reforms in technical education should precede the industrial reforms.

PRESENT TECHNICAL EDUCATION FALLS TOO SHORT OF EXPECTATIONS.

Only 30% are employable, so says a recent study.

The existing universities in India for various reasons have failed to cope with the demands from fast changing technological advances. Though the country possesses a massive infrastructural base in technical education consisting of a large chain of engineering colleges, vast pool of teachers and students, but it has not been so responsive to changing needs due to its inherent weaknesses. Universities have become 'Hamstrung' organizations unfit for nursing new ideas and technologies. They are far behind their counterparts in developed nations.

Though a large number of graduate engineers and technicians come out from Indian universities every year, yet the scientific and technological achievements of the country bear no relation to these vast number of S&T personnel. The quality, as well as relevance of education by world standards, is somehow missing today.

The need of the day is to undertake massive programs to educate masses and encourage innovations to country's need so as to provide a new direction to Indian economy and business. This cannot be achieved through the conventional universities, because of the simple fact that they are incapable of seeing these challenges. It requires exclusive treatment like agricultural universities to integrate education, with research and extension.

In liberalized economy, external pressures are mounting on Indian industry forcing them to restructure so as to become competitive. The industries which cannot cope with this change would become sick, and ultimately go out of business. It is seen that multinational companies in India are bringing latest technologies and recruiting competent manpower from outside / inside. So as to equip industry with able manpower and also to be competitive in future, it is imperative that the curriculum of technical education be charged with the spirit of research and innovation, without further loss of time.

Huge investments are made by both public and private sectors towards the industrial development. But because of inadequacies in technical education and consequently fewer competencies of engineers, they are less productive. Most of the industries are sick locking up huge capital in them. The productivity of industry now depends largely on the performance of personnel. The human resources produced by these institutes are an input to Indian industry and hence their capability is of vital importance to industry. Unless this manpower is globally competitive, the industry cannot prosper.

NEEDED - RESEARCH BASE TO GENERATE NEW TECHNOLOGIES.

Today technical education institutes are suffering from the deficiency of innovations. Many of these institutes have no research departments. Without Proper Avenue of research base, engineering education cannot grow and become up-to-date. It is seen that the basic premise of technology changes four to five time during the entire service career of a teacher. A teacher cannot teach the latest developments in the field of his specialization, if he is not exposed to the latest developments. He teaches yesterdays knowledge today. Technical education institutes now in changed situation have to provide competent manpower but also newer technologies to industry.

To cater to these needs, technical education institutes should be restructured. It is found that students learn best by doing research and hence, a strong research base to education institute is imperative.

The foreign collaborators have brought newer plans, products, and processes to Indian industry. The educational institutes and academicians in India have remained away from industry.

On the other hand, collaborators have gone closer to them. Time has come that industry and institute together jointly should bridge the gap and develop a system which would revitalize both on a continuing basis.

PATH SHOWN BY AGRICULTURAL UNIVERSITIES

Agriculture education, research and their application in India are looked after by the Ministry of Agriculture. Government of India, which is primarily responsible for growth and development of agricultural production also looks after education. The agricultural universities (set up after 1960) in various states receive their financial grant from the Ministry of Agriculture, and not from the Ministry of Education, Government of India. The directions and targets for education, research, etc are also monitored by this Ministry which provides matching grants too.

It is believed that this strategy has been the basis of India's success in alleviating its food problem, increasing food production (from 50 million tones to nearly 300 million tons). Had the agricultural education continued to be governed by the Ministry of Education, it would have never received the priority; funding and direction that it needed to address the nation's critical problem of food crisis. Medical Education is also looked after by health ministry.

To increase the industrial production substantially, it is necessary to integrate the technical education with industry. It seems appropriate to bring technical education and industry in the same ministry.

This strategy of putting engineering education, research and industry under one ministerial roof, is especially applicable to developing countries where industrial development plans are found to be going in one direction while technical education and research plans are going in another, as if one strategy has nothing to do with the other. As a result, there is much irrelevance in education and research.

It is seen that many engineers and educated people are unemployed on the one hand while people possessing required skills and knowledge are rarely available on the other. Huge capital investments in industry remain idle or underutilized making the industry unstable and allowing them to perform well below their installed capacities.

Allocation of fund to industry, as well as to education and research is important, but more important is the productivity of present spending. Fund productivity would yield better result if technical education and industry are strategically coupled.

Universities and education ministry, especially in developing countries, tend to be insensitive to market opportunities. They are ill equipped to understand and cope up with the high-speed environment of business. Universities sometimes have a lack of vision in relation to the speed and direction of industrial growth. They continue to work on more traditional lines forgetting the need for the students' community as well as industrial sectors. If teachers continue to teach what they know rather than what students ought to be taught, then the whole exercise of higher education becomes meaningless.

Therefore, a structural reform in funding mechanism as well as strategic control of industries and institutes is urgently required. If appropriate sectors of education and industry are brought under the same ministry, there will be a better coordination. This hypothesis has been tested both in the agricultural sector and health sector, Medical education also under Ministry of Health. It is yielding a positive response and, therefore, it is desired that such a trial be made in the area of engineering education also.

Michael Porter in his book, "Competitive Advantage of Nations" has observed, from comparative study of ten nations,that nations are industrially advanced where there are more technical universities. Secondly, Technical Universities are more productive, cost effective, than comprehensive Universities. Thirdly, where the policy of technical policy is compatible with the policy of industrial development, for which they need to be brought in one ministry.

SUGGESTIONS

Lateral expansion of technical education coupled with a strong research base along with judicious application of fruits of scientific developments be considered necessary in an integrated manner while setting up technical universities.

Following suggestions deserve serious considerations

- One of the Government colleges in each region need to be elevated to the university level which would not only avoid unnecessary delay but also reduce cost.
- Degree, diploma institutes and ITI in a region be brought under the control of a technical university, regardless whether these are private/aided or Government funded and steps be initiated to make them autonomous.
- Technical education need to be clubbed with the Ministry of Industry, Government of India, in the line of agriculture universities.

- A forum of leaders in industry and leaders in education need to be set up at the center and state.
- Industrial services department, innovation centre, and technology park be set up at each, university, so as to provide 'Technology Push' to economy and to reduce sickness in industrial sector.

CONCLUSION

So as to improve industrial competitiveness at this critical juncture of time it is essential to integrate education, with research and industry by establishing technical universities. To set up exclusive technical universities widening their scope to cover polytechnics, ITI is the need of the hour. Problems in technical education would remain unattended and industry would be unable to face competition globally unless this vital area gets utmost priority in near future.

Engineering colleges do not get the priority they deserve in the present university system. They have consequently remained far too behind. Any more neglect will however be too damaging. More so because the technology is now a major differentiating factor for a nation to win. Establishing technical universities or uplifting some of the engineering colleges including private unaided, to university status should therefore be on the national agenda. It is a very much ripe proposition and right way to capitalize on technology. IIT experience in this regards should be used to make implementation easy. Government industry and academicians should have to come together to make it happen. Establishing technical universities is the only way to build Indian industry globally competitive. It is the considered opinion of the author that higher and technical education today has to be far too advanced than yesterday. It is more complex, specialized and demands innovative strategies. It really requires a full time well qualified world class chancellor at state level. It is too important to be left in the hands of a decorative figure. A lead in establishing technical universities should have been taken long before, but better late than never.

The Innovation Makes Enemies of All Those Who Prospered Under The Old Order, and Only Lukewarm Support is Forthcoming From Those Who Would Prosper Under The New Machiavelli, the Prince, 1513

22

Higher Education : Lessons from Japan

Japan has made spectacular progress during the last forty years and the credit for this is attributed greatly to its educated and trained work force at all levels. A study entitled Japan's Intellectual Challenge by Lawrence P. Grayson of the U.S. National Institute of Education described Japan's strong commitment to education, particularly technical education. It details the expansion of scientific and technical education at all levels both to provide the engineers and technicians needed by the industry for growth and technical development and to produce the technically literate population required to facilitate the transfer and adoption of technology on which the nation's infrastructure has depended.

To illustrate the growth, in the last 45 years from 1955 to 2000, the number of bachelor's degrees in engineering awarded in Japan rose greatly. The US annual figure is surpassed in 1967. By 1982 on a per capita basis, Japan was graduating 2.3

times as many engineers as the US. Based on the figures supplied by US department of Labour, this report demonstrated a close coordination between the average annual rates of increase in engineering degrees and subsequent manufacturing productivity growth for both Japan and US over the years between 1950 to 2000.

Another noteworthy feature of Japan's education is that 21.6% of university students are in engineering. This proportion is the highest in the world. In USA engineering students constitute only 5.9%, UK 16.7% and Europe 15%. Almost half of graduates in Japan take up doctoral studies.

The number of students studying science on the other hand in Japan is far too few, only 3.2%, while in US they constitute 11.6%, UK 22.8% and Europe 13%.

The number of researchers per million of population in Japan is 360, largest in the world, USA has 310 and European countries 110 per million inhabitants.

TEACHING AND RESEARCH INTERFACE

Another feature of Japan is that on the periphery of universities there are several specialised research institutes to absorb the persons coming out of universities with new qualifications. Students get access to research in these Labs and researchers get access to teaching young students, which makes teaching, learning and research supportive to each other. Teaching and research in isolation i.e. when segregated from each other are found to be too weak and irrelevant. Besides, the application of new knowledge, new technology to manufacturing systems and various other professions and vocations is too slow. Teaching, research and extension are found to be more powerful and purposeful if coupled with each other. This is achieved in Japan by locating research laboratories on the periphery of universities. It is this strategy of producing large number of technically qualified people and bringing teaching and research under one roof and absorbing educated people in research activity of Japan which has been threatening European, US, and UK economies.

In India, although the population is almost nine times larger than Japan, yet the engineers graduating per year are proportionately less. The postgraduates and doctorate students in engineering are insignificantly small. The research is almost completely absent and consequently we are importing technologies at much higher cost. *Saving one rupee on research leads to spending ten rupees on import.* It is the collaborators from abroad which have contributed greatly for the advancement of industry in India and not the higher education institutes. The cost paid no doubt is much higher. Is this not like being penny wise pound foolish?

For priority courses like computer science, electronics engineering in which employment opportunities are abundant there is almost no funding from Government and students have to learn the new required knowledge at their own cost in self financing institutions. The youth as a result are being educated with scarce resources in inappropriate subjects and hence they remain unemployable. We are educating them in colleges, universities for old outdated skills which are not wanted. This is mainly because teachers teach what they know rather than what the students ought to learn. The situation is that what is wanted is not taught and what is taught is not wanted. There is a great mismatch because we have segregated research from teaching. Most of the research grants are going to CSIR Laboratories and they are not accessible to young students and teachers. Shall we not correct the situation by learning a lesson from Japan, and design systems to integrate teaching, research and industry?

THE EMERGING TECHNOLOGIES

Are we prepared to catch such hi-tech world market opportunities? Are we turning out enough number of system engineers with M. Tech. Ph.D. Degree? The question needs to be addressed and answered by all higher education institutes. This is a priority area with skill shortages and high pay off in world economy. We have youth with potential ability but for want of proper infrastructure and direction they tend to remain unemployed and opportunities missed. Universities and colleges ought to become more aware about opportunities arising out of emerging technologies which are short lived and attack them vigorously like a pack of wolves. Private institutes like APTECH, NIIT have shown a vision in starting a variety of courses, but the formal system of education like colleges and universities have lagged behind. Shall we in institutes of higher education become alert and responsive to opportunities and skill shortages in global market?

Japan with its vision, hard work and technical training to its people has been successful in pulling to it the center of gravity of economic activity from Western world. This has become possible mainly because of the fact that education development and industrial growth in Japan have been linked reciprocally. The increased quality and quantity of educated people have provided the manpower necessary for industrial development. In turn, economic growth has enabled the country to afford and create the necessity for the great expansion in the number of trained people.

Japan has installed research parks, technology parks, incubation centers on the periphery of each university. We have not done anything worthwhile in this respect. USA, UK, European countries have from 1980 installed a large number of such organizations and built bridges between industry and institutions, In this respect, we are far too behind the world. When shall we wake up? Otherwise brain drain will continue and we shall remain using imported technologies and perpetuating poverty.

In India, the Government, universities, institutes, enterprises and individuals, all need to become more aware about technological changes ahead of others and implications of not coping, which are quite serious, so serious that the situation will worsen and we will continue to remain poor most even in 21st Century. The present system, it is feared, will not be in a position to deliver the goods. Appropriate imaginative measures are called for urgently. This invites urgent attention of all people who are concerned with future of nation. The national knowledge commission in its report of 2006 has recommended overhauling of the system of Technical Education.

To sum up, we have to learn a number of lessons from Japan. Firstly, how to educate more people in engineering and divert more resources of Government to technical education. This will increase the productivity of available funds. Secondly, we have to learn to integrate teaching with research and industry by installing research parks and technology parks on the periphery of Universities and engineering colleges. Thirdly, we have to learn to budget more public funds for education and research. It is because the new emerging technologies of future need to be taught to youth instead of the old outdated technologies.

We Must Create Hi-Tech-Campus Companies, On The Periphery of Colleges Especially in Backward Areas

23

A Case for Initiatives in Technology Transfer

Foreign Collatorators Have Propelled thus far the Growth of Indian Industry. Now it is a Time for Indian Academicians.

Learning from the experience of other countries it can be said that technology transfer and marketing from higher technical education institutes to Industry and vice versa is the pressing need of Indian economy. Japan's multinational enterprises have, for long, established links for technology transfer and research and development (R&D) not only with institutes in Japan but also with institutes in United States, United Kingdom, and Europe. This is considered to be one of the important factors which have enabled Japan to become industrial leader. In India, thus far, it is more the foreign collaborators who have propelled the industrial growth. Academicians and technical education institutes have remained away from industry. Now time has come when they should stop working in isolation and move towards each other.

Technology transfer has become a major phenomenon in global economy. It is being considered a key to industrial competitiveness. Technology generation, dissemination, patenting, Intellectual Property Rights, are some of the current important issues before the nations.

Technology level of a nation has become the determinant of its economic wellbeing. Therefore, efficient organization and management of technology transfer in any nation more so in India, is the need of the hour. Performance of institutions dealing in technology in isolation ought to be discouraged. Fresh initiatives to integrate the working of universities with CSIR labs, engineering colleges, industrial estate, chamber of commerce, on the lines followed in Germany need to be introduced forthwith.

True that India is relatively a late starter in industry. It has traditionally been an agriculture based country. However, the Government now has taken a policy decision to build India a technology oriented nation and things are moving fast in this direction. Many engineering colleges have come up, and more than 2,00,000 engineers are passing out each year. Industrial Estates are being established even in small towns.

There is an atmosphere of enthusiasm in commerce, trade and industry. There exists a market pull which badly needs a Technology Push, which the higher education institutes ought to give.

Although essential, mere development of technology in laboratories and dissemination through usual methods of education, training, publication is not enough. The new technologies need to be transferred quickly and efficiently to industry to increase their productivity. Effective partnership between academics and industry in technology transfer is found to revitalize both the industry and the institute. They both thrive on each other's support. Today, in India there exists no technology transfer department in most of the academic and research institutes. However, the consciousness to set up such department is increasing. Technology transfer, usually known as "Extension", exists only in Agricultural Universities in India.

ENGINEERING COLLEGES/UNIVERSITIES AS TECHNOLOGY PROVIDERS

Engineering Colleges, IITs, polytechnics, ITIs, which so far remained away from industry have recognized that they have to contribute industrial development also. They have to play a leading role in innovation and entrepreneurship. So far the foreign collaborations have been transferring technology to Indian industry. They will keep doing so in future. But it is more expensive and makes us dependent. The Ministry of industry, commerce, trade and education have to consider worldwide developments like Technology Parks, Incubators, Entrepreneurship Centers and adopt them with modifications, if necessary, to suit our conditions. Japan and Germany have set up such institutes on the periphery of technical education institutes. Why can we not do that? Can our institutes not serve as a hub for area development?

HIGHER EDUCATION INSTITUTES AND INDUSTRIAL ESTATES

A large scale program is undertaken by central and state Governments to set up industrial estates, clusters and growth centers. Large investments are being made in them to provide infrastructure like land, water, electricity, etc. Huge amounts of loans and subsidies are being given to entrepreneurs in backward areas. Young enthusiastic people are taking up to entrepreneurship, working hard day and night with a dream to become industrialists. However, many of these enterprises in the course of time become sick. Some enterprises are born sick due to wrong conception, some choose wrong technology and their future in spite of big market and hard work is not bright.

The academic institutes, colleges, IITs and CSIR labs should show concern as to why many industries become sick.

What could be done to avoid this? The Government would have to dovetail the role of knowledge organizations, technical organizations with the establishment and running of industrial estates. With the increasing role of technology, the existing systems and procedures of industrial estates will have to be altered; it is not enough to have money and raw material to run an industry. Appropriate technology has assumed great importance. It is also not enough to have monitoring cells for industries in banks which give loans. Technology Audit has now assumed more importance than financial audit. There are doctors with various specializations to cure patients. Similarly, multiple approach to cure industrial sickness has become necessary.

Shall we, in India, not transfer this organizational invention to our industrial estates? As the maternity homes are necessary for safe child birth, so are the incubators and science parks necessary for safe start of companies.

We do have a few of them. But they are so few that in a big country like ours they hardly make their presence felt. The government has a central role in bringing together, the industrial estates and innovators. U.K. has implemented "Teaching Company Scheme" and European Commission has implemented "COMET" to improve competency of existing workforce in industries. Cost was shared by industry and government. Can such schemes improve the performance of Indian industry and reduce sickness? The benefits are far more than the cost.

VENTURE CAPITAL

Venture capital has been playing a vital role in promoting/ starting of new technology based firms in developed countries. In India government companies like RCTC, TDICI have made a beginning. The experience reported is, that the funds instead of being used for new untested technology, are being used by big companies for routine purposes. Will the VCF, companies reach the innovators? This is going to decide the innovation and growth.

A change in direction of usage of VCF is desirable. Academicians have to come forward to use them and to test their new ideas and products.

INTERNATIONAL CO-OPERATION

In the present time characterized by globalization, UNESCO and similar bodies have a crucial role to play. They ought to facilitate developing countries, to learn to generate New Technology. In India there exists a market pull and technology push is wanted.

CONCLUSION

The academicians and technical institutes in India have, thus far, remained away from industry. It is more the foreign collaborators who have gone nearer to it and propelled the industrial growth although at a high cost and with time lags. Now the two, namely, the industry and institutes would have to move towards each other to make India a technological leading nation.

Technology parks, incubators, entrepreneurship centers, patenting, etc. are some of the necessary boosters to transfer technology and improve the performance of industrial estates. Role of institute in establishment of industrial estates will have to be reviewed. Re-engineering of existing systems and procedures is desirable. In Germany, professors have to have two hats, one in the University and the other in industrial development agency.

Technology transfer in a developing country does not mean hi-tech to send a man to moon. It could be simple enough to increase industrial production and productivity. Engineering colleges, polytechnics, ITIs do possess such abilities. They are "Shakti Kendras" but for want of proper channels they remain unused Steinbeis centre scheme implemented in Germany by polytechnics is a good case to emulate.

Integration and pooling of efforts in a proper direction by all technical institutes, CSIR labs, IITs, Chambers of Commerce and industries, and taking helicopter view of technology transfer is the key to success for achieving industrial development. There is no doubt that the network of institutions, policies and procedures of government, matched with enthusiasm of industry will take the nation on the path of industrial, economic and social progress.

It is High Time that we Start,
"Teaching Assistantship" and 'Research Associateship'
Schemes Like in U.S.A. and Germany.
They are Economical and Productive Models.

24

Innovation and Technology Transfer Practices and Policies in Germany Lessons of Experience

Networking of Innovators on one Hand and Networking of Users on the Other is the First Lesson.

ABSTRACT

The chapter presents, in brief, the findings of a survey on "Management and Organization of Innovation and Technology Transfer" practices and policies in Germany. It indicates that although there are fundamental differences between Germany and India, in respect of culture, level of industrialization, framework of scientific and higher education institutes, yet selective proven models of technology transfer deserve to be considered for adoption, in India.

Technology transfer in Germany through interaction of professors with industry has a long history and is deep rooted. Institutional participation is however, of relatively recent origin.

New methods like patenting, licensing, Innovation centers, Steinbeis centers, research companies on the periphery of Universities are some of the important ones, in vogue today. The report presents a critical analysis of all of them and gives recommendations for consideration of Government, technical institute and industry. Foremost amongst the recommendation is that the policy on industry and policy on education both should be made compatible. They should lay emphasis on establishment of Technology parks, and Innovation centers, and jointly execute. The survey was done with a view to draw lessons of experience for India. But it could well be useful, especially to most of the developing countries.

NEED AND IMPORTANCE OF TECHNOLOGY TRANSFER

Technology Transfer (TT) has become a major phenomenon in global economy. It is being considered as key to industrial competitiveness. Technology generation, dissemination, patenting, licensing from higher technical education institutes to industry, especially small and medium scale enterprises are some of the current issues before the nations. Technology level has become the key determinant of a nation's economic well being. Therefore, efficient organization and management of technology transfer, technology development in any nation, more so in India, where there are ambitious plans of industrialization, technical education and research, is the need of the hour.

Merely development of technology in laboratories and dissemination through usual methods of education, training, publication is not enough, although essential. The new technologies need to be transferred quickly, efficiently to industry to increase their productivity. Effective partnership between academics and industry in technology transfer is found to revitalize both the industry and institute. They both thrive on each other's support.

Today, in India there is no technology transfer department in most of the academic and research institutes. However, the consciousness to set up such department is increasing. Technology transfer, usually known as Extension, however, exists only in Agriculture Universities in India.

The aim of this survey and study is therefore to draw lessons of experience from Germany and identify models which of them could be adopted in Indian environment to build a healthy and regenerative relationship between its industry and technical education institutes.

ABOUT SURVEY METHODOLOGY

The survey was not an exhaustive study, carefully developed and systematically administered, with carefully selected sample of respondents. Rather it was based on interviews of scientists, professors, administrators and students working at several German research Organizations, Universities, polytechnics, industry etc. Most of the respondents were from Karlsurhe region and a few were from Berlin, Stuttgart, Hamburg and Braunshweig. The interviews and discussions were conducted by the author himself. The author visited 3 research labs, 6 universities, 4 innovation centers, 2 polytechnics, 5 companies and 2 chambers of commerce. Many Professors, Scientists, Technology Transfer Officers, Students, and Administrators, were interviewed in sufficient depth, so that their responses contribute to the study. Whenever possible, interview were arranged with officials who would have broad perspectives and experiences. Some of the professors and scientists had visited India and had knowledge about the Indian Institutes and industry. One of them was Dr. Engleman who worked in India for ten years in Indo-German Co-Operation Project. Factual data regarding the size of programs, amount spent, number of licenses etc. were not readily available from many respondents and hence not used.

Some obvious themes and trends emerged from this study. They would be very useful to Engineering Colleges, Polytechnics, and other research institutes, which are contemplating to work in research besides teaching and be a major player in regional development. The way technology transfer is organized supported and carried out in Germany in an integrated manner by research laboratories, Universities, polytechnics, Innovation centers, technology park, Steinbeis centers and chamber of commerce have many positive aspects.

POSITIVE ASPECTS

German Government, both federal and State, have taken a positive view and given support to research at national laboratories, Universities, in-house research in industry, Polytechnics, chamber of commerce etc. and installed organizations to transfer research findings to industry, to develop new products and processes, so as to maintain Germany as a leading player in world economy. The Government has sanctioned significant financial resources of about 3% of GDP and human resources and put at the disposal of research institutes in both the public and private sectors. Government believes in "Public good" through applied research leading to new products, processes and techniques. Such innovations although at the cost of public resources are no doubt of significant value to the private companies or industry, but they also ultimately benefit the consumers and people at large. Innovation is the key to progress and prosperity so is understood by common man. *They believe that those who innovate will lead, and those who do not will lag behind.* It is this attitude and respect for scientific research which is reflected in funding scientific Institutions and other actions to promote research and its transfer to society.

The European commission with headquarters in Brussels has also been laying emphasis on R&D and technology transfer for maintaining competitiveness of European industry. They have devised a number of programs like Erasmus, Esprit, COMETT

Leonhardo-da-vinci for research education, training in new technology, and to avoid technological obsolescence. Germany being a member country has been also implementing a number of projects funded by European commission in various Universities and Laboratories.

It will thus be seen that there is a full support from top i.e., Government of Germany, and European commission for technology transfer which is a positive factor.

MULTIPLE APPROACHES

The activities of technology transfer are conducted by multiple organizations which work in a network and not in isolation. The industry interacts with appropriate organizations, one or more depending upon the type of industry, level of technology and field of specialization. The various organizations in Karlsruhe Technology region are depicted in the form of diagram as shown in Fig. 1 which shows various agencies, and their connections with each other.

It will be seen from the figure that there are various agencies generating and transferring technology to industry. All these agencies function in an integrated manner. They are mutually supportive to each other, and also competing. This is the second positive aspect of German system.

The University, and national laboratories largely involve in basic research while, Steinbeis centers, Innovation centers, Incubator and Fraun Hofer Gesselschaft Labs (FHG) involve more in applied research. Big companies are found by and large to interact with national laboratories, university and FHG, while small and medium interact more with Steinbis, Incubator, and research companies like FZI exclusively set up in the region. There is however, no hard and fast rule. It may appear that there is duplication of effort, many organizations doing the same work. But it is purposefully designed to be so to develop a competitive spirit among them, and avoid monopoly.

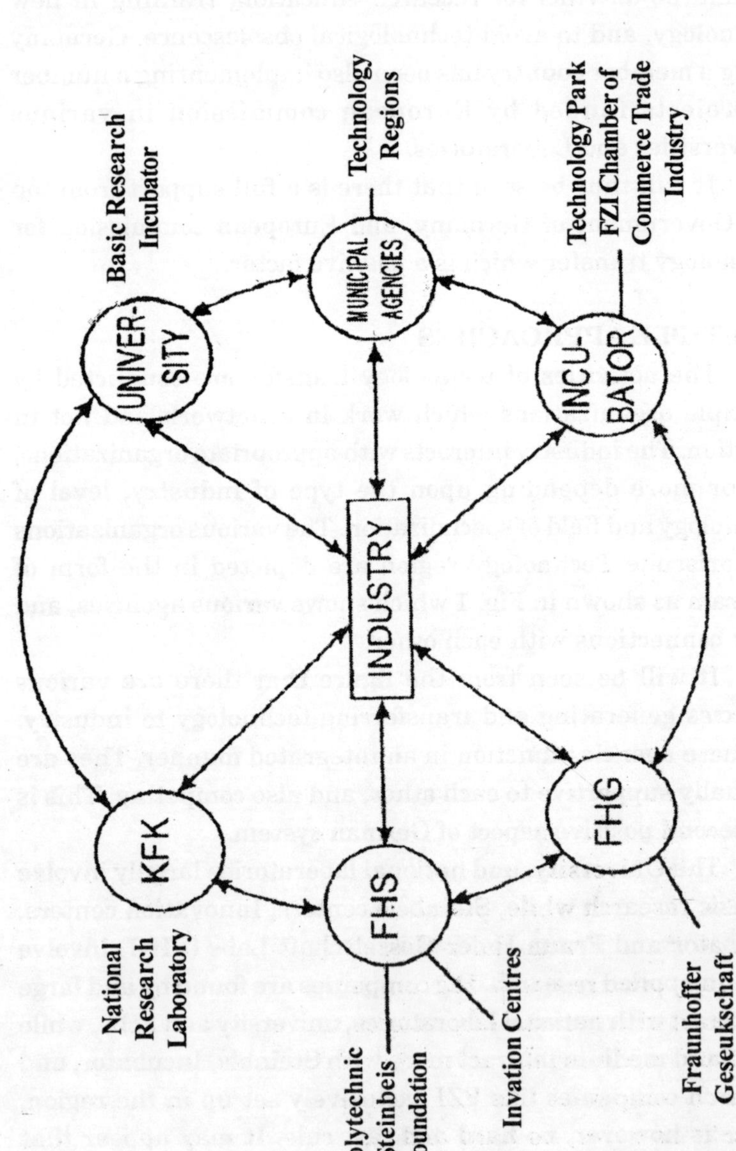

Fig. 1 : Various Agencies in Technology Region Karlsruhe and their inter Linkages

UNIVERSITY TECHNOLOGY TRANSFER OFFICES

There are 88 universities with science and technology discipline in Germany. Majority funding to Universities is from State Government. About 20% come from Central Government especially for capital investment like construction of buildings, equipment etc.

States have been active on technology transfer and have created technology transfer offices in most of the Universities. In Baden Wurtemberg State with a population of 1,02,34,000, there are nine Universities in which 2,21,000 students study, of which about 1,05,000 are in Science and Engineering. At University of Karlsruhe there is in addition an Intellectual Property Right (IPR) and licensing office providing service to all nine Universities.

The first of such offices was set up in the late seventies. In each office there are 7 to 10 persons, consisting of technical experts and supporting staff.

The mission of this office is to maintain industrial liaison, assessment of regional needs for new technologies and management of University outreach to the commercial sector by doing four activities, which are as under :-

(a) **IPR and licensing** – The office consults and supports members of Universities with a view to improve commercial exploitation of scientific research results. It offers.

- Confidential consulting to faculty in all questions relating to intellectual Property Right applications.
- Financial support for IPR applications.
- Commercial exploitation of inventions.
- IPR searches in international and national data bases.

(b) **Fairs and exhibitions** – Inventions, new projects and all services offered by University are presented in fairs, like Hannover, to inform about the latest results in science and research.

(c) **Research funding** – It facilitates obtaining funds from public and private sources, like European Commission to various faculty.

(d) **Advanced education and training** – It offers to companies information concerning continuing education programs to upgrade the competency of working engineers, scientists etc.

There is a history of positive working relationship between individual professor and industry. Most of the professors coming from industry at middle age obviously relate research and teaching best to the needs of industry. Some of them while working as professors in University work as honorary Directors in national or private research laboratories, and some of them have their own business. This enables them to find training places for students in industry and also jobs for outgoing students, the system is commended well by student respondents, University administrators, and professors. This relationship between professors and business has been at the back of good technology transfer in Germany. It provides professors an opportunity to do consulting in an industry relevant to their scientific expertise, and to receive a steady flow of real world research projects, topics for graduate and doctorate students, along with funds.

Till recently, it was assumed that inventions would be completed to the market needs only in company laboratory, seeds of which however would be shown in University laboratory. Now with global pressure on competitiveness Universities are taking projects to completion up to patenting and licensing. The trend of University staff is towards seeing the fruits of application of research findings in industry. It is believed that there is a greater charm for researcher to make new discoveries, but his pleasure is heightened when he sees that they have a direct application to practical life.

UNIVERSITY AS INCUBATOR

The Technology transfer office is maintaining close links with the innovators working in the University. The University is providing infrastructure to innovators to develop and carry out work on new ideas. One such case is of Dr. Sauter in Mechanical Engineering which deserves mention.

Dr. Sauter has done his Ph.D. on finite element method – application to optimization. He continued further research with a view to commercialize it, using University equipment, which he was permitted. Three more staff jointed him. Now he has developed a software, which has won prizes. He has also registered his own company and is planning to shift to innovation centre. He spoke very high about the role of TT office and the University which helped him in crystallizing his project into an innovative venture. He however, expressed about difficulties in obtaining loans from banks which insist on security. The venture capital fund scheme is not so developed in Germany.

Similarly, in machine design department, it is noticed that the department does lot of technology transfer to companies like Diemler Benz, Bosch, through students project work, contract research etc. They have obtained seven patents and many innovative projects in association with TT office. With the coming of Korea in market for I.C. engines it was told that German companies have become alert and contracting research more and more to this department.

There are many more cases of this type in University departments like chemical, electronics, civil etc.

TECHNOLOGY INNOVATION CENTRE (INCUBATOR)

This is a scheme from regional Government. It was introduced in the year 1984, and today there are more than 170 centers in operation in Germany. The scheme is meant for hi-Tech entrepreneurs, who have new ideas. The space and infrastructure are given on low rent, so that the entrepreneurs can concentrate more on their project ideas, rather than infrastructure development.

One such centre "Technologies Fabrik" is in Karlsruhe located adjacent to the University it is managed and maintained by the Chamber of Commerce. There are about 10 persons looking after the operation of centre. The entrepreneurs are provided here central facilities like Fax, parking, meeting room besides space on low rent. They are also given management and technical advice on demand. Presently there are 45 enterprises inside, and many are wanting to move into additional buildings which are under construction. The enterprises develop technology here and move out in a period of about 5 years.

It is reported by Dr. Stephen, Manager of the Chamber of Commerce that the scheme is very successful, The factors which contribute to success include nearness to University. The entrepreneurs are in close contact with the University for technical support. Many of the entrepreneurs are graduates from this University.

The Manager of the Technologie Fabrik mentioned that there is a pool of scientists and knowledge workers in Karlsruche who would like to have space in incubators. After five years, he said the enterprises have no difficulty in moving out, for at that time their requirement of space is much more, and the rent in fifth year as per agreement between them is also high. Management and control of incubator is with one agency namely the Chamber of Commerce. This is the other factor contributing to success. Berlin centre is found to be the best and other centers have varying degree of success depending upon leadership quality of the person in charge. This scheme is implemented in many countries and deserves to be implemented in India and other developing countries.

The author has visited three enterprises in the Technology Fabrik. All of them have expressed full satisfaction for having company in the Fabrik. They are getting more recognition by being in one place, and their image is brighter than if they were any where else.

They see no difficulty in shifting from this place after 5-6 years. Till then they are nursed well and need more support from this fabric.

Similar units known as "Technology Park" were visited by the author in Braunshweig, Harburg, and Berlin.

Braunshweig University has taken a lead in establishing the park adjacent to its premises. About 100 companies are functioning in this park in the buildings owned by University. It has been set up in the year 1984 and since then many companies have taken birth in this Technology Park, grown well and migrated to industrial estates. Such companies maintain links with the University professors and researchers.

The park of Harburg is also an offshoot of the technical University Harburg. This park has a huge premises of about 100 acres and three buildings. With the increasing demand for space in this park, the authorities have undertaken expansion. Harburg is relatively less industrialized area. This Technical University of Hurburg has been set up 15 years before along with the technology park with the aim of developing the area. It has been successful, so remarked the President of the University.

At Berlin, an authority known as WISTA has been set up after Unification of Germany to develop east part of Berlin. This authority has taken up establishment of Technology Park and Hombolt University in this area. Already incubator of Environment Technology and Electronics are completed. There are hundreds of companies in them. The programme is very ambitions aiming at transforming the economy completely. The M.D. of WISTA who has come from industry, is very optimistic about the success. This project deserves to be emulated in India.

The Fraunhofer Institute for Systemtechnik and Innovations Vorschungs Karlsruhe have done and evaluation of this scheme in Germany. They have reported that there are about 170 centres in the country and they are doing a good work. They have added value to the industrialization and improved income and employment. The regional economy by virtue of such centres has improved. The centres are further being expanded.

STEINBEIS TECHNOLOGY TRANSFER CENTRE

This is A SCHEME INITIATED BY Baden Wurtemberg State in 1983 through its ministry of science and technology. It is to function as a problem solver clearing house fro SMEs, utilizing the existing strong network of R&D institutions, Universities as well as individual professors and experts. Its winning strategy has been total identification with individual enterprises, tight formulation of projects which address their problems, rigorous search through its data base.

Today there are 220 centres, with about 3500 experts (full time and part time) doing service to 15274 enterprises. Most of the centres are based at technical colleges.

The underlying principle is to obtain intensive co-operation between academic, commercial and Govt. Institutions. It makes use of existing research infrastructure in FHS, University and other institutions. They have a financial independence but they must work as profit centres, and not as cost centres.

The author has visted six of them in Karlsruhe in the areas of computer, refrigeration, electronics and found them working successfully. The heads of centres are professors, employing 5-20 employee on full time basis. Students are also employed for whom this work is counted as project. The scheme gives a valuable feedback to professors, who in turn do more research or learn more and teach better in classes.

INSTITUTE FOR INNOVATION AND TRANSFER

It is an innovation centre setup in the polytechnic of Karlsruhe, as per the scheme of State Government it is operated in 25 other centers in the State. The unit has a head and fifteen other employees. They do only research and no teaching. The research is done mostly on projects given by companies on payment. The IIT earns the salary of 15 employees through contract research.

IIT makes full utilization of polytechnic infrastructure. Besides, it has some equipment purchased by itself from contract research projects on grants received from State. 11 Professors of the Fach Hoch Schule (FHS) are also working in this centre, for which they do not get extra money but a reduction in work load. Those who work in Steinbeis Technology Transfer Centers as consultants, get feedback from industry, and to cope with industry assignments engage themselves in research in IT, which is interdisciplinary.

IIT conducts Seminars on research done and participates in fair at Hannover. Presently 9 projects are in hand of which 2 are of long term nature.

Dr. Link the head, said the success of scheme depends on the ability of the leader.

FORSCHUNGS ZENTRUM INFORMATIC (FZI)

It is A private Limited Company, an offshoot of the University of Karlsruhe, in the area of information Technology. It was started in University and remained there for 1½ years and then moved to its won premises which is adjacent to University. It is supported by the State Government.

The Company undertakes research contracts in the area of I.T. It employs 120 researchers on full time and 250 on part time. Six professors of the University are honorary research directors. It has thus close links with the University and derives its strength from it. Many students and staff work in this company on part time basis.

It has competitors like Stainbeis Centers, FhG Lab, and other companies. This is a good model worth emulation in India.

FORSCHUNGSZENTRUM KARLSRUHE (FZK)

It is very big research laboratory, employed about 4000 persons of whom about 1000 are scientists. The Institute is financed by Government. It is involved in fundamental research, but also undertakes contact research.

The laboratory has Technology Transfer and marketing department in which 16 persons work. Dr. Just is the head. This office has granted hundred of license of technologies to private companies, FZK provides licenses and also training to personnel who are using licenses. SMEs normally do not go to FZK, it is only the big hi-Tech companies who go for licensing of FZK.

The Lab has very close links with the University. A few professors from Karlsruhe and other universities work have as head of research departments. Many Ph.D. and Diploma students visit his lab for project work.

This is a unique feature of German system brining about integration of Universities and research laboratories. It is missing in India and deserves emulation.

FRAUNHOFER SOCIETY

The Fraunhofer Society for promotion of applied research (Fraunhofer – Goselischaff - FHG) was founded in 1949 to "purse research and development in the spheres of natural sciences and engineering on behalf of Industry". FHG maintains 36 research labs at various location in Germany, one of which is in Karlsruhe, covered in the survey. FHG has a staff of 5000 of whom 1500 are scientists and engineers. About 30%, budget comes from Government (90% from central, 10% State), the balance 70% is earned through contract research sponsored by agencies of the federal Government, the state and by private industry. Over the past ten years, industry sponsored project research has been the major growth factor for the society, while basic support from Government as a percentage has decreased from 45 to 30, the total FHG budget increased almost two times.

Expansion of Grant funds through Federal Ministry for Research and Technology (BMFT – Bundes Ministerium Fur Forschung and Technology) for projects that jointly involve industry and academics for market oriented technologies.

Applied research is supported by Federal Government principally through BMFT, and to a lesser extent, through ministries, Approximately 40% BMFT's grants go to applied research and collaborative projects in research area of high economic priority, known as Market oriented technology promotion. Such projects are implemented in co-operation with many Universities.

RECOMMENDATION

In India, there are Indian institutes of technology, council of scientific and industrial research laboratories (30), National Institutes of Technology and about 350 Universities, which engage in education and research. Only a few of them have in the recent past, (from 1990) started Technology Transfer foundations/offices. There are 12 Science and Technology Parks and six incubators installed at the initiation of the Department of Science and Technology, Government of India. The schemes are however going slow. Universities and Engineering Colleges do not have Technology Transfer departments. However, all the Agriculture Universities have Extension Departments, carrying technology from Lab to land.

Most of the Engineering Colleges (about 1700) are like Fachhoch-Schule which are teaching oriented and have very little research. About half are in private and the other half in public sector. There are over 1200 polytechnics, which offer 3 years course and they are also teaching oriented.

Industries in India, (SMEs) rationally do not do research. They mostly make more profit by improving marketing, management and saving on taxes and importing technology, Innovation in technology by and large is not seen as a means of necessary profit.

Many industries are sick for various reasons. Many industries depend on foreign collaboration for diversification and progress rather than on any academic or research institution within the country. It can be said that it is more the foreign collaborations that have propelled the industrial growth.

It is however, increasingly realized in free liberal world economy, by younger generation that partnership between industry, research and technical education institutes is necessary. It is increasingly being viewed as an effective means for revitalizing both, it is the need of the time that this complementary relationship between institutes and industry be achieved for which the following recommendations are made:-

1. The Indian economy and industry are suffering from a deficiency of "Innovation and Technology Transfer". To make up the same it is recommended that a committee consisting of experts from industry and academics under the Chairmanship of a industrialist be set up by State / Central Government. The Committee should prepare an action plan for implementation.
2. It is necessary to integrate the efforts of technology transfer between CSIR labs. Universities, Engineering Colleges, Polytechnic etc. Government of India, considering the trends in world, should design a scheme for exchange, circulation of personnel, with incentives like in Germany that the professors have to have two hats, one is university and the other in laboratory. This will improve productivity of research expenditure. Professors should be permitted to go in CSIR labs. IITs and industry. So also industry people should be invited as adjunct professors in institutes.
3. Set up technology transfer offices in each college, polytechnic, university. Today, not many institutes have such offices. Improved methods of technology transfer like licensing, patenting, consultancy, will have to be introduced, if we have to go with the world.
4. More funding from Government for R & D and Technology Transfer is badly needed. The Government would have to look financial figures of R &D in other countries, like USA, Germany and Japan. Today, it is spending amount 1% only and that too mostly in public sector. Productivity of R & D expenditure in public sector is lower than in private sector, and therefore a joint project, market oriented will have to be thought of by the Government of India and State Government. We may have to reconsider

the industrial policy to promote R & D in Engineering Colleges and not only in CSIR labs. Today no R & D money comes to college, and youths are not provided access to research. This will have to be revised to build India as a technological nation.

5. Research companies private limited like FZI: Set up private companies like FZI on the periphery of Universities and engineering colleges. The model of FZI in Karisruche is worth emulation. Committees may be appointed to prepare project reports with a view to propagate hi-tech and to provide opportunities to talented people within the country, organizations like this are necessary. This will be help to avoid brain drain. It will build indigenous capability in hi-tech and reduce imports.

The leading Engineering Colleges and Universities should step in this area, so as to make application of high tech at a faster rate. The highly educated persons in subjects otherwise find it difficult to get chance to use their knowledge and they tend to migrate elsewhere. Such companies would help Universities to bring about regional development.

Alumni of the institute may be involved in setting up of such companies, by taking shares. The case of Wisconsin Alumni Research Foundation which gives grants to University for research and obtains patents on research findings, licenses the patents to COS and earns income which is put back into research is a good model like FZI.

6. Establish Incubators: Innovation centers adjacent to the higher education institutes like technologic fabric in Karlsruhe.

The various State Governments are implementing ambitious plans of industrial development. They are spending through agencies like Maharashtra Industrial Development Corporation huge amounts on establishing Industrial Estates, in large, small and medium size towns. They are providing infrastructure in the form of land, water, roads and electricity.

When the scheme was prepared there was no scheme like incubator. But now MIDC scheme would have to be redrafted in the light of such new schemes.

A look at the enterprises in the industrial estates indicates that many of them are sick for various reasons. One of the important reasons is that the technology they have chosen is outdated; it is less productive, when more productive ones are available. Now it is not enough to have money, raw material and market to run an enterprise. Proper technology is very important.

It is proposed that 'incubator' also called as 'Nursery for industries' to provide proper technologies as a part of MIDC scheme be taken up. As is maternity home necessary for safe child birth, so is a incubator necessary for healthy start up of companies.

Government should design a scheme of incubators for various areas out of industrial development budget. It will increase success of industrial estates. Now that VCF is available, in India, the chances of success are greatly enhanced. VCF without incubators weakens the scheme of VCF. Like Karlsruhe University, the Institutes have to extend their infrastructure to innovators, and the whole institutes function like an incubator.

7. Start scheme like Steinbeis : The Steninbeis foundation of Germany has signed an agreement with C.I.I. for the implementation of the scheme in India.

C.l.l. has thousands of member industries in the country. A message from C.I.I. to industries to tap expertise of Engineering Colleges, Polytechnics, is very important. It is a forward step to develop "Market Pull".

Now it is for the institutes to participate and cope up with the requirement of industries in respect of new technologies. The technical education department, Government of India, should whole heatedly cooperate; equip its staff and labs to a great extent.

The scheme empowers the professors and avoids bureaucracy. The scheme should have :

- Exchange of personnel – visit to Germany for 2 – 3 weeks for about 100 key people from academics, industry and Government.
- Private colleges may be involved first who would be more devoted and flexible.
- Exchange of students should be included in this scheme.

8. Reform system of Higher Education: Presently, professors have no research grants. The labs are not equipped. Research programs for scholars should be started forthwith leading to Ph.D.

Professors must also exert more to obtain research grants from industry, DOE, DST etc. They would have to prove worthiness and attract grants from industry to be appointed as professors. Research would have to be stepped up greatly in Colleges, for without research there is no value for these institutes, and no patenting, licensing etc. If professors miss this in early young age, they miss it forever and remain professors by title and not by work. No doubt professors would have to be provided adequate incentives, like in Germany, freedom to work, research, to do private practice, etc. Research assistant's posts be created on full pay to attract best talent of scholars. ISTE should play a vital role in establishing the rights and privileges of professors in India.

9. Last but not the least – develop awareness for market pull amongst industries and Technology push amongst institutes by conducting seminars and conferences jointly for industry and academic personnel. One sided effort by only industry or by only institutes is not enough. Both have to move to each other, for which it is recommended that academicians in association with Confederation of Indian Industry and similar bodies should organize seminars, and invite experts drilled in the minds of persons who matter most, without which it is difficult to build bridges between industry and academics

25

Technology Revolution How To Make Most

What happens to those who are left out of technology revolution?

World experience tells us that now the economic development is technology driven. The limiting factor for growth and prosperity of a nation is not oil, nor minerals, nor land, water but is the scientific and technological capability of people. This is a bold writing on the wall which the people and its Government have to read. Any neglect is however, likely to be too damaging for generations.

Nations like Japan, Germany, and U.S.A. by virtue of their technological superiority are found capturing the world market and emerging as epicenters of our interdependent world. The ever emerging technologies are giving both support and shocks to the economies of most of the nations, and it is no wonder if Indian economy is affected. The tremors are experienced with intensity depending upon the level difference, more the level difference bigger it is.

There is a vast ocean of opportunities at national and global levels arising out of emerging technologies. In today's rapidly changing techno-economic environment ability of people, especially engineers to innovate, learn and relearn newer technologies have become a determinant factor.

The professional status of engineers and rewards to meritorious depend on their learning rate, and those who cannot cope with may have to face problems. The researchers, students and teachers have to learn at a much faster pace to be able to reap the benefits from technology revolution.

This is a world full of opportunities that too of high pay off, which, however, are available to only those who can master the latest technology. Acquisition of technological capability on continuing basis is found from world experience to be the only way to acquire economic and political power. It is therefore argued that the engineers of today have to be more innovative, imaginative, and of world class standards.

The fault is not so much with the political system, bureaucracy or social system as much it is with the system responsible for educating people in scientific and technological subjects. The transformation of society to healthy status can be achieved by only upgrading the efforts of Science and Technology education.

INTRODUCTION

In today's high velocity environment, Engineers are a matter of great significance. It is obviously because they are the ones who are generating and assimilating new technologies and using the same to make the lives of people more comfortable. They are working hard to provide water to thirsty, food to hungry, houses to homeless and illuminating lives by providing electricity, constructing roads, Bridges and producing various kinds of industrial goods. They are in fact taking away miseries form the lives of millions of people. They are the ones, who build projects for prosperity and endure the same for generations. The engineers certainly deserve to be proud of their key role in changing world.

This is an age of discontinuity, so said the famous management expert, Peter Drucker, things world happen much differently than they occurred in the past. This is coming to realization when we notice that a revolutionary change in social-economic and political systems is taking place all round the world. There is fast upsurge in the aspirations of people accompanied by political interference especially in developing countries. The environment in which we live is no more static, but is fast changing, due to variables which are too many and unpredictable. In an indeterminate environment the main driving force shaping the civilization is however, noticed to be the, 'Technology Change". Engineers are called upon to take into account all the variables both favorable, and disturbing, and yet steer the progress of projects in proper direction. The factor 'Technology Change" is to be noted specially, studied carefully and adopted, for making most.

ENGINEERS ARE PRIME MOVERS

Engineers are considered to be the engines of growth. They are the prime movers. It is they who largely determine the future of a society and function like insurance against obsolescence and backwardness. A society which is comprised of more number of engineers progresses faster. Japan has highest number 170 per thousand population, India has hardly four. It can thus be imagined how scarce and important the engineers are to the Indian society.

More and more engineering projects, complex in nature, with massive investments are taken up for implementation during the five year plan periods. The responsibilities cast on engineers both working for public and private sector are quite heavy and time bound. It however, needs to be viewed as an opportunity to prove capacity and to serve the people. Engineers have been accepting them gladly and equipping themselves with knowledge, skill and attitude to discharges them in a professional way.

Besides engineering, they have to display skills in human handling a spirit of co-operation, working together and carrying with all others associated with diverse background, which is so essential, because of mass awakening of people and frequent political interference.

Once Pundit Jawaharlal Neharu went on visit, to Nagarjunsagar Project, he was happy to see the execution of works in full swing. He went near a worker carrying stones on his head, and asked what he is doing? The worker replied, 'He is carrying stones". The worker was not able to say where the stones are used and for what purpose? Pundit Nehru called his supervising engineer and told that he is not a good engineer. He was surprised to hear the comment. He said he has done his B.E. with first class distinction, designed the works properly and is executing in time, as per schedule. Pundit Nehru said, this is good but not enough. You have to educate your workmen in what they are building and explain to them what contribution they are making in nation building, which brings about emotional integration of an individual with the project. The role of engineers in projects is to carry all the people, officials, non-officials, workmen, contractors with, to educate them and to enable them to have pleasure in participation of the process of development. Engineers ought to have higher negotiating ability with imaginative will and skill and harness the energies of other for the cause, without feeling as interference.

Engineers are not only technologists they have to be much more than that, as 'Change Agents'. Change managers, who love change and shape future. They manage change from low productivity to high productivity, from low technology to high technology from low income to high income. They convert negative energy into positive.

TECHNOLOGICAL REVOLUTION OFFERS BOTH OPPORTUNITES AND PROBLEMS

Presently, we are passing through a period of Technological revolution. Technology change is faster than ever before. The previous industrial revolutions increased only the mechanical power/muscle power of human kind. Steam engine, diesel engine enhances the capability of man to do mechanical works.

The present revolution is characterized by computers, genetic engineering etc. which provide an auxiliary brain to human kind to enhance the brain power and raise the intellectual capability. They are bringing about almost a complete transformation of human civilization. It is said that, the revolution is likely to be much more powerful than could be imagined at this juncture of time. Shall we not like to use this new power for the welfare of our society?

Every change offers opportunities to those who are capable for and poses serious problems to those who are sluggish and caught unawares. Best engineers become leaders in technology and stand to gain while others are bound to loose. With the onslaught of technology AUTOMATION/ROBOTZATION/CAD/CAM is becoming the trend of time. Work methods tools, knowledge and skill required on the part of engineers are under going a complete change. Many new jobs like software engineers are being created but people are not to be found to fill them up. At the same time old types of jobs are becoming obsolete and employees clinging to them are tending to loose them.

ABILITY TO CHANGE MATTERS MOST

The change is so fast that many people and many nations find it difficult to cope with the CHANGE. Technology change has in fact led to restructuring of the economy of the entire world. World Bank Report 1989 has expressed grave concern that due to 'Technology Change' huge resources are flowing from developing world to develop world; and have risen a question 'Can this ever be reversed?' Unless it is done so, the third world countries have no good future. There is almost a complete shift in employment pattern, from manual to computerized producing much greater output but requiring higher knowledge and higher capacity on the part of engineers.

DOES HI-TECH LEAD TO UNEMPLOYMENT?

A Myth is prevailing that hi-tech is pushing production and productivity but at the expense of employment. People wrongly feel that hi-tech takes away jobs. Unions were found to obstruct computerization and automation. This is partly true because in advanced age they do not wish to learn new things, and wish to keep doing what they did for years although it is irrelevant and at the cost of production and productivity.

The employers also have a resistance for change. New technology means new plant, new machinery requiring additional funds. They have a tendency to keep using old out of date, less productivity lines and feeding consumers substandard goods at high price. This however does not and cannot continue for long for other companies overtake them and those who do not change with time become sick, throwing many people out of jobs. On one hand efforts are on to create new jobs for unemployed, while on other hand existing jobs are being lost due to incompetence of employed people, and inflexibility to adopt to technological changes.

Joblessness is found to be more rampant in countries which do not use hi-tech, Joblessness is less in those nations which are innovative and use hi-tech. For example Japan, where 95% of world's robots are employed in production, it is producing goods of superior quality at cheaper price. They are able to capture markets all over the world and feed more work to their people and generate surplus for further employment. To illustrate, we all are using Casio calculators. The calculator market of India is not available to Indian manufacturers and does not provide jobs to Indian workers, but it has become available to Japanese only by virtue of their superior technology.

Sheltering the industry form foreign competition is found to lead to sluggishness and incompetence. Therefore Government of India and several countries in the world have adopted now a liberal approach. Countries where engineers do not keep pace with advance technologies cannot stand world competition. They may be Gold medalists once, but to remain so all the time which is not easy, they would be loosing their value and demand in profession, and are susceptible to go out of business if they don't upgrade.

INDUSTRY IS NOW TECHNOLOGY DRIVEN

The industry today has become technology oriented; what is means is that the "Technology" is the prime factor for successful performance of and industry. Availability of funds, markets, raw-materials etc. are all secondary. Some deficiency in them is tolerable but no deficiency in technology is tolerable. The gains arising out of technological up gradation are far more than the gains out of any thing else and hence government of India have resorted to all round modernization, for example, sectors like steel, fertilizer, sugar, construction, increased world wide communication has made it possible for others to sell their goods in India, so also for us to sell our goods abroad. The nations are becoming more interdependent. There is a political disturbance in Iraq and we in India get economic shocks. Globalization of economy has crept in, trade and commerce providing hints to engineers that they would have to be comparing themselves to their counterparts in other countries

Becoming engineers, getting jobs and timely promotions, although important, are not enough. We have to learn to raise our head high for high quality, reliability and finish yet cost competitive by world standards. This demands that we aspire and put in hard work to become World Class Engineers.

INDIAN SCENARIO

A little comparison between India and the developed world is worth noting. The national scene is gloomy, although improving but still a look at facts may enable us to understand where we truly are. It may inspire and give force to our thoughts and actions.

Our population is more than 100 crores which is 16% of the world's population. We have the third largest S&T personnel, abundant raw materials and huge markets, yet our industrial production is less than 1% of world production. The import is much more than export, leading to adverse situation in balance of payments. The share of India in export market is continuously going down from 2.25% in 1950 to 0.25% in 2008. The export is largely consisting of software and raw materials like iron or raw-cotton, and not much of value added goods. Although export is increasing in absolute figures yet in terms of the % of world trade it is going down, which simply means that others are exporting faster than India. India's share in sunrise technologies like computer at world level is lees than 0.0001%. Our income per capita per year is 500 dollars, one of the lowest in the world. The Human Development Index of India is 4339 rank 134th in the world while that of Japan is 13,135. Out put of industrial goods of Japan, with eleven crores population, is 50 times more than India of 100 crores people, we are quite rich in natural resources like iron ore, coal, minerals, land, water etc. but they are underutilized, and wasted.

The productivity in various industries is too low. On an average it is 1/29th of Japan, 1/10th of Korea, and 1/9th of China. The time and cost overruns in project implementation are too high, and their capacity utilization is also too low. We are constructing for example 100 crores project at 400 crores, and subsequently using it as if it is a project of Rs. 25 crores. This is largely on account of incapacity of our organizations and engineering personnel. If we examine multinationals operating in India, in the same environment, the capacity utilization is found to be more than 100%. This speaks about low capacity of Indian companies. The cost of steel produced per ton is the highest in the world, the electricity consumed per ton of steel produced is almost double than in Japan, man days consumed are three times more. This is true in almost all other sectors.

The above comparison is presented hear simply with a view to understand dispassionately where we are. This is not to say that we are not progressing at all. It simply means that other countries like China are progressing faster and we need to double up.

Can and Should We Anticipate and Prepare for Technological Change?

India has all along been importing technology from foreign countries. We are clearly a technology follower so far. We have never been a technology leader. We have much foreign collaboration in India. Paradoxically we have been exporting engineering talent, 'Brain Drain' to U.K., U.S.A. Can the situation be reversed for the better? These are some of the questions which we first grade fellow engineers have to address to ourselves.

'Sunrise Technologies' usage is the urgent need but is not an easy job.

A serious attempt of research, permitting continuously theory to influence practice is the need of time. Without our own research it is not possible to anticipate and prepare for the technological change. It demands establishing research cells at more places and earmarking more funds especially for mixing of scientists at international level. It requires collaborative research, mutual co-operation between various Government Departments, private and public sectors, industries and above all willingness to learn and adopt a change. It demands conceptual ability and vision on the part of higher ups. There is a saying where there is no vision people perish. We have to learn to develop vision of this Changing World.

New technologies like Bio-technology, CAD, CAM, CIM, computers, Micro electronics, genetics engineering offer tremendous opportunities to younger generation. They are however, in today's fast changing world short lived. The Product life cycle has become munch small due to rapid change in technology, How a country anticipates and responds to the rate of change of technology and the competitive environment now decides its health and viability. There is a saying '*An early bird, catches worms.*' Can we engineers be smart enough, fast enough, and innovative enough to take full advantage of the opportunities offered by technology revolution? Do we perceive the challenges? Do we accept them and prepare for them? Otherwise we will have no future.

Bright Future Awaits Innovative Enterpreneurs

Privatization is becoming the trend world over. It is obviously because privatization is found to make more productive utilization of resources. The systems and subsystems structurally tend to be more efficient; as compared to those in Government.

Privatization, however, demands decentralization entrepreneurship among the engineers. Now it is not enough for engineers to be good in design and technical things. They must learn and master the art of synthesizing and bringing about a fusion of various kinds of resources like men, materials, machines and money.

The 'Winds of Change' all over the world indicate that more opportunities are exploited by private sectors. The technology change provides many opportunities at national and international levels. It is for engineers to see in advance and avail for which, however, they would have to become entrepreneurs. In large size organizations, the engineers would have to be innovative, imaginative and doing the work with latest knowledge and technology. Such engineers are known as Intrapreneurs. They work within a corporate structure with the same spirit as entrepreneur works.

Many schemes providing incentives are designed by Government to promote entrepreneurship. Venture funds scheme is introduced for innovative and academic entrepreneurs who can use untried technology in production at the risk and cost of venture capital firm. Incubators, technology Parks are being established it is time that the experienced engineers make a note of the winds of change and resort to establishing professional companies instead of working as employees. Academicians are reported to be more successful I knowledge industry.

MODERNISE MEN TO ACHIEVE EXCELLENCE

Government of India have launched the programme of modernization of almost all sectors of economy, like Textile, Steel, Fertilizer, Power, Jute etc. Modernization means new jobs, new skills, new products, huge capital investment, and displacement of labor. Among all the factors the most important is the displacement and reemployment of people. In-service persons tend to become surplus and persons with new knowledge are required. This has to be managed very skillfully. Otherwise the technology for no fault of its own goes in dispute. Modernization of men must precede the modernization of plant and equipment, to avoid problems. Chairman of Sony Corporation Akio Morita in his book Made in Japan has said when the technology was changed from Analog to Digital we retrained our men, and they made Sony a forerunner in the world. From where else we would have got such experienced persons.

This problem is faced not only in India but in every country where new technology is being adopted. Hi- Tech certainly leads to regeneration of employment. But there is a shift in the pattern of employment. New jobs requiring higher intellectual capability, training and knowledge are generated. The old type of jobs requiring hand skills are saying goodbye and new jobs are coming in at a much faster rate. This has been proved amply by experiences in U.K., U.S. etc. where jobs in coal, textile and steel have gone out and new jobs far in excess in Electronics, Computer have come in. In India the output of computer software engineers has shot up. India is supplying software engineers almost too whole world. This is a good sign. India Government has adopted a liberal policy to sanction new institutions.

This is a time characterized by rapid, 'Technology Change'. Those who change and learn faster stand to gain, if a country attempts to shelter its old production lines instead of exposing them to global, competition, it cannot succeed.

CONCLUSION

The nation's future is linked to the speed with which, the people, learn and relearn science and technological subjects. Faster the adaptation of newer technologies in professions and vocations, faster is the technological and economic development. It is therefore imperative that earlier the nation realizes this, faster it can rise. Government of India has adopted this philosophy and is permitting many institutes to start.

Hi-Tech promotes only efficient industrialization and generate productive, high quality employment. Expansion of Continuing Education Programs to reduce adverse effect on adoption and implementation of hi-tech is the need to the hour. We have to learn to swim on the ever emerging ideas of technological change and competition. Engineers have to keep their eyes wide open to see the developments taking place world over and with their intellectual ability assimilate and adopt them to our situations. It is a high time that we give a new direction to our thinking, raise our head high in international society. The nation looks at all engineers with high hopes. There is no doubt that with our skill and will we shall be able to make most of the technology revolution.

Engineering colleges, polytechnics and universities are expected to produce not only new generations of scientists and engineers but also new knowledge, new technology and new companies; that drives new changes in our economy and society.

26

Technical Education for Tomorrow

Technical Education Costs, But Costs of Not Giving It Are Prohibitively High

The article presents in brief, some of the latest concepts in technical education, which in the present context of large scale unemployment of youths on one hand and acute shortage of technical personnel on the other have achieved significant importance. Technical education has a potential to bridge the gap and help to achieve the much desired, well being of the people. It argues that expansion in technical education and diversification of courses is very essential especially for enabling the youths in rural areas to get opportunities in globalize world to fulfill their rising aspirations and face the unknown challenges of tomorrow more boldly and resourcefully.

INTRODUCTION

In this age of science and technology the role of technical education in various walks of life, vacations and professions is achieving significant importance. It is influencing so greatly that the social, economical and political culture of the world is under going almost a complete change. High paying jobs in the fields of computers, electronics etc. unheard of a few years before, have come in existence.

It is realized that the basis of development of any country today, lies in its educating people in technology. More the education more is the development, which in turn depends on technical education of its personnel, besides the availability of raw- materials, minerals etc. It is also being realized that economic, political and military power of a country depends upon its technological power, where once nations measured their strength by the size of their armies and arsenals, in the world of future knowledge will matter most, so says bill Clinton, former president of USA In India, although we have the third largest scientific and technical personnel in absolute terms, we have only 3.8 people per 1000 population, while countries like Japan have 170.

Technical Education is important, more so because of certain recent developments that are taking place in the international situation of transfer of technology. The developed countries like U.S.A., Japan day by day are becoming more and stricter and not permitting their latest technology, like nuclear technology, to cross their borders. Of course, they are giving after making us bow down in deals. This has been the experience especially in the fields of electronics, computers, automobile etc. We have been consequently, forced to pay heavy cost.

"Global network of educators and students enriches human civilization."

The second industrial revolution which is characterized by micro- electronics, robots, space technology, solar energy, computers, bio-technology etc. is picking up momentum. If we miss this train as we missed the first industrial revolution the dangers are far graver. We are likely to be left permanently behind and our future generations may not pardon us. Therefore any neglect of technical education is going to be disastrous.

Technical Education Alone Can Help in Converting Raw-materials into Usable Goods and Services

It is said that India is a rich country but inhabited by poor people. It is quite rich in terms of natural resources like land, water, minerals etc. The population of the country is very large and hard working but it is not equipped adequately in terms of knowledge of science and technology. The only active resource of any country is the human resource, other resources like minerals, land etc. are passive and inert. They do not do any work by themselves. Due to the lack of technical capability of our personnel and scarcity of technological knowledge our rich resources are unexplored, and underutilized.

Consequently, we have been exporting raw materials, like iron ore at very cheap price and importing finished steel at a very high price. Right from the beginning we are at the receiving end, buying technology at all the items. India is a richly endowed nation, and what we suffer from is not so much the paucity of resources but the inability to make most of them. Our problem is not so much of in adequacy of resources but their productive utilization, for which technical education alone can help.

TECHNICLA EDUCATION IS A JOB CREATING AGENCY

An engineer by virtue of his education and training in the latest concepts in science and technology, is always an asset, His chances of employment or self employment are much brighter as compared to other graduates. Once he is gainfully employed or self-employed he is found, from past experience to create jobs for seven diploma engineers, 20 skilled craftsman and 50 other personnel in tertiary sector like transport, trading etc. If we try to find out as to how the jobs are generated, it will be seen that it depends more on the capability of the men in the country. It of course depends on the availability of money, raw materials and planning for development but at the back of which is again the human resource, which matters most. It may therefore be interpreted that if we have less number of engineers, the generation of jobs in the proportion of (1:77) is forgone. Joblessness, in fact may be viewed in our situation as resulting on account of shortage of innovative engineers.

When more and more people take to engineering education the competition in the profession grows. The requirement of knowledge level for employment or self employment goes up. Only those who reach to the level of employment get it while others have still to work hard to reach to it. This, however, is a short time phenomenon but is essential for up gradation of the overall performance. Once we reach to the international standard, the industry is then able to produce goods and services of good quality at competitive price to find market all over the world.

World experience says countries have developed when they could export goods and services to other countries. It is only the export oriented growth which can give stable economy and prosperous life to its people, which obviously demands technical education of high standard. With high level technical education they become more mobile and take jobs or be self-employed any where in the world. Let us therefore give technical education to our youths, like the strength in the wings of birds, and they will not ask jobs but give in return to many more.

Engineers take jobs in both the private and public sector. Doing a job in public sector is relatively easy, while in private sector, jobs are more tough and uncertain.

LACK OF TECHNICAL EDUCATION

The productivity of Indian industry is said to be hopelessly low, only 30% of their counterparts in developed countries, although the availability of raw-materials is plentiful and cheap. The proportion of sick industries is very large, about 40% locking up a national investment of thousands of crores. The reasons are very many. But one of the important reasons is that they are using obsolete technology.

Up gradation of technology, and modernization is the single most important factor which can improve the situation, towards which innovative technical education contributes.

IMPARTING TECHNICLA EDUCATION COSTS BUT THE COSTS OF NOT GIVING IT ARE PROHIBITIVELY HIGH

Government has to incur expenditure to establish facilities and impart technical education. Due to the limited funds at the disposal of the Government an attempt is always made to keep this expenditure as low as possible. A Question, however, arises as to whether it also costs when technical education is not imparted? The personality of the youth would remain dwarf, its potential unfolded. The costs are invisible, hidden and in terms of foregone opportunities, Can we close our eyes towards these unseen costs? If no, should we make a comparison and decide which between the two is more beneficial. There are a large number of projects in India which are required to be slowed down because of the non-availability of appropriate technical personnel. Time and cost overruns and under utilization of capacities in the projects is so frequent that the employment and income generation and the resulting benefits from them are greatly delayed.

Import of know how and equipment from foreign collaborators in projects like water and land management, power generation, Electronics is frequent. Royalty at high rates goes to developed countries. Major benefits arising out of our projects such as income and employment generation go to the developed countries; right at the start. Besides, with continued dependence on them, they keep on selling while we keep on buying. Thereby, we are also loosing an opportunity of exporting. It is said that, we have been not only building huge fixed assets inefficiently but also under utilizing them subsequently. Simply put, we are investing Rs. 100 crores in a project whose worth is only Rs. 25 crores, and producing goods from these projects just as in an industry worth Rs. 10 crores. This is largely because we are investing too low in our human resources which are supposed to design and implement the projects. If we have therefore to reverse the trend for the better, we must lay stress on Technical Education and convert our potential human resources into more knowledgeable and competent personnel. This is the Basics of Knowledge society.

A project for imparting technical education is a worth while project form investment point of view. The study conducted by the World Bank on education projects reported that the rate of return (R.O.R.) is of the order of 80% as compared to the usual 40% in a commercial project. An investment of one rupee in research, in technical education is an investment in two things, first it goes to produce engineers and scientists, and secondly it goes to produce new technology.

Technical Education to youth goes much beyond the commercial viability. It enables the youth to make most of their capabilities. In fact, the experience in the world tells us that engineers are far more creative in difficult and challenging situations. Today in India Engineers being in short supply, get jobs easily without any problem in general and their full capacity is not put to test. A little unemployment amongst them may, as in other countries make them more efficient innovative and competitive which is good for them in ultimate analysis.

TECHNICAL EDUCATION RECEIVES HIGH PRORITY IN HOUSEHOLD BUDGET IS IT REFLECTED IN GOVERNMENT?

It is experienced all over the country that career engineers are in great demand. People are ready to pay higher fees for obtaining education is engineering colleges. At times they postpone buying a house T.V. or refrigerator, in favor of technical education of their children. Is this priority reflected in the national and state budget? A glance at it indicates that the budget of technical education is very small about 1% of the total budget. Should we perhaps and cater fully to educational needs? This is a matter for consideration. Investment from Government is only 03.37% of GDP which 4 times smaller than in developed countries.

MANAGEMENT OF ENGINEERING EDUATION MOVES FROM GOVERNMENT TO PRIVATE SECTOR

The recent expansion in the facilities of technical education, in private sector in Maharashtra raising the intake capacity of colleges form 2000 students per year to more than 55,000 students per year is welcomed by the students' parents, Industry and Government. The students are happy obviously because without these colleges they would not have been able to get admission.

The teachers were never so much in demand as they are today. Rightly so they are likely to get higher salaries and better conditions of work. The industry will have now a wider choice in selection. The Government is not required to spend any thing except for planning and monitoring.

The institutes which have recently started have made reasonably good progress. For this much of progress all over the state in government sector, it would have taken much longer time and a lot of money. These colleges are likely to be more sensitive to the needs of the society. The institutes which have been opened in rural areas have the following advantages.

(1) Land cost is comparatively less,

(2) Cost of construction is also less,

(3) Cost of living for both students and teachers is less,

(4) The students have no other attraction, so they could possibly study better,

(5) Dissipation of the knowledge of technology to rural areas, which is the objective of government, is likely to be achieved through these institutes. These institutes would have many handicaps especially in getting competent teachers and in maintaining standard. This should, however, be a temporary problem.

In the newly established Institutes non-availability of qualified teachers is experienced to be a major constraint. Procurement of equipment, furniture, construction of building etc. is much easier. But the lead time required in preparing teachers being much larger, getting qualified teachers is difficult. However, it is occasion to review our methods of teaching and learning. With the advent of video films and other audio-visual aids is it possible to use available teachers more productively? Use of video tapes is essential especially in newer subjects where teacher would always be in short supply.

A few years ago, When, Arts, Science and commerce colleges were opened in private sector the same thing was experienced. With the passage of time these problems have been solved. Now the colleges are in a stable position. Likewise it is hoped that engineering colleges would also get streamlined. Universities have, however, to be strict and particular to see that the standards do not fall.

DIVERSIFICATION OF COURSES IS THE PRESSING NEED OF THE HOUR.

The courses started in various colleges are not in conventional fields of civil, mechanical and electrical engineering but in specialized areas like electronics, water management, production engineering, petroleum technology etc.

Often discussions are held on whether it is beneficial to have a general degree or a specialized degree. With the general degree the advantage appears to be that the employability is on a wider basis. While it is felt with the specialized degree it is narrower. But with very general and same syllabus many engineers learn the same thing without achieving the excellence which is the need of the hour.

This is an age of specialization and only general training is not enough for specialized jobs, with ever changing job demands requiring higher and specialized knowledge, retraining by way of specialized courses may have to be organized. A suggestion is often made that we should have a general degree at the undergraduate level and specialized degree at the post graduate level. This is the conventional approach. It involves more time, expenditure and effort on the part of students, besides, all can not acquire specialized knowledge so well.

Instead of this, if the students are given a specialized knowledge at first degree level, they could reach to a much greater depth of learning and right up to the frontier of the subject. To avail the employment opportunities arising out of new technology, excellence in specialized knowledge is desirable. The technical knowledge is growing so fast that with general degree our youth will always remain trailing and not be able to harvest the benefits of science and technology. Hence well planned diversification of courses is must.

ROLE OF ENGINEERING INSTITUTIONS

As in the heart to our body, so is an engineering institution to our industrial society. It has the role to provide blood, (Qualified engineers) and purify (Retrain) time and again to keep the various organs of industrial society functioning with efficiency. It is high time that the colleges engage themselves in imparting technical education not only to youth, but to practicing engineers to keep abreast of the latest technologies, because the rate of obsolescence is observed to be the highest in technology. There may be administrative difficulties in doing so. However, they must be over come. Otherwise the industrial organizations are likely to be sick and inoperative.

CONCLUSION

Experience in the world indicates that the socio-economic and political development of a country depends on its industrialization, which in turn depends, to a great extent, on technical education of its citizens. Only those countries have developed and have become more competitive internationally which have invested greatly in technical education.

Technical education converts a liability into an asset. Engineers create jobs and convert raw-resources into usable goods and services, so essential for raising the standards of living of our masses. Technical education enables the youth to become what they are capable of . With the vast majority of the Indian population in rural areas, there is no denying the fact that this potential tool of development must be taken to the rural masses without which the overall development of the country is not possible.

The existing facilities offering technical education are far too meager and have failed to meet the needs of the Indian society. That is why sudden starting of new Institutions, it being easier in private sector has resulted. Institutions offering Engineering ought to reduce their near total dependence on Government funds and mobilize resources from private sector so as to meet the educational needs of the society.

Technical education in private sector may make it more relevant, purposeful, flexible and cost effective. The enthusiasm shown by philanthropic organizations, individuals, industrial houses needs, however to be shaped well. They are showing a new light and direction in the pattern of establishment of engineering institutions with their financing in a collaborative way and with modern methods of teaching and learning. The institutions in rural areas when well developed may prove to be the change agents and transform the complete economic and social scene of the country.

27

The Challenge of Globalization for Indian Universities

Indian Universities by world standards are far too behind their counterparts in developed countries. They still operate on old lines as if they are an extension of high school system. Whereas universities in developed countries like USA, Germany, and UK are primarily research universities. Research output, especially need based, is their main contribution and education, is their by-product. Bush Commission report, *Science - the Endless Frontier (1945)* gave this philosophy to universities of USA and which is also adopted in other developed countries. National Science Foundation of US has reprinted this report in 1990, and re-circulated it.

The report prescribed that universities' main output should be research, patents, new technologies, intellectual property rights. Higher education should be their by-product. Students learn best by researching, and then it is relevant and up to date. It is because of this philosophy that the education in universities of US is observed to be innovative and creative in nature. Without research, it is believed that education remains stale and outdated. Normally two-thirds budget of a university goes to research.

Characteristics of Universities Abroad

On the campuses of universities like Madison, Cambridge, Edinburgh what we notice is that research companies are flocking round them. Incubators, research parks, innovation centers, patent and intellectual property rights bureaus are distinctly visible. Venture capital companies have opened offices in campuses in search of new technological ideas for commercialization. Universities in developed countries have become like magnets that attract not only scholars but also industry, entrepreneurs and VCF companies from across the world. They are globalizing their operations to meet the world needs both of education and of technology. Students from many countries, so also industries from across the world are coming to their campuses and they feel proud of the same. By virtue of strong research base they are a source of latest knowledge in education and a source of new ideas, enabling companies to win. It is well realized in those countries that new knowledge, that is to say new technology, is an important source to bring about economic change. USA has doubled its industrial output from 1909 to 1949 and that 85% of the credit is attributable to technology change, according to Nobel Laureate Bob Solow.

Universities like Madison are producing patents as many as 100 per year. The university sells patents to companies and earns an income by way of royalty as much as 40% of its budget. They generate wealth through research, which is believed to be the mainstay of high-income economies in the world. According to World Development Report (WDR, 1999), they spend about 4% of GNP on research. Low-income economies like India spend very less, even less than 1% of GNP on research. The employment generation and income generation is attributed mainly to research in Universities.

Young scholars along with the in-service personnel carryout research, which is disseminated best through teaching in classes. Innovation and research are considered as 'well springs' of economies.

Helping Business to Win

Every university has a patent and technology licensing department engaged in technology sale. The author during the period of his recent three months visit to Germany, UK and USA, sponsored by the UGC, studied in depth the organization and management practices of universities along with their visions and missions, systems and procedures. Universities in general have huge campuses, with student strength in the range of 20 to 80 thousands and faculty strength from 1000 to 10,000. For example MIT, Boston has around 30,000 students and 3,000 professors, Karlsruhe University in Germany has around 25,000 students and 1,000 professors, all teachers possess Ph.D. and post doctoral qualification. Faculty represents a wealth of talent and knowledge, which is exploited to benefit both faculty and university financially. In India faculty with Ph.D. qualification are very few less him 10%. Our bright students are thus being taught by lowly qualified and less experienced teachers.

Spin off of companies from universities is a common phenomenon, so also spin- off technologies. The companies like Apple Computers were conceived and born in universities. Project ideas were based on their PhD thesis. A foundation is set up in MIT, Boston with the facility of venture capital fund enabling professors and PhD scholars to start new ventures based on technologies; they develop during the period of their research. Every year as many as 15-20 new technology based firms (NTBF) are born in MIT Boston. The university gives consultancy on retainer basis to as many as 3,000 companies. This is not unique with MIT only. It is true with almost all universities in developed countries. They have created

Technology Incubators to enable raw project ideas to be innovated to marketable stages. The entrepreneurs and professors are thrilled when they see their theoretical ideas being converted in to practical projects. Thereby they are earning wealth for themselves so also for the university besides credit and satisfaction. Universities have thus become *'Maternity Homes'* for safe birth of new enterprises. Such enterprises that are based on brand new technologies help to reduce mortality rate and sickness of other industries.

New Model for Universities

Does Indian economy need such universities? Can we do without them? At what cost? Without such innovative schemes our investments are being made in sunset technologies. Obviously they can not be competitive globally. National Council for Applied Economic Research, New Delhi has published the results of a survey which found that of the 657 Indian companies in the study sample that started up in 1997, 57% were manually operated and 38.7% were semi-automated. In the same period, according to the study, 80% of the start up companies in Japan was fully automated and 20% were semi-automated. It seems then that substantial investment in India is being made in companies which are based on less competitive technologies, and which are therefore handicapped right at birth. Such companies can not hope to be competitive on global scale. In USA, 36% of capital investment is in new technology based firms (NTBF) where as in India NTBF are almost non existent.

However the shift from old technology to new technology industrial base is not easy to achieve. It presents many technological, social, economic problems, as well as resistance from trade unions. People must unlearn old methods and skills and adopt new technologies and knowledge. Universities must reorient themselves; prepare to offer courses and interest people in learning and becoming more competent. Without this strategy by universities, industries and industrial estates will languish and become sick, which would be looking for foreign collaborators. *Can Indian universities dream of propelling industrial growth?* They must do so forthwith. Otherwise universities may become dysfunctional and economy will run into difficulty. The rate of absorption of new technology in various walks of life depends much on knowledge of people and their scientific and technological capabilities.

New Vision for New World

What Indian universities lack today, is the new vision of new world? They ought to develop connections with best known universities in the world and correct their priorities and strategies. It is no doubt a long journey. Yet, it must begin somewhere. Is it not that thousand miles journey begins with a single step?

Prof. Terman of Stanford University in USA observed in 1950 that industry so as to remain competitive globally needs access to first class research in universities. So also the first class researches in the universities need access to industry so as to commercialize their research findings. This is equally applicable to Indian universities at this juncture. They can not become and remain competitive without the support of each other. Will our universities care to follow today what others did years before?

It is important to know how universities are conceived and started in those countries. The author visited a newly started Harburg University in Germany. This university started 35 years before under collaboration from 15 best universities in US, UK, Japan and Germany. Today this university has 10 thousand students and one thousand professors. It started with a research park, which today contains around 500 research-based companies adding strength to the economy of the region. University is not planned in Germany without an industrial estate and industrial estate is not planned without a university.

The author also visited Harriot Watt University at Edinburgh, which is located on 600 acres of land and has

Research Park on 600 acres surrounding the university. The University of Madison (USA) has a strong Alumni Association known as Wisconsin Alumni Research Foundation [WARF], which is managing and maintaining a big research park.

Taiwan has set up a *'Science Town'* at Hsinchu with some 13000 researchers in two universities, 6 national laboratories and around 150 companies specializing in electronics. Tsukuba Science City near Tokyo is another example of university technology park collaboration.

On the other hand Indian Universities are engaged more in teaching as if they are schools. The vector direction of our universities is wrong. They are largely teaching and examining bodies without research base and hence they are not effective to cope with challenges. Will they learn themselves and adopt what best universities in the world are doing? Will they do correct bench marking?

Universities abroad have opened continuing education departments, more from 1980, for in-service personnel. They are offering short-term refresher courses leading to PhD The research work done by people in their work places is counted for the award for degree. They have a flexible model Cafeteria Approach in which students can choose a wide variety of options. A combination of economics, engineering and music is also possible.

The credit transfer system, from one university to another is common. A student can study for the same degree course in a number of universities. The credits earned in one university are approved in another. European Commission encourages the mobility of students and professors. It has drawn a program known as Leanhardo-da-Vinci to provide financial support to promote such mobility. The students are allowed to get degree from any one university, which they have visited.

Life Long Education

Continuing education has become so common that the in-service part time students studying in universities are ten times larger than the full time students. We see three generation students in campus. Learn while you earn life long is very common. It is observed in an OECD study that Europe, Japan and USA together represent 80% industrial global outputs. The main contributing factors to this dominance include continuing education policy and practices of universities in developed countries. Continuing education facilities and better management of technology adds significantly to economic success.

Many Indian universities yet do not have continuing education departments, patent and technology licensing departments. Technology Park and incubators are conspicuously absent. They have almost no connection with industry and industries have almost no confidence in universities. The industrial progress in India is propelled by foreign collaborators. Indian Universities have not gone nearer to them, nor have industries established links with universities. Universities have become corporate offices bureaucratic and political in nature. Consequently what is taught in universities is not wanted and what is wanted is not taught. There is serious mismatch between demand and supply. Rather than motivating and preparing students for the world of work the universities have become organizations which tend to thwart and impede the potential of their students. The National Education Policy (NPE, 1986) recommended autonomy to colleges to enable them to respond to the needs of industry in terms of research, training and technology transfer. However progress has been slow.

The traditional affiliating system of universities has become a problem rather than a solution. It has stifled the innovation potential of academics and the public is unhappy. Attempts for improvement are being made. The lack of mobility of Indian academic staff and research staff to world class centers is seen as major problem. Why is India unable to upgrade its universities? Do we realize that the cost of mediocrity is higher than the cost of upgrading? Why do Indian institutes not transfer technology to industry through the use of patents and IPRS?

To conclude, globalization of Indian universities is the pressing need of time. Redefining their scope, missions and visions in the light of worldwide changes ought to be carried out forthwith. Restructuring the organization, methods, systems and procedures, revising the university acts, making colleges autonomous should become the first item on agenda. Research in universities is the most cost efficient and cost effective model for employment and income generation. It should therefore become the focus of university activity.

Universities to a nation are like heart to our body. Outdated universities are more costly than cost of their modernization. They should therefore be revamped urgently. There are no doubts many problems in adoption and implementation of new policies and practices. How to manage the change is certainly a big challenge before Indian universities. They need to take in to account the experience of IIT along with experience from abroad. The speed and direction of change in universities in coming years matters most to the wellbeing of the people. It is hoped that with the given will and skill of leaders in academics, leaders in industries and politics, we will be able to achieve desired goal.

28

Vision 2020 and Institutes of Technical Education

Professors and principals should spend most of their time on envisioning and on crystallizing the visions

NEED AND IMPROTANCE

It is a proven theory that where there is vision people flourish, and where there is no vision people perish. In the knowledge driven economy of today 'vision' has achieved significantly high importance. Vision ignites minds for creative action. Indian economy, in spite of abundant resources, it is said has, so far lagged behind because of a lack of vision. About 25% of the people are still living below the poverty line. Per capita income is only around 450 dollars, whereas that of Japan is 30,000. How do we explain this big difference? Do they work hundred times more? Certainly they do not. It is mainly their technical education system which has moved the economy forward. A country like Japan of eleven crore population from the last 50 years has been producing two times more graduates than India. They adopted vision to build knowledge - society long before.

The Govt. of India has recently announced the national goal to become a developed nation by the year 2020. Prime Minister Hon. Atal Bihari Vajpayee in his address to the nation on 15th of August 2002 has proclaimed to have conceived this goal and expressed commitment to build India into a technology oriented nation. India aspires to be free from poverty, and to sit in line with G-8 nations. Our President, Hon. Dr. Abdul Kalam wrote,

"A developed India by 2020 or even earlier, is not a dream. It need not even be a mere vision in the mind of many Indians. It is a mission we can all take up."

In order to achieve this goal, the Technology Information and Forecasting Council (TIFAC) of the Department of Science and Technology, Govt. of India, has been preaching that *technology* has to be the driving force for development. The council in its reports of 1998, has underlined the need and the importance of creating knowledge society, for which reorientation of technical education is an essential prerequisite. TIFAC has recommended to AICTE to revamp technical education system so as to realize the dream of a developed India by 2020.

The Vision to Build World Class Institutes

The important questions that must be addressed are how long should students go abroad for higher education? And can all go abroad? Thousands of students from India have been going abroad every year for higher education. The trend is increasing year after year. In the year 2005 as many as 66,836 students left the Indian shores. This figure is higher by 22% than previous year. Those who do not get admission in premier institutes in India tend to go abroad. Indian brains are in search of quality education within the country, but the supply is inadequate. The trend to go abroad is continuing from pre-independence period. How many more years should this continue? Foreign universities from countries like England, America, and Australia are also coming here to attract the students. What do these trends mean to our institutes? Should they be welcomed or opposed? What is in the interest of our students and of this nation? We have no alternative than to face competition. We have to acquire better polices and practices, systems and procedures from our counterparts in developed countries. It is now not an option but compulsion. Education institutes, except IITs are far too behind their counterparts. Can we not build our universities like IIT MIT, Oxford and Cambridge? We have not been able to do so, thus far.

This was largely not on account of the lack of resources but more due to a lack of vision. Now, here is the required vision.

The key to accomplish this vision does not lie in collaboration, and waiting for foreign aid. Some times the aid is counter - productive. The key lies in creating motivated education entrepreneurs, professors, principles and vice-chancellors. Previously, colleges and universities were designed at best to become technology followers. Now we have to redesign them to become world leaders. India now upholds a vision to become a developed nation by 2020, free from poverty, and on par with G-8 countries. Technical education has a key role in achieving the same.

Vision to re-engineer Universities, Colleges, and Polytechnics - to Lead a Change

Can India hope to become competitive with the existing old model of technical education? Should we throw out the dysfunctional model of affiliated colleges and adopt a new model where educational institutions are more autonomous in nature? How can the institutes become enterprising, setting up innovative activities like patent center, Research Park, etc. and integrating them with education and research? How can we go about using new technologies, virtual classrooms, and sharing development efforts with private agencies? We need to set up more technical universities, and if so how many?

It is the agriculture universities which have solved the food problem of India. We need to emulate their model to solve the problem of industrial competitiveness. Starting many engineering colleges is good, but not enough. Without setting up technical universities, such a move will not bear the expected fruits. This is the opinion of 98% of respondents in a study conducted recently. Innovation is the origin of progress. Policies, practices, and also an overall climate favorable for innovation are the essential prerequisites for growth and prosperity. Institutes legitimately are the crucibles of reformation and advancement. They are the centers from where economic and industrial reforms should originate. They should earn the status of initiators of change, and function like spark plugs to release the energy for reformation. This has to be borne in mind by the education planners, administrators and professors. Accordingly these institutes need to be equipped to enable them to lead the change. More importantly, the institutes themselves have to *deserve* to become the drivers of change.

It is relatively easy to bring about road development, housing development etc. in shorter periods. But it is quite difficult to bring about development of universities and colleges worth the name. Pandit Nehru on the occasion of laying the foundation stone of IIT, Mumbai in 1959 said, 'It is easy to install and run a big factory but it is more difficult to establish and run a small higher education institute competitive by world standards.'

Future of people undoubtedly depends on what vision we adopt today. Implementation of vision needs resources. There is a well known saying, "Where there is a will, there is a way." There are resources available now, and many more will follow, running of mediocre institutes' turns out to be more costly than the cost of their up gradation.

Where do our Universities and Colleges Stand in World List?

According to a world-wide survey, only IITs, and IISc, Bangalore stands in world list. However, the students in many other colleges like Mumbai University Delhi and Pune University are world best, students get into them after stiff competition. Many institutions are very good in dissemination, but they are functioning like Departmental Stores. They are borrowing knowledge generated else where, which is acceptable only up to a certain point. We need to contribute to increase the pool of knowledge, and teach from our own firsthand research.

The areas, in which we lag, are low level of faculty research and low visibility. Generation of new theories, new knowledge is almost absent. Best minds can be attracted and nursed well only through active involvement in research. Recognition to institutes comes from the quality of its alumni. The infrastructure of most of the institutes is good. What is lacking is the proper direction to their working. We have to be world class in research. Then, and then only our institutes can become world-class in education. Teachers should not fall behind in their research commitments. Good teaching skills go hand in hand with good research capabilities. Teaching without research involvement results in mere dissemination of obsolete and irrelevant material.

It is the research output of an institute that creates its reputation. Management and Government should invest more in research. This makes education cheaper and better. If the institutes acquire research capabilities, there is no reason why they cannot become world class.

What we notice in foreign universities is that research companies are flocking round the universities in search on new technologies. The institutes on their periphery have units like Patent and Intellectual Property Rights (IPR) Centre, Technology Incubator, Innovation Centre, Industrial Services Centre, etc. Venture capital companies open offices nearby for early commercialization of brand-new technologies. Spin-off start-up companies are born one after the other. The Institutes attract both scholars, and companies from the world over. Thus the technical educational institutes have become a source of new ideas enabling them to win. All these multifaceted activities have a positive effect on education. Students get access to these centers of research and technology transfer. They feel happy to take active part in the research activities and thereby elevate their capabilities. It is such schemes that have turned the universities into well-springs of new knowledge. It is mainly innovative activities such as these that are attracting scholars and industries from the world over to US.

Adopting an Inquiry-based Learning Model

This is a model that is currently being followed in some of the world's best universities like Oxford, Cambridge and MIT. This model was recommended by the Boyer Commission in USA in 1998. In this model, students are introduced to research right from the first year. They learn both through discovery, and transmission. The important characteristic of this model is that all persons, namely professors, senior and junior students, lab assistants etc. are learners, researchers, and discovers. They all have a shared vision to achieve a common goal of inventing new knowledge, which bind them together. What matters most is the skill of the professor to synergizing the efforts of individuals to create a community of learners. The first year is the most vital of the formative years and hence senior professors choose to address them.

The model is recommended for innovative institutions which aspire to excel. The institutes which possess a commitment for creating new knowledge and new technologies are fit for the purpose. They ought to appoint professors who have research capability and who can create an environment favorable for innovation, such institutions prefer international market orientation and invite scholars from the world over, junior students work with their seniors under the guidance of professors to generate new technologies. The institutes integrate the education of their undergraduates with research projects.

Such Institutes do not function like departmental stores. *It is this approach which is found to result in continuous supply of eminent scientists and professors to the economy.*

Reverse Brain Drain: Time is Ripe Now

Shall we not realize and implement the schemes like research parks, which are well proven elsewhere in the world over a period of about 30 years? When shall we realize our strengths? MIT is earning about 100 patents every year. 20% of the institute's budget is met out of technology sale. Here research is observed to subsidize education, and education to subsidize research. Research and teaching are like the two ends of bow. Neither gets force with out the other. Shall our institutes not adopt this logic and become a Lighthouse for industry? This is the trend worldwide which India ought to emulate. When institutes elsewhere in the world could do this, why can we not do so in India? Should this not be the vision for the nest 20 years? Who will provide this vision? The institutes would have to adopt modern vision to bring fruits of globalization to its people. China has been successful in attracting its brain back with huge FDI.

How to Abolish Limit to Growth

The question is: Have we put upper limits on ourselves by worthless systems and procedures? Private universities, although new to India, have existed in the USA for over hundred years. Almost half of the universities there are private. They are managed and maintained by the church, Industry, or philanthropic organization. The standard of education in them and the quality of research vis-à-vis to that in state controlled universities is frequently found to be superior. The best institutes like MIT are private. USA has progressed well and due credit must go to private institutes. Many important inventions and innovations have taken place in them. Today a large proportion of patients and IPR are earned by private

universities. The human civilization would not have progressed so well, if there were no private universities in the world. On the other hand, all universities in India are state funded and hence state controlled. Their performance due to inherent weakness of the model is however far below expectation. They are over centralized, bureaucratic, and monopolistic, thwarting and impeding ideas of students and professors. The appointment of vice-chancellor is politically motivated. Does the answer lie in setting up of private universities? The state universities need to be supplemented by private universities to pose competitions. The systems of accreditation and ISO have now been introduced world over, which assure recognition nationally and internationally.

Are there risks in starting private universities? Are there greater risks in not starting private universities? Do the private universities deserve fair considerations? US universities have overtaken European universities because of privatization. Private universities do not need not to toe the Government line of thinking. They do not become routine, like government departments. On the other hand they become innovative and generate new knowledge and provide the same to Government to improve administration. They are in search of truth, working for high ideals and enrichment of minds and lives of students. They have to have academic freedom to think, and the freedom to act. Then only can they do justice to their existence. For, independent and free thinking privatization helps. Hence we have to learn to believe in privatization and strive to make it s success. The private institutions will not fail to tap the talent regardless of whether they have money or not. The institutes will install scholarships. New vision and insights are necessary in privatization.

Life Long Education

"They know enough, who know how to learn." Learning only once in the initial stages is good, but not enough. One has

to learn again and again nonstop. Continuing Education for increasing the competency of in-service personnel has assumed high degree of importance. There exists a gap in knowledge level between the Indian engineers and their counterparts in foreign companies, which has made survival difficult for the Indian corporate sector. Indian companies are being merged, amalgamated and purchased by foreign companies. Many persons in mid-career are being thrown out of jobs. They have to learn new technologies and acquire new skills to get re-employed. A learning organization with learning individuals alone can win in the world economy. Many people are re-learning at their own time and cost.

Have companies in India given sufficient thought about training of employees? Employing persons, giving them high salaries is good, but not enough. It is essential to provide them an opportunity for lifelong learning, to increase competency to the level they are capable for. It is reported by International. Association on Continuing Education that it yields more than 100% return on investment. It brings back sick units to good health. Motorola observed that when it invests one dollar in training it generates 30 dollars in three years. 60% productivity gains it has realized through training of employees. Only 5% of employees in India get a chance to receive training, where as in Finland 90% do. Countries like France, Finland and China have made legislation and made training obligatory for both the companies and individuals. Continuing Education activity in India is insignificantly small. A wave in this is perhaps needed. Will the institutes, Govt., and the industry not come together? Who will show them the vision? Higher Education Institutes will.

Arrival of the Digital Light

Education today is in the wonder-world of Internet economy. With the advances in communication technology, World Wide Web and personal computers, the traditional methods of learning and teaching have been threatened. Virtual classrooms and virtual universities are coming into existence. IIT Mumbai, MIT, Boston, and several other universities are launching programs which can be attended at home and at leisure. The academic community is having a fear that the emerging technologies will undermine what many deem best about traditional instructional practices and academic experiences - that is the personal contact between learner and teacher and among students. Many others feel that the arrival of new technology will bring instruction to them at cheaper cost. What lies ahead for universities and other sectors of education? What consequences will technology have on the institutional mission and mandate of universities? An extreme view has been offered by management sage Peter Drucker that traditional universities would not survive. Higher education is in deep crisis. Already we are beginning to deliver more lectures and off campus classes via satellite or two way video at a fraction of the cost of traditional courses. The colleges' campus would not survive as a residential institution. Today college buildings are hopelessly unsuited and totally not needed. The university colleges however should have to evaluate how fast this can happen? Should the institutes welcome new technologies? Undoubtedly yes, and accelerate their arrival. India should exploit new technology to the benefit of masses.

Finance for Innovation

The Govt. has created many schemes for financing industrial development IDBI, ICICI; IDCs etc. have been providing finance and support: this is good, but not enough. It is the scientific and technological innovation which need a boost. The Govt. would have to create "Innovation finance" in universities and colleges.

The industry, bankers and institutes would have to come together in this common cause. Innovation finance has modernized both the institutes and the industries in foreign countries. When they could do this, why can we not do so in India? Such financing has become essential a prerequisite to cope with demands in competitive and dynamic economy. Does the connection exist properly in India, between the industry and institutes? Without such interaction, the education and the economy of India will be crippled. The key person's viz. policy makers, administrators and professors would have to expand their thinking, and open up to new possibilities and global opportunities arising out of ever emerging technologies. They need to adopt a new agenda for the thought and action that would enable them to become more capable leaders. Not all the inputs given in this article are applicable to every college. They can choose what suits them. Who will show the way to create innovation finance? The learned professors will. At least 2% of industry budget should be diverted to innovation to make fruitful investment in industry.

Preserving the Global Culture and Heritage

Ability to communicate well is essential in the present era of globalization. In this interdependent world, familiarity with foreign languages and foreign cultures, tolerance towards other faiths, an awareness of the benefits and differences in civilizations assumes importance. One of the objectives of education is that it helps to preserve the sanctity of human civilization. Education is directly concerned with moral power. In the past, institutes have neglected this aspect. It is only through moral education that we can work through, and find solutions to the problems of unemployment, poverty and terrorism. Most of the time, religions have been educating the people in improving morality. That is necessary, but not enough.

Corruption has grown beyond limits. Disparities between the rich and the poor are increasing. Educated people hold the key to progress. It is they who spend most of the budget. Unfortunately, they in general, do not have a good image in society. Introspection needs to be done. How the educated people look at the situation would decide the future of the world. Should education institutes not take a note and apply corrective measures? Imparting technical skills and knowledge are essential, but making them good human beings should not be forgotten. Deliberate and well thought-out effort needs to be made in every institute to hold human civilization together.

Creating World-class Technology

The questions are: can academics in India propel industrial development? Industrial goods from China and several east-west countries are flooding the Indian market. Many domestic industries are finding it difficult to survive the global competition. India ranks 43rd in world list of competitiveness. Some of the industries are becoming sick; some are being amalgamated, and purchased by foreign firms. Unemployment is rising. Can the Indian industry compete in a globalised market without modernizing the higher education? There has to be a close bond between the two. Gone are the days when Indian industry development plans used to be propelled by foreign collaborators. In those days it was believed that technology can be generated only in foreign countries and after testing, it could be imported at high cost. Now it is proved beyond doubt that technology can be generated in India on par with that abroad and that too at half the price. It is no more necessary to knock at the doors of foreign countries for technology India should hold the vision to propel the industrial growth indigenously.

Government Funding of Education

There is a school of thought that, if the state spends more on education, there will be a faster rate of growth. That if it is does not, growth will be slower.

Education is a wealth generating mechanism. Even in the hours of financial crisis, increase in budget to education is advocated. This is because it increases competency of people to utilize physical and financial resources. Nobel laureate Dr. Amartya Sen advised government to increase budget allocation to 6%. When asked by Mr. Yashwant Sinha, the then Finance Minister, What should be the first priority in budget, he replied 'Education.' What should be the second priority? He replied 'Education.' What should be the third? He replied 'Education.' Indian has failed to grow faster so far, in spite of enormous promise only because of its weakness in education in general particularly, technical education. Many countries like Indonesia and Philippines are more advanced because of education.

Education alone can move a nation forward. The future belongs to those who understand this. We need a cultural and attitudinal revolution in favor of education.

There is, at present a wide gap between urban and rural areas in both social and economical development. *Poverty anywhere is a threat everywhere.* The people in rural areas do not have access to education. It is the scientific and technological capability of the people which enables them to strive and reach to higher income.

Adopting Internationally Proven Policies

The education should not depend on short-sighted whims and fancies of politicians. It should go on and on, uninterrupted, non-stop, regardless of the ruling political party. Academicians should be allowed to think and act freely. Higher education is more important and should go ahead even in times of war and peace. The earlier it is liberated from the vested interests of politicians and bureaucracy the better will it be for the state. Arrival of professionalism in education is hindered so far by politics and bureaucracy. Bringing policies and practices, systems and procedures from developed countries and adapting them to local situations is the crying need of the hour. People's minds need to be prepared for autonomy. The universities which are supposed to lead a change in favor of autonomy are found to be actually obstructing the process solely based on narrow selfish interests. In the wider national interest they should in fact dedicate their efforts to the cause of reformation in education.

The author suggests that the Chancellors of universities in the face of rising challenges and increasing complexities in higher education essentially should have an independent office. The chancellor should be an academician working full-time, the present system in which the Governor of the state is the ex-officio Chancellor, needs reconsiderations. The bottleneck today is at the top. The problems are being ignored and not attended to. The chancellor who is a Governor of the state remains too busy in his other legitimate duties and responsibilities. Any person, howsoever efficient may he be, cannot do justice to both. The origins of ills in higher education today, lie at the top. The situation demands urgent correction.

Universities as Maternity-homes For Safe Birth of New Enterprises

It is necessary for the universities to establish Patent & IPR Centers, Innovation Relay Centers, Research Parks, Incubators, Industrial Services Centers, Entrepreneurship Centers, Venture Capital Fund, Technology Transfer Office Etc. The above mentioned centers are commonly seen in all universities abroad. Companies like HP, Apple, etc. were born in university incubators. It is these centers which have taken their countries ahead of others. But they are conspicuous by their absence in our institutes. If the state of Maharashtra takes this vision to set up such centers and succeeds, brain drain will be converted into brain-gain. Poverty will be wiped out, and employment generation for vast masses will take place. The schemes are known for income and employment generation.

Scientists from labs will have to be offered chairs in academic institutes and professors be offered chairs in laboratories. The practice of exchange of academic leaders prevails in Germany and many other countries. Networking of innovators on the one hand and the technology users on the other hand, to obtain push-pull effect will have to be done.

A committee must be appointed to prepare project reports and monitor implementation of establishment of such centers. The committee must be comprised of representatives from industry, laboratories and institute. Bhatnagar award winning scientists, Noble laureates, NRI professors be specially invited to work on these committees. Innovation culture will not come automatically in the academic institutes and the state. It will have to be deliberately planted. Hence is this recommendation. 93.03% respondents in a study, recommend the establishment of such a committee.

Total Quality Management Techniques

According to a study conducted recently, 91% respondents recommend use of TQM in education institutes. 88% say investment with out TQM does not improve quality. 97% respondents say TQM should be made compulsory where public funds are utilized. 96% say use of TQM will lead to improvement in quality and productivity. 91% say that there should be a state council for quality assurance. This will ensure higher efficiency in the state level systems. Due to the lack of TQM approach, our resources are wasted and are not available where they are needed.

Accreditation has been introduced at the national and state levels. This is a good scheme. But it has to be implemented in a right way. It has to be realized that accreditation is the last step of Quality Assurance. The preceding steps of Quality Assurance are not cared for. Benchmarking, identification of systems, inputs and outputs, use of statistical methods, making a survey on how satisfied the students, the faculty, the employers, and other stakeholders are, must precede and become a part of accreditation. Doing accreditation has unfortunately become a cosmetic exercise. The spirit is forgotten. The norms and standards prescribed by accreditation board are backward by world standards. Mediocre are being declared excellent. It has become like conducting of examination without the prior conduct of lectures and practical. This is precisely contrary to the principles of Quality Assurance. There is a plentiful of scope for improvement. In universities in UK that receive grants-in-aid, quality assurance is compulsory.

ISO headquarter at Geneva first arranged education programs and created a cadre of LEAD ASSESSORS, THEN gave them authority to educate persons in industry, to install Quality plans, Quality manuals. The exercise of training personnel in an enterprise continues for a year or two, and after they are prepared, they make application for ISO certification. Some such preparation of the institutions will essentially have to precede accreditation. Shall the NAAC/NBA devise mechanism to install quality assurance?

Industry-Institute Interaction

American industry has helped institutes to transform them into Power Houses of economy. Can Indian industry not do this? Industry and institutes can achieve peak performance only if they go hand in hand.

According to the study 93% say that there should be a committee at state level to plan and implement industry-institute interaction. It is a well proven theory that industries in isolation from institutes cannot progress and become competitive, so also the institutes. In order that they are productive they must marry with each other. The proven theory says new technologies must be born in institutes and they should be transferred and used by industry in production of goods and services. The efforts of both needs to be synergized. There is a University Industry Science Partnership Program (UNISPAR) of UNESCO. Funds and guidance are available Maharashtra state has appointed a Director for Industry-Institute Partnership. This shows vision on the part of Govt. of Maharashtra. What remains is to activate the Directorate, to forge links between the industry and institutes. Who will show the way to activate it? The academicians will.

CONCLUSION

What then is our vision for the year 2020? The vision is to make India a destination of world class technical education. The vision of India is to become a world class fountain-head of S&T, a well-spring generating and disseminating new technology to small, medium and large scale enterprises, both in India and abroad.

Can India hope to become a developed nation with the old outdated model of technical education?

Certainly not! We need to throw out the dysfunctional college-affiliation model and grant autonomous or deemed-university status to them. This has not happened so far. The bottleneck lies at the top. There is a need of full-time Chancellor.

Government in associations with ISTE would have to carry out restructuring of existing education and research organizations. This will make the institutions more productive, putting idle resources to effective work. However, there remains a need to increase the Govt. budget up to international norms, i.e. 6% of GDP.

We shall have to bring world best policies and practices like in MIT, Oxford and Cambridge to our Institutes. Institutes will have to acquire a vision to become world leaders in technology. However, moral education must no be forgotten.

We envision starting technical universities, not only to award ME and Ph.D. degrees but also to become lighthouses for industry. The models of private university, virtual university need be given a fair chance. The youth must be given full access to research in public and private labs.

Education must be made research-based. Installation of Research Parks, Incubators, Patent Centers, Venture Capital Foundations, and other centers of excellence deserves high priority. Education has to be made innovative. Creating a culture in colleges and polytechnics that favors creativity and new ideas is the patent need of the hour.

Appointing state level and national level committees to achieve technological innovation, industry-institute interaction etc. in a proper way must be done.

Upgrading the skill sets of vast masses so that they may perform jobs in modern industry to earn higher pay will have to be given priority. Centers for continuing education to fit people to job requirement will have to be established. Many jobs in India and in the world market are lying unfilled due to non availability of proper people.

All aspects of this vision are not for all institutions. What will colleges and polytechnic look like in the year 2020? If the vision stated above is implemented in letter and in spirit, they will be much different. The Indian economy will then quickly grow stronger.

It is hoped that the leaders in industry, academia, religious, social and political systems will come together, work together, use collective wisdom and give a proper shape to build India into a developed nation by the year 2020.

Conclusion

The higher and technical education institution, in the coming time, although will undergo substantial changes, driven by new learning technology, harsh financial constraints, changing public demand, globalization and growing intellectual opportunity, it must keep learning and especially student learning at the heart of its mission. Campus of today indicates larger society of tomorrow. With this in view institutes need shaping. How would the winning institution in 21st century look like? An institute which has characteristics as under is more likely to win. An attempt should therefore be made to upgrade institutions to acquire following characteristics.

- The successful Higher and Technical Education institution of 21st century will be that which will maintain institutional autonomy, lively faculty, Independence, and vigorous academic freedom, but will enjoy strong, impartial, public governance and committed institutional leadership. All good institutions, world over, are essentially autonomous. Professors ought to have freedom to be innovative and creative. They should not be over powered by non educational persons. They themselves can ably steer the direction of academic pursuits. There should be almost no interference in academics from outside. This is in larger interest. Autonomous status is a prerequisite to succeed. This should be accorded in letter and spirit. Faculty and staff should be allowed developing taste by mixing with their counterparts elsewhere in the world.

- The winning Institute of 21st century will be that which is compatible to the opportunities and challenges in globalization. Indian institutes are yet not aligned and tuned to world dynamics. They have in the recent past progressed well quantitatively but are yet poorly equipped and woefully unsuited to the quality demands of globalization. Transformation to world class status demands more of intellectual capital inputs besides financial.
- The preferred institution will be increasingly privately supported but publicly accountable and socially committed. Privatization of technical education is certainly good. But there are some risks, which need to be guarded so as to make most of it. Private institutions in India are mostly managed and maintained by political persons. They should keep in mind the deeper purposes of education. Students should not be exploited but helped. It is hoped that governing authorities would show statesmanship and use the institutes as means to build a national unity they seek, and to develop the human resources needed by economy.
- The successful institution will be technologically sophisticated but community dependent. Quality of Education does not depend only on instructions in classroom and laboratories. It depends more on building synergy in institutes and industry. Indian institutes need to learn commercialization of new technologies. It needs multi facetted activities like Entrepreneurship, Technology Incubators, Patents and IPR, Lifelong education centre for grownups, Research parks, Enterprise development centers which bring about a marriage between industry and academics. They are new in India and should be set

up as early as possible. Only class room teaching although essential is not enough to improve quality, and relevance. Only pumping more money and appointing more men in institutes is not enough. National Knowledge Commission has recommended establishment of above centers of excellence, as integral components of the institutions. They have a deeper impact on quality of education. Solution lies in sensitizing institutions as well as industry in the potential synergy between the two.

- Each successful institution in 21st century will be competitive, not only by national standards but by international. The visions and missions of the institutions, policies and practices, systems and procedures should be made responsive to the changing world. Indian Universities, colleges and polytechnics till recently were ahead of their counterparts in China. But now they are far too behind. Do we realize this? Only those who realize, do benchmarking will improve.
- The successful institution will be campus rooted but internationally oriented. The professors in the past did not have adequate opportunities to go abroad and see what their counterparts are teaching. They are practically disconnected from rest of the world, and are not familiar with the global developments. In order that they become equal to world class professors they need to be granted increased international mobility. Sachin Tendulkar could not have become world class cricketer if he was not allowed to play international cricket. Cost of providing international exposure to professors is high but much less than the hidden cost of not providing, which is borne by the society.
- The successful institution will be academically independent but constructively partnered. If the institution is to meet the increasing range of social needs, it will require new alliances within the academic community and new

partnerships outside it, with communities, local, state and national agencies, corporations, libraries, museums, publishers, professional associations, scholarly societies, and other institutions. It will establish closer cooperation with other "providers" and "users" of knowledge including commercial vendors of educational hardware and software. Institutions will be successful who nurse public private partnership, [PPP]. Success of an institution will depend on how many partners it is able to carry with.

- The successful institution will be knowledge based but student centered, research driven but learning focused. There is an acute need of establishing technical universities. It is they who can focus better on technological research, and to become "lighthouse" for industry. Universities should go beyond puppet like teaching. Students should not become teacher puppets. They should aim to become pace setters in changing world. They should create an atmosphere of competition and avoid monopoly.
- The successful institution will be producing new technologies in its laboratories. By importing and following the technologies from abroad, India cannot hope to be a technology leader. Institutions should aim at producing new knowledge, new technologies, and leaders in industry. Can Indians become technology pioneers? They should aim to produce Indian brands in technology and industry.
- The successful institution will be that which acquires new vision of the new world. The industries need continuous input of new knowledge and new Technology, so as to remain competitive in global market. Institutes and Universities should acquire this new vision of the new world. They should include corporate development and enable industry to win. Institutions will be successful who provide new technologies to industry.
- Indian institutes will be successful which produce balanced output of BTech, MTech, and PhD. Present output of PhDs

in Engineering is 0.5 per million populations. The corresponding figure of USA and Japan are 30 and 28 / million population. With this abysmally low figure of PhDs can India hope to win in the world race?

- The successful institution will be quality obsessed but procedurally efficient. Many institutions in India are spending money far in excess but due to lack of TQM approach they do not excel. Implementation of TQM does not require additional money, it results in saving. The Governing boards, AICTE should prescribe use of TQM.
- The institutions will be successful, where the chancellor of universities is competent academically. Governor of a state is presently the ex-officio chancellor of universities. This system coming by tradition is defective. Now when education has become so vast and complex, stakes involved are so high, the chancellor of universities cannot be a decorative figure. He needs to be an academician with wide open experience in the world of academics. Today the problems in higher education remain improperly diagnosed, inadequately analyzed. Hence solutions are not forth coming. A separate office of chancellor with qualified staff is the need of the hour. If this is not done foreign institutes will find it easy run over and capture the vast Indian education market.
- Institutions will be successful which give birth to new technologies, patents, hi-tech startups. Do we want imported brands of technologies or generate Indian brands? Then industry and institutes should look to each other's support for growth. Youthful talent in institutes is a great force. Synergy between institutes and industry is the only way to achieve peak performance. Industry should change their mindset and learn to support technological research in institutes. They should jointly undertake activities like research parks, innovation centers, technology incubators etc

- Industry should take a long range view of the interaction with institute. It cannot do all the research all alone by itself needed for becoming globally competitive. It must think differently and align with institutes for research. With this approach it is much cheaper and better to develop indigenous technology and/or absorb technology coming from abroad.
- The skill set of the vast population of India is far too low by international standard. It needs up gradation forthwith. Both young and adults in urban as well as rural areas should be uplifted in knowledge and skills. They need to be enabled to become globally competent. Lack of skills leads to unemployment, increase in poverty, nexalite tendency, crime rate and in turn forced for investment in security measures etc. Shall we then not choose to invest in favor of education rather than building prisons?
- Institutions will be successful only if the Mechanism of governance at all levels i.e. governmental, university and college levels is modernized by using scientific approaches. It should be made flexible, participative, and responsive to the aspirations of youths. Government is devising policies and practices so as to make it inclusive. Universities and colleges should bring them in practice.
- Higher and technical education in India will be successful only if the recommendations of National Knowledge Commission [2006-7-8], and Yesh Pal Committee [2009] in respect of grant of autonomy to Institutions should be urgently discussed debated and implemented. Innovative and creative budding minds demand autonomy. Nations where institutions are autonomous progress faster.
- Institutions will be successful which identify internal weaknesses, revise structures, systems and procedures. A world proven theory says that some of the authorities in chair and politicians in power may obstruct even sabotage and slow down the process of transformation.

Resistance to change, inertia of the system is natural. This is usually done to keep alive their personal vested interests putting public interest in danger. This is human tendency. Therefore transformation of higher and technical education should not be left totally in the hands of authorities in chair. An independent body to plan and monitor reforms must be constituted. Implementation of recommendations of NKC and Yeshpal committee-2009 should not be left to authorities of universities and colleges like in the past. A separate independent task force of dedicated educationists, industrialists, and social reformers is necessary to be constituted at state and national levels for the purpose. Recommendations of earlier education commissions, like Kothari commission, New Education Policy 1986, Radhakrishnan Commission [1959] have not been seriously implemented because of lack of independent taskforce.

- The institutions will be successful which replace traditional bureaucratic approach in governance and management of academic institutes. Bureaucracy in institutions is no more relevant today, it should be abandoned forthwith. Indoctrination of ideas, rigid frame work, and inflexibility has no place in academics. They throttle emergence of spontaneous, breakthrough ideas.
- Higher and Technical education will be successful if it gives go bye to the present degraded policies and practices and pulls up from the ruts and takes up to higher orbits. Without which the economic security of India in globalised world cannot be ensured.
- If the reforms are delayed, foreign institutions are likely to establish education hubs in India and exploit the vast education market. Indian academics will then go in service of foreign masters. Consequence will be that Indians will be branded inefficient, incompetent and less knowledgeable to govern institutes in global context by

themselves. They will become subservient to foreigners. Education may slip out of our hands in favor of foreign, which is too detrimental.

- Foreign universities once they come in India they will not remain limited to education but interfere in industrial, social and political affairs of the country. Thus, in turn the sovereignty is likely to be in danger. India will tend to become like Afghanistan and Pakistan.
- Institutions will win which view Professors as researchers, discoverers, innovators and creators. They should be enabled to grow to the level they are capable for. They are a great force in pulling the nation forward. They are an insurance against obsolescence. They should be encouraged and enabled to discover new SandT, write books, research papers, obtain patents etc. How many of our professors have travelled abroad? How many have written books? How many have published articles in journals? How many have obtained PhD, patents and IPR? Then how shall we inspire younger generation to be innovative, creative? A saying goes" if there is no water in the well from where it will come in bucket"? A change in mind set of people who govern is the need of the hour.
- Institutions will succeed which empower Professors with necessary freedom to think and freedom to act. This is essential in the interest of public at large. It is they who design and shape the future of the younger generation. They create tomorrow's leaders today. This is a very important job. This should be borne in mind by professors, planners and administrators. Institutions must have to be manned by high quality devoted people.
- Higher and technical education will take the nation forward where Professors are differentiated from government servants. They are think tanks. They are like horses of race not like horses pulling carts.
- Institutions will be preferred which value acquisition of knowledge and storing it in brains but learning innovation

skills, creativity and discovery skills are given higher priority. Students should learn to learn to capitalize on technology, and knowledge.

- Institutions will win which make a paradigm shift in the teaching methods in the institutions making use of modern technologies like Computer, telecommunications distance education etc. This is found to bring down the cost yet improve effectiveness. Should we not permit more experimentation?
- Nations win which increase the public budget allocation to at least 6% of GDP. India needs to increase from present 3 % of GDP to 6 %, which has been announced by government way back in 1991, but not yet done. It should be realized that spending on education is far more rewarding. Not spending is a false economy, and certainly planning for failure. Not investing in education is more costly. Do we realize this? It is the education which has failed India. But for education India has lagged behind. India in world eyes is a less educated country.
- Modernization of Education costs but mediocrity costs far more. Do we realize this?
- If you do not upgrade the Higher and Technical Education, the economy will weaken gradually, and outside elements may exploit. Let us remember that the institutes create the future. Bright future could be created only if institutes are made world class.
- Institutes will be successful which establish Technology Transfer offices. The knowhow possessed by these colleges is very much needed by SSI's and SME's. The institutions should not run after only big industries that have their own R and D centers.
- Technical education Institutions, students and professors must adopt global perspectives, global mindset. They should attract talent and ideas, like magnet from every where and anywhere in the world. They must remain constantly in touch with their counterparts.

- The World experience tells us that high tech industries are flocking around the institutions which are able to generate new ideas and new technologies. Scientific institutions are a pre- requisite to industrial development. This model is being replicated in China, Japan, Philippines, and all over the world.
- Institutions will win which harness the strength of their alumni. Alumni associations play a critical role in modernizing the institutes. No world class institute exists without active alumni association. They bring fresh ideas to institutes to remain in tune with world. So much is demanded from college that all alone an institute cannot give. It must be backed by ideas from alumni who are their ambassadors, scattered the world over.
- Regions/ Nations / cities will develop faster and better where the institutions are excellent. Regions with out them even if endowed with plentiful natural resources do not develop well. Regions/ nations do not develop where scientific and Technological capability of institutions and people is limited.
- Putting more money and putting more men on the job is good but not enough. What is essential is using current and appropriate strategies, adopting flexible rules and regulations.
- Nations will succeed more where innovation fund for students studying in colleges is provided. A national level as well as state level committee is constituted in education to give boost to innovation. Potential of innovation in youths in colleges is high but is unexplored. Education charged with spirit of discovery and innovation alone can move India forward. Future belongs to those who realize this.
- Nations will be progressive which establish new polytechnics and colleges by following principles of scientific project management. This ensures optimum

utilization of resources, in achieving the institutional objectives. The age old method of sanctioning resources, in government in a piece meal manner is wasteful, besides missing Institutional targets. The old out dated practice should be abandoned forthwith.

- Higher and Technical education will be in top demand where teaching and research are treated as inseparable. Every teacher will be a researcher and vice-versa.
- Nations will be winning in global competition where Government makes it a national agenda to educate "every one –life long- nonstop" and earmark budget for the same. Keeping skill set of people up to date is of paramount importance.
- What is then the vision of India for the year 2020? A developed nation? Then we need to throw out old dysfunctional college affiliation model and resort to autonomy. So as to achieve this dream, institutions must have to become fountain heads of S and T, a well-spring generating and disseminating new technology to small and medium enterprises.
- Nations will be successful where exclusive well focused technical universities exist. They are spear headed organizations capitalizing on technology. It is these universities which can take the nation forward at a faster pace. Earlier they are established better it is.
- Nations will win which recognize that education the world over is getting deregulated. It is more due to distance education, open course ware on internet, reducing monopoly of universities, for profit institutions etc. Multiple approaches in private and public sectors will grow.
- Last but not the least; nations will be successful which nurture today the young minds for entrepreneurship, so as to ensure that they become global players.

Today's government leaders were students yesterday. Tomorrow's professional pacesetters are today's graduate students. The future leaders of India and the world stroll today across our college quadrangles; future lawmakers, judges, chief engineers and CEO sit in university classrooms. The task in which institutions are engaged- the pursuit of learning-is not the passive conveyance of information; it is the passing of torch, the sharing of the flame. It is igniting the spirit of entrepreneurship and innovation. If the institutions trivialize that responsibility, if they reduce it to distributing the stale food of disarticulated information or limit it to sharing lifeless elements of technical competence, they will fail those who have entrusted them with responsibility, who have upheld their freedom, who have provided them resources, and who have supposed they were meant about doing a greater task. India disparately needs institutions which will provide new generations' creative, inclusive, inquiring, engaged and enabling leaders that will come out of the higher education institutions. Brave India of tomorrow is being created today in these temples of knowledge. It is this prestigious institution that must be challenged and enabled to play an increasingly influential role in preserving traditional knowledge, and rewriting the book of new knowledge.

Bibliography

1. Abhiji Das, "A bridge too far"? A robust economy can only be built on the said foundation of education and training E.T.

2. Abheek Barman, "Fund a Lab and grow" Economic Times, 2.5.1997. The economic growth depends on technology fillips so said Francis Becon in 1605, Govt. would have to fund basic research, since nobody else would. Kealy another scientist said "government money for science displaces private funding and private funding works better". Nobel Leaureate Bob Solow observed that output of U.S. from 1909 to 1949 doubled, and that 85% of growth was attributable to technological change. Kealey disputed that Government funded basic research drives technology. He feels, generally R & D takes place in industry.

   Only 10% of innovations from 1975 to 1985 originated in University, 90% came from industry labs.

   Private Hi-tech, labs are the efficient users of technology. If they wish to retain their market edge by innovating new products they will have vested interests in maintaining scientists efficiency and vested interest drive hard to scientific breakthrough.

Industry in USA has overtaken Govt., in R& D funding. Research done in industry remains secrete not available to others and hence less growth takes place. R& D remains the province of Government. Industry for vested interest and government for open distribution should involved. Private cos. should focus on innovation – application.

3. Association of University Technology Managers (AUTM) Technology Transfer Practice Manual Vol. I – III, 49 East Avenue, Norwalk CT 06851 USA.

   * It is a document prepared for non profit technology transfer professionals, contains 40 subject areas. In during patent, intellectual property, managing technology transfer office, technology licensing, technology association, marketing, soliciting invention disclosure, royalties, preparing agreements, intellectual property protection, pertinent laws and regulation etc.

     It prescribes establishment of a technology transfer office in each college, university. This is going to augment income to the institute and build interaction with industry. Such offices are existing in USA. Germany from the last twenty years.

4. Alvin Toffler, "Future Shock" Bantam Book New York, 1981.

5. Bibek Debray, Reforming the academic world 18.10.1994, Financial Express (F.E.).

   The state academic world now is such that it is difficult to find individuals who stand head and shoulders above their peers.

6. British College Students face new Test Tuition Fees – News Item in Times of India, 10 August 1997.

   For the first time U.K. plans to impose tuition fees on all college students abandoning the long held commitment to free higher education for every one. This will deter many students from going to higher education. Unions feel "the state should pay because you will give so much back to the state by getting a better job and paying more in taxes. Universities are in financial crisis and that could be addressed either by raising fees or taxes." Change is essential, we can not defer action to next generation.

7. Branson W. Murrill, "Faculty Entrepreneurs" helping universities earn while students learn, Journal of Industry & Higher Education Aug. 1996 (P-238).
   Recommendations – promote faculty entrepreneurs and closer relations with industry. It will create richer campus environment. Faculty will thereby remain technologically uptodate, Industry will gain new ideas, students will get relevant education at reduced cost. This approach is not without risks. First academic integrity must never be sacrificed for profits. Potential conflicts must be resolved ethically, benefits outweigh the cost.
8. Chris-Johnson, Innovation is the key.
   Times of India dt. 26.11.1997.
   The National University of Singapore is testing students ability in innovation. Innovation and flexibility can occur when you have hunger for growth. In a controlled domestic environment there is no need to innovate.
9. Chairman of Zerox corporation wrote a book "Winning the Brain Race – A bold plan to make our schools competitive". He says we cant have world class economy without a world class work force, from senior scientists to clerks, and we can not have world class work force without world class schools.
   If our country is going to get stronger and more competitive, our college and universities simply must become a national priority. Modern industry can be built if competent manpower is available.
   Providing excellent education will cost more, but the cost of mediocrity is much more although invisible. Employing mediocre people and then training them is more costly.

10. Claire L. Zepka and Kevin Warwick, "The vital role of cybernetics in Industrial Development". Industry and Higher Education, June 1996, (P-170).

Changing role of Universities – Not only Universities are cheaper than consultancies, they are more up to date.

11. C.S.Prabhakara "Intellectual capital goes one – up on" machinery and labour, Financial Express 28 Feb. 1998.

Recent studies show that R.O.R. in skill, knowledge improvement is more than twice that of investments in plant and machinery. Substainable competitive advantage lies in IPR.

According to UNESCO data bank India has 5th largest pool of technical manpower. But a considerable number of them are engaged in non research and non developmental areas. The innovation from them is dismal. India spends a paltry 0.75% of GDP on R&D. The weaklink lies in factor creating mechanism such as Educational Institutes.

12. Competing beyond Technology, "What Strategy can Do for Technology," by Kim B. Clark, Harward Business Review, Nov. Dec. 1989.

13. Customers drive a Technology driven company. An interviewwith George Fisher, Harward Business Review Nov. – Dec. 1989.

Every one of Motorola has a talk directly with customers to better understand business.

14. Computers and the coming of US, by Charles H. Ferguson – HBR, July-Aug 1990 (P-80).

- We try to bridge the gap between our company and the institute that supply us with people. We are entering an era of partnership with established Universities. We give them feed back on the courses they teach and even on their faculties. Motrola is running a University which is presently open to its employees, suppliers, customers and educational partners.

15. Directory of Foreign Collaborations in India. Published by N.K.Vyas Publishers, Ahmedabad 380 009.
16. Dr. S.R.Valluvi, "Day of reckoning for Indian Industry" E.T. 19.03.1994.
Economic liberalization will sound death knell for licence culture and demand a strong R&D base to compete globally. It is the top management of Indian Industry which has not been giving direction to R&D. They have to do this industry competitive.
17. Dr. V.S.Vaidya, "Teacher Effectiveness", The Indian journal of Technical Education, Vol. 18 No.2, April-June 1995.
18. Dr. R.Natrajan, "The multiple Functions of Engineering Teachers".
19. Dr. J.P. Srivastava "A Critical Review of Present and Future Post Graduate Technical Education in India". The Indian Journal of Tech. Education, Vol.18, No.2 April-June 1995.
20. Education, training, research – The obstacles to transnational mobility – supplement 5/96 Bulletin of European Kuion, Green paper –
European commission encouraged mobility of students, engineers and researchers during and after the studies. They have drawn out programmes like leonhardo – da – Vinci to finance mobility, and transfer of credits from one university to another. It identifies the obstacles to mobility and has drawn out lines of actions. Edith Cresson, member of the European Commission, a is taking lending part. She believes that mobility of ideas across the world, enriches the human civilization.
21. F.A.Van Vught, "Dangerous Curves – An international analysis of participators growth and higher education policy in seven countries". Journal of Industry and Higher Education, Aug 95, (P-1198).
Private funding makes institutes less dependent at Govt. funding, and therefore allows to greater autonomy.

Increase in private funding leads, higher education for poor and deserving in grave danager.

22. Financing Innovation, Innovation and Tech. Transfer Vol. 6/97, P-8.

New companies start up get 26% share in USA where as in EU it is 5.7%

The return of investment in R&D depends upon full and rapid exploitation of results. Current Research Information system (CRIS) will be critical in enabling companies (SMES) to make productive use of technological resources.

23. Fourth World Conference on Engineering Education, October 15-20, 1995, Minnesota, USA.

Investment in people should be a high priority, for Governments, organizations, industries and of course individuals.

- We ant engineers who are highly skilled in their disciplines.
- We want engineers who can work and communicate across functions.
- We want engineers who understand the global nature of business and markets.
- We want engineers who are curious and think innovatively.
- We want engineers who welcome change, and who know how to lead and how to be team players (P-175).

24. Grahm Guest, The learning organization – its principles and practice, IACEE, news letter Vol.7, No.4, writer 1998.

They know enough, who know, how to learn, Unless you try to do something beyond what you have already mastered, you will never grow. It is not only educational institutes or companies that are learning organisations the concept can be successfully applied to labs, towns, countries, offices etc. An Individual has a capacity to learn, what is the difference between a traditional company and a learning company. In traditional company only selected people are sent to training. In a learning company, every one learns from every one and responsibility is shared by all. Learning is satisfying to both individual and company.

25. George P.JK. 1993, Continuing Engineering Education concept and Practices, Indian Journal of Tech, Education, Vol 16, No.4.
26. Greg Tegart "The Co-operative Research Centres Programme". An Australian initiative to link research to commercialization. Journal of Industry and Higher Education, June 96 (P-160).
They involve collaboration between research groups and users of research. It required support of Govt. in initial – 7 years.
27. High Tech Management consideration, Oxfort IBH, Publication, P-113, P.D.malgaonkar, 1989.
28. International Technology Park at Patandur Agrahar Gate, while field Rd, Banglore-66, E.T. 17.12.1997.
29. IEI Report in Journal of the Institution of Engineers (India) 8 Gokhale Road, Calcutta.
"Technology Transfer and Development for most developing countries Industrial Development is and will continue on imported technologies. Technology Transfer process is often too costly and ineffective. The buyers may lack the professional skills to select a technology that is suited to local conditions, and to acquire on favourable terms. The real challenge is to bring about technological change and catching up.
30. International Association on Continuing Engineering Education (IACEE). Report No. 8, 1997. Thejoy of learning, Published by IACEE, DIPOLI, P.O.BOX 8000 FINLAND, hut.
Learning Technologies will be demand driven, Universities will have to be more flexible, companies must share to become learning organizations, basic initial education and continuing education will be viewed in an integrated manner. Use of multimedia, new technology in education

will dominate. Only those organizations will win which transform themselves creatively and continuously. The average length of job tenure is decreasing and greater variety of working relationships and organization structures are coming into existence. Trade unions will have to share the goals with industry and education providers.

31. Indo British Seminar on Industry Institute Interaction. March 6-7, 1995 Organised by C.I.I. New Delhi.
    - In the agriculture sector, education and research are under agriculture Ministry. The ministry gives funds for both agricultural production and research. In industrial production such an arrangement is needed. (P-2)
    - Education and Research flow into one another and feed of one another. There is an obvious satisfaction in teaching something that the teacher has discovered by his own research, rather than by the scholarship of studying what others have discovered or invented.
    - Research strategy with institutes is going to become increasingly move important (P-123).
32. Innovation Relay Centre, Innovation and Technology Transfer, Vol. 6/97 (P-9)
33. John Opel, an industrialist said "If you want modern industry tomorrow, you have to have modern institute today. Success in international competition depends on turning intellectual strengths into marketable commodities". If India is to compete internationally, we must co-operate nationally. We need to integrate people, ideas, opportunities, markets and capital in new and effective ways.
34. John Lorriman, "What can we learn from 25 years of life long learning in Japan", Journal of Industry and Higher Education, August 1995, P 248.

    The Japanese, over the past 20 years, have studied the best practices elsewhere in the world and have then carefully adapted them for their own circumstances. They invited experts, who were best possible in world, and paid them offen more than Japanese prime minister, so keen were Japanese to learn. They invited British experts in Electrical Engineering Prof. Henry Dyer, Edmund Merel, US experts Edward Morse and Erwin Baiz from Germany. Japanese have learned so much but Japanised it, the lessons other countries should take "Japanese are the best educated people in the world, and its success in international market owes to this aspect". The most important role of managers in Japanese is to coach and develop their staff. They maximize the skills development of their staff. On the job training in Japan as compared to other nations, for present and for future is very high 34.2% as compared to 1.5% in U.K.20% to 50% of time of managers goes in coaching. All employees share experiences in learning half a day per week.

35. Japan's Research and Development Corporation (JRDC) JRDC promotes development of engineering technologies. It is not only a financial source, but an organizer of R&D projects. It provides interest free grants which must be refunded only in the case of successful development. Japanese Government have forward thinking, proactive policies to assist companies in developing new technologies to make them more competitive. (P-234).

36. Michael Porter, "The competitive Advantage of nations" The Free Press, New York.
Many advanced nations (Germany, Sweden) have no such special R & D incentives and yet their firms are aggressive investors in R & D. It is because R & D Generates profit more then the other products can generate (P-634)
German technical Universities are more prestigious than regular Universities. (P-629). University research offers a number of benefits in stimulating a rising level of productivity in an economy. First new generation of

scientists are trained. Second, diffusion is facilitated in a open manner. Third, Universities are fertile incubators of new businesses. (P-632).

Nations succeed in fields where they have well developed educational systems in Engineering. (P-270)

37. Malaysia, out to create Harvards of the East F.E. May 16, 1996.

Under the new private education act, which came into effect this year, major Malaysian corporate enterprises will be allowed to establish their own Universities. The new legislation will also permit established overseas Universities to set up branch campuses at the invitation of education ministry. Not every one in academic community in happy with the decision.

38. M.M.Ansari, "Bridging the Missing links" F.E. May 9, 1996

India has been investing much less in education than several Asian countries. The Commitment of 6% of GNP has not been fulfilled. It is around 3.5% only. As a result, the share of public expenditure on education to the total expenditure has been the lowest for India. 11.2% as compared to Korea 22.4%, Thailand 20%, Malaysia 19%.

39. M.V.Rangnath, M.V.Shivram, "Indian Experience of CEE-Developing" a model for developing countries, Int. Journal CEE Vol. 1 No.2, 91 P.151.

India's 300 colleges, 500 polytechnics are currently underutilized.

40. Modern Temples of India, Selected Speeches of Jawaharlal Nehru, Edited by C.V.J. Varma & K.R.Saxena Central Board of Irrigation and Power 1989.

While laying Foundation stone of IIT – Mumbai on 10th March 1959, Nehru said –

"Those nations which have more of educated men knowing science and technology progress faster. More engineers we produce more will be their demand. By producing new engineers we are not producing just able men and women but we are buildinga new India, a whole new world. It is relatively easy to put up a factory or a plant. It is much more difficult and it takes much more time to train human beings, that will run that factory or put up another factory or plant, P-114.

41. National Security and our Technology Edge by Simon Ramo, Harward Business Review Nov. – Dec. 1989 (P-120).

    The real answer to our competitiveness problem is education in all its phases. We need massive public backing for educational reform. We must make funds available for education to pursue innovative approaches.

42. News item E.T. May 24, 1997.

    Of the 255 electronic patent applications filed in India, 226 are from MNCs, like Motrola, IBM Deewoo, and only 29 are from Indian innovators like CSIR labs, individuals etc. The Indian Patent Act 1970 allows both product and process patents in electronics.

43. N.B.Sunder, "make global learning local" Economic Times 20th Sept. 1997.

    It says students need curriculum choices enriched courses, specialised studies and wide access to resources. The trend word wide is to use Interactive Distances learning based on ATM technology at low costs.

44. National Policy on Education, 1986, New Delhi, MHRD, Govt. of India.

45. North American Universities capitalize on property values journal of Industry Higher Education Aug. 95, P-195.

    Land is leased to a shopping mall, residential development, a research park, 1100 unit retirement community, hotel conference facility in University of Guelph.

46. Narender Pani, "Academic Protectionism" Times of India 13 Sept. 1997.

    At a time when various sectors of Indian Economy are being asked to stand up to foreign competition, why should academics be the exception.

47. Penny wise corporate starve R & D, Times of India by Antara Nanda, 9 Aug. 1997.

Advanced Countries are now curtailing the flow of technology. Investment on R & D of cos. In India is hardly 0.45% of gross sales. Though most companies agree that upgradation of technology boosts competitiveness they are reluctant to bank on in house R & D support. Indian corporate sector is already a few decades behind in terms of the technological progress achieved in the developed world. Technological self reliance is the order of the day. And unless Indian cos. make a sincere effort to achieve that objective, they will find themselves out of the race even before they began.

48. P.H.Waghodekar & B.V.Tekwade, "Industrial Training : The Hub of a curriculum wheel". The Indian journal of Technical Education Vol 20, No.4, Oct-Dec. 1997.

49. Pradeep Kumar Panda, "Innovative Entrepreneurs Issue, Policy initiative in development efforts", Economic Times 19.08.1993.

The current thought is increasingly oriented forwards encouragement of innovation and entrepreneurship to faster balanced development, rather than traditional elements of Land, labour and Capital. India should learn from experience of U.S.A., U.K. Canada, Japan from projects like research parks, innovation centres, venture capital and encourage entrepreneurship, to faster industrial development.

50. Proceedings of the Seminar on "Restructuring of Technical Education System for Better efficiency and effectiveness, December 5-6, 1997, ISTE Chapter V.R. Siddharth Engineering College, Vijaywada 520 007.

51. Proceedings of XXII Annual Convention, December 26 – 28, 1993, I.S.T.E. Kamataka Regional Engineering College, Surathkal.

52. Proceedings of "International Conference on Technical Education in 21st Century" – Challenges and strategies in global Perspective, 8-10 January 1998, D.T.E. Bhopal Madhya Pradesh.
53. Proceedings of the 4th internaional conference on continuing Engineering education, held in Bejing China, 17-19 May 1989.
54. P.R.Dubhabhi, "Privatise Higher Education", Economic Times 28th August 1997.
He says "with Govt. support comes Uniformity and centralization. The U.G.C. set down uniform qwualification, uniform scale of remuneration, fixed load of work model syllabi and the institutions became prisoners of uniformity, mediocrity followed. The idea of Uniform fee structure has no merit. The quality of teachers, infrastructure, for students is bound to vary. The fees should vary accordingly. To insist on uniformity in fee, uniformity in pay, standards of education is to kill entrepreneurship. He recommends establishment of private universities, like in USA and other countries, so as to make most of the intellectual capital in the country.
55. P.V.Inderesan, "A whole overhaul", Economic Times.
Indian Industry has been all along neglectful of technology development. To correct this malady competition will be enforced and protection withdrawn.
56. Rangnath M.V. 1993, Continuing Education Project for working professionals, Indian Journal of Tech. Education, Vol 16, No.1.
57. R. Natarajan, The nature and scope of continuing Education for Engineering manpower, XXIII ISTE convention 1993 of K.R.E. Surathkal.
58. R. Ramchandran, "Render into R&D its case" Economic Times 1.8.1997.
In order to foster indigenous R&D DST Govt. of India have set up "Technology Development Board", and

allocated 30 crores as a first installment. This is besides venture capital Fund of IDBI, which is given in the form of equity for brand new technology development. The fund for Technology Development & Application (DTDA) is too small for the purpose.

59. Raymond J.G. Wells, Malaysians' Johor Technopolis, A Strategy for Technological deepening, Journal of Industry Higher Education, Aug. 1996, (P-227).
    Such an infrastructure "Technology park" for technological deepening is Universally required although different countries have different models.

60. R.Bhaskaran, "The need for closer interaction between industry and academia in the light of economic liberalization and globalization", The India Journal of Technical Education, Vol. 20, No.4, Oct-Dec. 1997.

61. Rajiv Raghunath, "Varsity Education Vital for industry growth", F.E. 26.11.1997.
    Corporate organizations are wanting to play a proactive role in the development of professional education. The industry is quite concerned about the poor standards. From a survey it has been found that insularity of university education from ground realities is what has contributed to poor quality of manpower.
    UNESCO has initiated a programme, "UNISPAR" University Industry Science Partnership. It aims "to match engineering education with industry needs, transfer research findings, retrain engineers, and reorient university curricula. Prof. Moegiadi from UNESCO is incharge at Delhi Office. He said there are "co-operative research centres in Universities in Australia." Universities should sit together with industry and prepare proposals, and develop a model for linking industry with higher education.

62. "Silicon Surrey", is now known for its enterprising university and small hi-tech business development.

"US survey finds that investing in people paysoff" – The survey commissioned by president Bush and designed at University of Pennsylvania came to a conclusion that 10% improvement in educational Qualification produced 8.4% increase in productivity while 10% in crease in capital stock increased productivity by only 3.4%.

63. Shobha Ahuja, "who will foot the bill" Economic Times. She says, "Even developed countries change only 40-70% of tuition fees, the rest of covered through grants subsidies and endowments." "She recommends that industrial houses should run institutes like". Thaper Institute of Engineering and Technology. Fees in self finance colleges may vary from institute to institute. The scheme given by supreme court that the payment category student pays for self and one from free category is a sort of subsidy to poor and deserving students.

64. Science and Technology Entrepreneurs Park – Economic Times, 20th Sept. 1988, by B.M.Naik.

65. Soumya Bhaskar, "I[grade of Perish" F.E. May 5, 1996. Distinguished Scientists A.P.Abdul Kalam, R.A. Mashalkar, FICCI Secretary Amit Mitra etc. have emphasized the need and importance of domestic R&D. Access to foreign technology, in liberalized economy, has become difficult, and costly. India should provide on priority, better environment for indigenous R&D to flourish. A survey conducted by the council of Applied Economic and Research and Friedrich Stiflung Germany that out of 657 units,56% are manually operated, 38.7% semi automatic. When compared with Japan 78% are fully automatic Indian cos. spend more on advertising than on R&D is the tragedy.

66. S.P.Sukhatme, "Restructuring the undergraduate Curriculum in Engineering in an Indian University". The Indian Journal of Technical Education, Vol. 18, No.3, July-Sept. 95.

He has compared the curriculum with U.S. University and suggested that

- Emphasis on drawing and work shop practice should be reduced.
- Humanities and social science should be increased.
- Patent laws, legal aspects of technology be introduced.
- Giving autonomy to colleges be seriously considered.

67. Soumya Sarkar, "Continuing Education comes of Age" Financial Express 10.10.1997.
Indira Gandhi National Open University (IGNOU) courses offer flexible opportunities for working professionals to upgrade their skills. The focus of courses in various other Universities is the Young students yet to enter job market. For people already in service, the continuing education courses, like in IGNOU are very few. The management programmes have opened up opportunities for most professionals.
68. The Evaluation of COMETT, Final Report Commission of the European Communities, Aug. 1991 square de Meeus 25, B-1049 Brussels Belgium.
Scheme was launched by European Commission in all member countries. It had developed University Enterprise Training Partnership (JETP) centres to upgrade technological competency of work force. It is still continuing more vigorously to build Europe more competent.
69. The management of Intellectual property by Satyawrat Ponkshe, A Bhate and Pankshe Publication, UBS Publishers, Distributors Ltd., 5 Ansari Road, New Delhi.
70. The Technopolis stregegy, Japans 26 emerging silicon valleys IInd International Technical Innovation & Entrepreneurship symposium proceedings Sept 1-4, 1987, Birmingham, U.K. 1987.
71. T.H.Chowdhary, "Competition is the key", F.E.May 16, 1996.
Demonopolization, and Debureancratization are a must to stem the trivilization of S & T education. Denmark,

Sweden, Finland have 20 to 30% of their population with S & T Qualification, while Japan has 12% India has less than 0.5%. We don't have good base for R&D. The reasons are in trivilzation of science and technology education.

72. University – Industry linkage, Graduate Resource Integration program (GRIP) prepared by HRD branch, HEPD, UNIDO, May 1996.
The gap between skills needed and skills supplied is a major reason for unemployability, low productivity. GRIP aims of bridging the gap by making surveys in various countries. It has formed committees of leaders in Industry and leaders in academics to analyze the problems.

73. Venture Capital Funds – A risky business, Economic Times 30th May 1991.

74. V.K.Bhansali, "Entrepreneurship Development in Technical Education. The Indian journal of Tech. Education Vol. 18, No.3 July-Sept. 1995."
He recommends that entrepreneurship should be the integral part of engineering education. This will solve problem of unemployment and provide a much needed boost to hitech industries.

75. World Development Report 1997
    - For centuries access to natural resources was considered the prerequisite to development. Much of Africa, Asia, America was colonized to acquire these resources, and countries went to over them. Gradually, however the thinking changed, and machines, capital and equipment was held to be the key opment, but now technology, knowledge and ideas are considered to be the keys. (P-29)
    - Privatization – no matter how dedicated, hardworking, or public spirited state officials are, they can not anticipate all the public goods and services that citizens desire (P - 116).

New knowledge can make drastic difference in peoples lives.

76. World Education Report 1997, Indicate the ranking of the universities in the world. Indian Institute of Science Banglore figures in this list as 18th, IIT Mumbai 101st. The other universities like Delhi, Mumbai are much down below, it is only the American Universities which are in first twenty.

Index

A

Abdul Kalam, Dr. APJ, former
    Ind Pres., 264, 266, 358
Academic
    Autonomy, 148
    Council, 37
    Freedom, 29, 68, 83-84, 87
    Institutions, (AIs), 24, 29, 35,
        59, 72, 82, 142, 147, 214,
        219, 232
    Leaders, 80
    Leadership, 21, 67
    Missions, 173
    Standards, 174
Academy of Sciences of USA, 133
Accreditation, 183, 371
    Agencies, 185
    Measures, 185
Administration, 32, 35-36
Advanced Education and
    Technology, 314
Affiliation, 286
Affiliating System, 25, 33, 35
    Abroad, 71
    Huge Waste—, 25
Afghanistan and Pakistan, 382
Agra College, 25
Agriculture
    Education, 289, 290
        Universities at Parbhani,
            133
    Universities in India, 309
    Universities, 72, 250, 289,
        321, 360
AICTE/UGC, 183
All India Council of Technical
    Education, (AICTE), 34, 68,
    71, 82, 140, 143, 153, 160,
    194, 250, 256, 358, 379
Ambani, Dhirubhai, 266
American
    Council on Education, 27
    Economy, 37

Federation of Teachers, 258
Industry, 372
System, 37
Universities of Europe, 79
Apple Computers, 61, 266, 351
APTECH and NIIT, 298
Art Technology, 45
Aston Science Park, University of Birmingham, 205
Attendance System, 277
Aurangabad University, 65
Aurangzeb, 67
Australia, 181
Australian Universities, 61
Author's Visit to Labs/ Universities, 309
Autocracy, 22
Automobiles/Robotization/CAD/ CAM, 331
Autonomous
Institutions, (23-24
Structure, 21-22, 24-25, 37-38
Autonomy, 173, 187, 203, 245
Academic, 30
and Funding Structure, 31
and Privatization, 28
Concept of-, 22
Financial, 30
Institutional, 31
Policy for Higher Education, 21-40
Powers, 25

B

Backward Region-Marathwada, 129-137
Basic Literacy, 42
Behavioural Skills, 268
Below Poverty Line (BPL), 59
Benchmarking, 162, 163, 165, 185, 193, 270, 371
Berlin, Stuttgart, Hamburg and Braunshweig, 309
Bhatnagar Award, 371
Bill Gates, 108, 225, 266
Biotechnology, 340
Biswas, Kanti, 25
Block Grants Scheme, 32
Board of Studies, 37
Bob Solow, 350
Book Writing, 126, 165
Boyer Commission, US, 362
Brain
Drain, 93, 182, 200, 201, 335, 335, 363
Power, 67, 174
Power Factors, 209
Race, 158
Brand New Technology, Commercial Exploitation, 145
Braunshweig University, 317
Budget Allocation to R&D
in China, 66
in India, 66
Bulgaria, 30
Bureaucratic Culture, 22
Bush Commission Report, 174, 349
Business
Incubator, 141, 266
Park, 196

C

CAFETARIA Approach
  Courses, 68
Cambridge
  Education Centres, 234
  Research Centre, 150
  University, 198, 233
Campus Companies, 171
Career Planning, 225
Casio Calculators, 332
Central Advisory Board of
  Education (CABE), 25
  Terms of Reference, 26
Centralized Organizations, 39
Centres of Excellence (CE), 93
Corporate Education Centre, 93
  Incubators, 93
  Industrial Service Centre, 93
  Innovation Relay Centre, 93
  Patent and IPR, 93
  Product/Process Innovation Centres, 93
  Research Parks, 93
  Technology Park, 93
Chamber of Commerce, 313-316
Change of Technology, 254
Charitable Trusts, 232
Chhatisgarh, 178
China, 32, 50, 101-102, 104, 127, 147, 363, 377, 379
  Association of Continuing Engineering Education, 102
  Association of Science and Technology, 102
  Concept of Continuing Engineering Education, 101
  Continuing Engineering Education in-, 102
  Higher Education in-, 32
Chinese Universities, 61
Civil and Political Rights, 46-47
Classroom Management, 260
Clinton, Bill, former US Pres, 340
Coaching Industry in India, 57
Cochin University, 52
COMET, 304, 310
Commercial
  Exploitation, 62, 147
    Of Researches, 221
  Projects, 80
  Trends in Education,
    Unethical Trends, 70
Commercialization, 86, 350
Communication Technology, 365
Company Training Program, 115
Computer
  Aided Teaching, (CAT), 104
  Industries, 208
Confederation of Indian Industry (CII), 64, 286, 324
Continuing Education, 116-117, 354, 364
  Centres, 117
  Program, 338
Continuing Engineering Education (CEE), 99-110
  Progress, 110
  International Association of—, 100

Master Plan, 102
Traditional Methods, 103
Corporate Education Centre, 141
Council of European Conference, 29
Council of Scientific and Industrial Research, 130, 251, 297, 302, 303, 305, 321
Laboratories, 201
Counseling Sessions, 170
Cultural Revolution, 46
Curricula, 29, 275
Curriculum, 280
Of Courses, 279
Customer Focus, 161

D

Daimler Research Centre, 214
Decentralization and
Autonomy, 32
Privatization, 24
De-Licensing Policy, 266
Designs System, 161
Diversification of Courses, 346
Dream Big, Jump Start Clusters, 54
Drucker, Peter, 132
Duke University, 52, 61, 219

E

Economic
And Social Development, 53
Competitiveness, 76
Development, 47, 101, 218, 230, 327, 338
Freedom, 23
Growth, 42, 120
China, 120
Hong Kong, 120
Japan, 120
Power, 29
Shocks, 333
Economies of Europe, UK, and USA, 297
Economy, 35, 42, 44, 46, 66, 78, 92, 113, 117, 120, 198-199, 211, 220, 249-250, 280, 338, 342, 357, 367, 372
Education
And Training in Universities, 15
And Training, 22
Barons, 70
Commission, 25
For Economic Development, 46
Loan Scheme, 175
Market, 59
Market, (India), 170
System, 277
Educational
Ecosystem, 57
Entrepreneurs, 237
Infrastructure, 43
Institutions, 289
E-Governance, 47
Electronic—Industries, 197
Electronics Engineering, 297
Electronics—Biotechnology, 213
Elphinstone College, 25
Employment, 139, 155, 197, 198

And Income Generation, 61
Generation, 140, 195
Engineering
Colleges, 283
Education Institutions, 243, 248
Education, 251, 273-281, 345
Objectives, 274
Institutions, Role of-, 347
Profession, 112
Objectives, 112
Professors, 271
Teachers/Professors, 120
Engleman, Dr., 309
Enrolments, 42
Entrepreneurship Development
Centre, 141, 145, 148
Environmental Technology, 317
Erasmus, 310
Esprit, 310
Essentials of
Principals, 123, 124
Professors, 121
Europe, Japan and US, 355
European
Commission (Brussels),
304, 310, 311
Patent Office, 154
Universities, 177, 364
Evaluation of Program, 22
Executive Council, 37
Export of Books to Least
Developed Countries, 127

F

Faculty Appraisal, 256
Fairs and Exhibitions, 313
Financial Grants, 28, 289
Finland and China, 365
Food Problem in India, 249
Foreign
Education, 167
Universities, 59, 67, 139,
143, 158, 361
Entry of –in India, 170
In India, 37
Universities in India, 250
Fraun Hofer Gesselschaft Labs
(FHG), 311, 320
Fraunhofer Society, 320
Functions of Faculty Members,
254
Fundamental Rights, 31
Funding, 313
Mechanism, 291
Funding, Private and Public, 48

G

G-8 Countries, 219
Gandhi-Nehru Period, 171
Gautam Buddha, 230
Geographical Positioning
System (GPS), 233
Georgia Technical University, 65
German Research Organization,
309
Germany, 29,48, 105, 181, 213,
311, 315
And Japan, 250
Continuing Engineering
Education, 105

National Laboratories, 311
Science and Technology Universities, 313
Technical Universities, 71
Global
Competition, 120
Competitiveness, 127, 218
Economy (ies), 47, 302, 308
Markets, 43
Network of Educators, 340
Standards, 244
Globalization, 30, 35, 41-45, 49, 51, 54-55, 59, 106, 222, 232, 247, 305, 375
And Liberalization, 286
Challenge for Indian Universities, 349-356
Challenges of-, 30
Job Opportunities in-, 51
Of Economy, 49, 333
Goal Setting, 261
Governance
and Leadership, 231
of Education in India, 193
Governing Boards, 86
Government Projects Designs, 278
Govt. Funding of Education, 368

H

Harburg University Park in Germany, 150
Higher and Technical Education
Crisis, 247
Institutions, 375
Higher Education
And Technical Education, (HETE), 139-155
Innovation and Entrepreneurship in-, 139-155
Institute for Employment Generation, 139-155
Accountability and Privatization in Private Sector, 27
Autonomy Policy for-, 21-40
Decentralization, 36
Establishment, 30
Financial Autonomy, 30
Financial Resources, 79
Financing, 87
Good Health for-, 28
Governance, 29
In India, 34
In US, 27
Institutions (HEIs), 28, 30, 32, 36, 42, 53, 54, 79, 86, 136, 139, 141, 147, 195, 197, 220, 298, 365
Internationalization of-, 177
New Role of-, 50
Privatization of-, 76, 80
Reform Agenda (HERA-Vietnam), 31
Role of Higher and Technical Education-, 41-56
Role of-, 218
System, 31, 33, 41, 140, 170

High-Tech,
Employment, 217
Entrepreneurship, 209
Industries, 196, 212, 284
Skills, 30
Hindu College, Calcutta, 25

I

IAUP (International Association of University Presidents), 27
Recommendations, 27
IDBI, 131
Import of Know How, 343
Imported Technologies, 284
Incentives, 163
Incubator Centres, 298
Incubator, 141, 171, 350
India,
A Technology Oriented Nations, 91
And US, 76
In Export Market, 334
Third Largest Technical Manpower, 113
India's
Growth Rate, 72
International Competitiveness, 218
Share in Sunrise Technologies, 334
India-Canada Project, 148
Indian
Economy, 42, 171, 221, 234, 269, 327, 352, 357
Education Market, 139
Engineering Schools, 61
Engineers, 264
Engineers and Industry, 120
Higher Education
Institutions, 50, 140
Industry (ies), 14, 55, 141, 284, 286, 288, 342
Institutes of Management (IIMs), 33, 34, 36, 224
Ahmedabad, (IIM), 27
Institute of Science
Bangalore (IISc), 61, 141, 154
Institute of Technology (IITs), 50, 58, 65, 141, 198, 204, 224-226, 303, 305, 321, 359, 360, 366
Kharagpur, 52
Mumbai, 52
Institutions, 239, 246
Market, 93, 141
Society of Technical Education (ISTE),
Program, 125
Standard Codes, 275
Students, 60
Traditional Researches in-, (ITR), 52, 62
Ayurvedic Medicines, 52, 62
Basmati, 52, 62
Haldi, 52, 62
Wheat, 52, 62
Universities, 61, 171, 175-177, 234, 287, 349-356
Indians in Silicon Valley, 142
Indira Gandhi National Open University (IGNOU), 106

Indo-German Cooperative
Project, 309
Industrial
Belts, 209
Development, 92, 195, 199, 204, 266, 288
Development Plans, 67
Estates, 131, 199, 208, 302, 303
Exhibitions, Hanovar, 62
Goods of Japan, 334
Growth, 284, 301
Leader, 301
Management, 135
Revolution, 285, 331
Services Centre, 141
Sickness, 200
Slowdown, 146
Training, 165
Industrialization, 124, 200, 209, 211, 213, 305, 308, 347
Industrialized Nations, 218
Industrially Advanced Countries, 177, 201
Industry (ies), 48, 68, 92, 93, 112, 160-161, 169, 171, 174, 182, 221, 229, 232-233, 238-239, 245, 248, 249-250, 267, 278, 288, 292, 308, 321, 333, 350
And Education Institutions, 109
Conventional, 198
Manufacturing, 114
Information Technology, 130
Infrastructure, 145, 146, 148, 152, 182, 196, 221, 267, 298, 314, 361
Development, 211
For Patents, Technology Transfer—, 136
For Technical Manpower, 124
Of Indian Institutions, 238
Innovation
Centres, 137, 145-146, 148, 149, 171, 196, 213, 229
Infrastructure, 229
Relay Centre, 370
In-Service Program, 125
Inspector Raj-License Raj, 36
Institute of Engineers (New Delhi), 117
Institutional Autonomy, 27
Intellectual
Capital, 43
Property Rights, (IPR), 41, 62, 68, 72, 73, 136, 182, 207, 302, 313, 363
And Licensing, 313
Property Rights Centre, (IPRC), 63, 145, 148, 153
Property Rights Royalties, 173
Internal
Quality Audit, 163-164
Services, 131
International
Association of Continuing Education, 365
Association of Technology Parks, 209
Framework, 30
Market, 207, 212

Organizations, 42
UNESCO, 42
World Bank, 42
Reforms, 49
Standards, 263
Trade and Commerce, 49
Internationalism, 127

J

Japan, 31, 51, 103, 125, 133, 182, 197, 340
And Germany, 303
And US, 296
And USA, 271
Continuing Engg Education in-, 103
Corporate Education in-, 31
Engineering Students, 296
German and US, 327
Germany, UK, 52
Higher Education, 295-299
Korea, 334
Japan's
Economic Growth, 197
Economy, 37
Education, 296
Intellectual Challenge (Study), 295
Multi-national Corporations, 301
Japanese
Economy, 182
System, 37
Jefferson, Former Pres of USA, 25
Job
Generation, 109
Market, 44
Joblessness, 332, 342

K

Karlsruhe University in Germany, 38, 65, 351
Knowledge
And Decision Making, 23
Based Economies (KBE), 35, 41, 42, 46
Based Economy (ies), 30, 47
Based Organization, 244, 245
Commission, 76
Economy, 75
Society, 4, 46, 53, 91, 97, 344
Korea, 172
Kothari Commission, 381
Kothari, Dr DS, 25

L

Leaders, 22
Charismatic, 162
For Economy, 44
In Education, 55
In Industry, 44, 55, 142, 249, 253
In Technology, 142, 263
Political and Social, 117
Visionary, 44
Leadership, 24, 31, 58

Institutions, 231
Private Sector, 24
Skills, 43
Legislative and Regulatory Reforms, 31
Liberalization, 247
Privatization and Globalization, 221
Liberalized Economy, 247, 248, 288
Lifelong Education, 37, 118, 228, 354
Centres, 376
Limerick University Research Centre, 150
Literacy, Scientific and Cultural, 45
Local Inspection Committee, 36
Lord Clive, 210

M

Maharashtra State Electricity Board, 116
Management
Competency, 114
Courses, 115-116
Development Program for Officers, 115
Of Education, 32, 111-118
Of Education, For In-service Engineers, 111-118
Of Education, India, 114
Of Education, Why, 113
Of Technology Transfer, 308
Skills, (Managerial), 111-112
Strategies, 232
Manmohan Singh, Indian PM, 178
Manufacturing System, 296
Marathwada, 129-137
Development Board, 136
Market Orientation, 126
Medical
And Engineering Courses, 81
Education, 291
Mediocre Institutions, 130
MFUCTO, Association of Professors, 25
Minerals, 113
Ministry of
Agriculture, 289
Education and Training (Vietnam), 31
Education, 289, 290
Health, 291
Mission Statement, 242-243
MIT, 52, 65, 100, 150, 159, 193, 213, 359, 362, 363, 366
Boston, 51, 61, 169, 196-197, 200, 270, 351
Electronic Lab, 208
Technologies, 208
Mobility of Academicians, 151
Modern
Institute, Agenda, 95
Teacher Aids, 260
Modernization, 333, 342
Of Laboratories, 147
Of Sectors of Economy, 337
Monitoring and Evaluation, 259
Monopoly Regime's End, 169-180

Moral Education, 367
Motorola Company, 108, 365
Multi-faculty Universities, 72
Murthy, Narayan, 225

N

Nagarjunasagar Project, 330
Nalanda, 57, 58
NASSCOM, 64
Nation's Infrastructure, 295
National
  Accreditation Board, 160
  Economy (ies), 72, 77, 80
  Education Commission, 173
  Education Policy, (NEP-1986), 25, 106, 355, 381
  Funding for Education, 88
  Institutes of Technology, 321
  Knowledge Commission (NKC), 26, 106, 224, 234, 253-255, 377, 380, 381
  Productivity Council, 115
  Research Laboratories, 248
  University Singapore, 65
Natural Resources, 113, 141, 200
Naxalite Movement, 71
Nehru, Pundit (Pandit) Jawahar Lal, 91, 231, 330
New
  Industries in Aurangabad, 131
  Organizational Structure, 113
  Science and Technology, 382
  Strategies, 239
  Sunrise Knowledge, 226
  Technology (ies), 50-51, 60-61, 91, 93, 99, 111, 147, 153, 211-212, 218, 226, 233, 254, 284, 288, 296, 305, 308, 332, 337-338, 359, 361, 362
  Technologies in Industry, 198
  Technology Based Firms (NTBFs), 50, 51, 58, 61, 95, 129, 141, 147, 151, 152, 172, 199, 204, 210-211, 220, 234, 266, 351-352
  Based Industries, 41
  For Industry, 131, 140
New Zealand, 181

O

OECD, 150, 211, 355, 42
Online Business University Part, 150
Openness and Transparency, 47
Operation Manual, 158, 160
  Purpose, 160
Organizational
  Management Capability, 78
  Structure for Modern Institutions, 96
  Structure, 58, 164, 205
Outdated Know How, 276
Oxford and Cambridge, 359, 362

P

Participative Decision Making, 162

Patent (s), 33
And Intellectual Property Rights, 50-52, 54, 58, 60, 65, 122, 129, 137, 141, 143, 152-153, 169, 176, 217, 221, 223, 228-229, 234, 266-267, 350, 355, 361, 370
And Technology, 84
And Technology Licensing, 355
And Technology Transfer, 52, 139, 148, 149
Centres, 52
For Sale, 62
Performance
Appraisal System, 256, 258
Appraisal, 260, 261
Philanthropic 363
Organizations, (PO), 48, 169, 173
Placement of Engineers, 161
Planning, 242, 259
Performance, 253
Strategic, 237-246
Policies and Practices, 58, 60, 69
Political System, 30, 46, 328, 329
Poona College, 25
Private
Institutions, 77-79, 81
Self-Finance Institutions in India, 77
Universities, 84, 158, 169-180
Why, 170
Privatization, 47-48, 76-78, 80, 85, 28, 173, 336, 364
Of Education, 70
Of Technical Education, 376
Policy in Education, 237
Professionalism, 77, 82
Project Planning, 279
Projects, 130
Industry, 130
Irrigation, 130
Roads, 130
Public-Private Partnership, 378
Punishments, 253, 260

Q

Quality
Assurance, 184, 371-372
Assurance System, 30, 181-194
In Higher/Technical Education, 181-194
Audit, 18, 162-163
Cell Creation for Quality Audit, 162
Circle, 187
Improvement Program (QIP), 125, 146
Management, 187, 191
Principles of-, 184
System, 193
Manuals, 371
Of Education, 376
Of Leadership, 66
Of Technical Education, 146
Planning, 163

. Plans, 371
Policy, 161-163, 189
Procedure, 189

R

Radhakrishnan Commission, 381
Radhakrishnan, Chairman UGC, 179
Raw Materials, 93
Regional
Development, 54
Resource Development Centre, 106
And Education, 67
Research, 82, 93
Assistantship, 64
Based Education, 59
Centre, 196
Funding, 313
Grants, 126
Park in Herriot Watt University Aston, 201, 205, 353
Park in-, 220, 221
China, 220
Japan, 220
Taiwan, 220
UK, 220
Parks, 50, 66, 96, 145, 148, 149, 171, 212-214, 218-219, 231, 266, 298, 299, 350, 354, 370
Triangle Park in North Carolina, 196, 197, 200, 219
Universities, 133
Researcher Park, 196
Rewards, 253, 261, 328
Right to Information (RITs), 47
Rights of Intellectual Property Rights, 30
Robots, 340
Rural Development, 118

S

Satellite, Impact on Education, 103
Scheme of
Autonomy, 158
Contract of Teachers, 68
Science
Council of Canada, 214
Park, 195-215, 201, 203
Generates Wealth/ employment, 195
Park at Bradford University, 205
Town (Taiwan), 354
Science and Engineering Education, 58
Science and Technology, 100, 102, 111, 195, 127, 129-137, 213, 221-222, 234, 273, 339-341, 358, 385
And Economic Development, 132
Centres, 137
Education and Research, 133
Entrepreneurs Park (STEP), 52, 201

Institutions, 135
Investment in-, 130
Laboratories, 135
Park, 199, 204, 321
Personnel, 287, 334
Projects, (STP), 130
Internal Services, 130
Research Parks, 130
Science City, 130
Technical Universities, 130
Technology Incubators, 130
Technology Parks etc., 130
Research Innovations Centres, 137
Transfer, 46
Universities, 131, 201
Scientific
And Technological Capability, 133
And Technological Facilities, 129
Infrastructure, 219
Management Practices, 80
Sector,
Automobile, 233
Corporate, 82
Industrial, 290
Information Technology, 80
Sen, Dr. Amartya, 66
Shivaji, 67
Sickness of Industries, 100
SICOM, 131
Silicon Valley, (SV), 52, 63, 197, 213, 219, 263
Corporation, 209
Model of USA, 132
Adoption by Japan, Korea, 132
Sinha, Yashwant, Fin Minister, 66, 368
Skills and Innovation and Patenting, 66
Small Scale Industry, 203
Social
And Economic Development, 116
Reformers, 136
System, 46, 328
Socratic Oath, 122-123
Software Industry, 61
Solar Energy, 340
Solob, Bob, MIT Boston, 133
Space Technology, 340
Special Economic Zones (SEZs), 67, 131, 267
Staff Appraisal System, 256
Stanford University, 52, 196, 200, 219, 353
And California Universities, 52
State Universities, 172
Steinbeis Technology Transfer Centre, 317
Strategic
Audit, 242
Planning, Process, 239
Plans, 239, 245
Structural Reforms, 291
Sunrise
Knowledge, 64, 69
Technologies, 64, 143, 217, 335

Technologies and Industry, 92
SWOT Analysis, 106, 239
System
Manual, 165
Software, 197

T

Tax Collection, 78
Taxshila, 57, 58
Teacher, Performances, 255, 258
Appraisal, 255
Teaching
And Research, 29, 70
And Research, Quality of-, 23
Assistantship, 64
Company Scheme, 304
Profession in India, 57
Development, 274, 295
Education, 75-89, 120, 222, 228, 267, 288, 292, 295, 299, 339-348
Identification of Risk Factors, 75-89
Job Creating Agency, 341
Privatization of-, 75-89
Reorganization of-, 287
Education and Research, 308
Education Institutes (Institutions), 75, 91, 222, 289, 301, 308, 309, 357-375
Institutions in India, 305
Technical
Manpower, 200
Skills, 273, 368
Universities (TU), 72, 208, 250-251, 284-286, 291, 292, 360
In Germany, 150
Industry Oriented, 283-293
Techno-Economic
Development, 120
Environment, 328
Technological
and Industrial
Development, 220
Society, 96
Technologies, 147, 219, 263
Technology, 32, 55, 62-63, 65, 91, 106, 113, 141, 174, 196, 234, 340,
Absorption, 95
Audit, 304
Based Industries, 196
Change, 212, 219, 329-330, 335-336, 338
Generation, 302, 308
Incubators, 131, 266, 228, 352
Innovation Centre, 315
Innovation Relay Centre, 141
Leaders, 95
Licensing, 161
Licensing Office (TLO), 65, 150, 270
Management, 214
Oriented Nation, 200

Park (s), 54, 131, 137, 199, 201-210, 249, 267, 298, 299, 305, 317, 355
In Cambridge, 201
Functions, 206
Leads to Technical Knowledge, 204
Means to Poverty Eradication, 204
Methodology, 207
Organizational Structure, 205
Steps for Establishing-, 210
Revolution, 327-338
Role of-, 304
Sale, 87
Transfer (TT), 51, 137, 141, 201, 229, 244, 248, 301-306
In Germany, 307-325
Practices and Policies in Germany, 307-325
Techno-Polis
in Japan, 196
Strategy, 197
TEQIP (Technical Education Quality Improvement Program), 146, 153, 158, 167, 224
Terman, Prof., Stanford University, 52
Test House, 96
Textile and Steel Industries, 198, 208
Thailand, 27, 172
Think Tank, 46
TIFAC (Technology Information and Assessment Council), New Delhi, 62, 153, 154, 358
Toronto University, 219
Total Quality Management (TQM), 181-184, 186, 187, 189, 193-194, 224, 232, 371, 379
In Education, 371
Steps in Implementation, 191, 193
Trade
and Commerce, 333
and Industry, 303
Traditional
Affiliating System, 355
Courses, 366
Instructional Practices, 366
Lines of Teaching and Learning, 218
Organization Structure, 287
Regulation by Universities, 35
Training, 279, 280, 308
and Development, 120, 124
and Employment, 271
Program, 162
Transfer
And Adoption of Technology, 295
Of Technology, 128, 196
Transparency, 30
Triangle Park North Carolina, 52
Tuition Fees, 28, 47, 87

U

UK, 31-32, 45, 47, 50, 125, 128, 181, 197, 198, 203, 208, 285, 286, 371
And US, 171, 337
Engineering Students, 296
Higher Education, 31
Science Park Association, 213
USA, 335
USA and Australia, 170
UNESCO, 99-100, 102, 105, 250, 305, 372
Unification of Germany, 317
Universities in-, 38, 66
Australia, 51
Germany, 38, 51, 66
India, 61, 64
Japan, 248
UK, 38, 66
US, 38, 248
Universities Visited By the Author (UVBA), 64
China, 64
Germany, 64
UK, 64
US, 64
University
Acts, 71
Aurangabad, 65
Education, 105
Grants Commission (UGC), 34, 68, 71, 82, 140, 143, 194, 255, 351
Industry Science Partnership Program (UNISPAR), 372
of Karlsruhe, 313
of Madison, 101, 354
of Madison, Cambridge and Edinburgh, 350
Massachusetts, 28
Oxford and Cambridge, 159
Poone, 52
Roorkee, 117
System, 179, 292
Technology Transfer, 313
Texas, 101
Ulm, 214
West Indies, 103
Up-gradation of Technology, 342
URR Parks, (University Related Research Parks), 142
US, 45, 47-48, 50, 59, 63, 77, 79-80,121, 125, 127-128, 147, 150, 174, 181, 196-197, 200, 213, 219, 231, 258, 285, 286, 340, 349-351, 355, 362
And Japan, 136, 177
And UK, 51, 205, 247
Companies, 51
Competitiveness, 61
Continuing Engineering Education, 101, 104
Dept of Labor, 296
Economic Performance, 28
Economy, 33
Engineering Students, 296
Fees Paid by Students, 87
Financial Resources for Science and Technology, 133
Germany and UK, 349

Japan, 379
National Institute of Education, 295
National Science Foundation, 349
Produce Leaders, 145
Software Business, 60
Technical Universities, 71
UK and Europe, 301
UK and Japan and Germany, 353
Universities, 51, 60, 169, 173, 174, 364

V

Vajpayee, Atal Behari, former PM, 358
Venture
Capitalists, 271
Companies, 171, 361
Venture
Capital
Centre, 145, 148
Companies, 361
Firms (VCF), 66, 234, 266, 271, 304, 324
Foundation (FUND)(VCF), 141, 229, 304, 305, 350, 370
Video Film Making, 126
Vietnam, 31
Vision 2020, 357-374
Vision Statement, 189

W

Warren Hastings, 210
West Indies, 103
Wisconsin-Foundation (WARF), 354
WISTA, 317
World
Economic System, 46
Economy, 44, 58, 214, 221, 230, 284, 298
Market, 158
Operation Manual, 159
World Bank Financial Aids to—, (WBFA), 148
Congo, 148
Zambia, 148
World Bank
Project, 148
Report, 45, 93
World Class
Industries, 92
Institutions, 34